12 STEPS TO MASTERING THE WINDS OF CHANGE

12 STEPS TO

MASTERING THE WINDS OF CHANGE

PEAK PERFORMERS REVEAL HOW TO STAY ON TOP IN TIMES OF TURMOIL

Erik Olesen

RAWSON ASSOCIATES

NEW YORK

Maxwell Macmillan Canada

TORONTO

Maxwell Macmillan International

NEW YORK   OXFORD   SINGAPORE   SYDNEY

Rawson Associates
Macmillan Publishing Company
866 Third Avenue
New York, NY 10022

Maxwell Macmillan Canada, Inc.
1200 Eglinton Avenue East
Suite 200
Don Mills, Ontario M3C 3N1

Macmillan Publishing Company is part of the Maxwell Communication Group of Companies.

Library of Congress Cataloging-in-Publication Data
Olesen, Erik, 1954–
    12 steps to mastering the winds of change : peak performers reveal
how to stay on top in times of turmoil / by Erik Olesen.
        p. cm.
    Includes bibliographical references and index.
    ISBN 0-89256-357-5
    1. Change (Psychology)   2. Life change events.   3. Stress
management.   I. Title.   II. Title: Twelve steps to mastering the
winds of change.
BF637.C4054   1993
158'.1—dc20   92-39486
                                                               CIP

Macmillan books are available at special discounts for bulk purchases for sales promotions, premiums, fund-raising, or educational use. For details, contact:

                        Special Sales Director
                        Macmillan Publishing Company
                        866 Third Avenue
                        New York, NY 10022

10 9 8 7 6 5 4 3 2 1

Printed in the United States of America

To my wife, Mary Lee,
who copes beautifully with
two dynamic kids,
a career,
and a husband who dreams too much.

Contents

5   STEP TWO: BUILDING COMMITMENT THROUGH GOALS AND PASSION

6   STEP THREE: STAYING COMMITTED WHEN THE GOING GETS TOUGH

9 STEP SIX: BEING OPTIMISTIC

10 STEP SEVEN: USING HUMOR TO COPE WITH CHANGE

11   STEP EIGHT: LEARNING FROM MISTAKES   *141*

12   STEP NINE: MAINTAINING PERSPECTIVE   *157*

Foreword

All my life I have been fascinated by the relationship between change, stress, and success. Why do some people seize the opportunity presented by stressful change and go on to win, while others choke under pressure or simply give up? Why do most people stop trying in trying times, while others thrive in the face of adversity?

My good friend and mentor, the late Hans Selye, M.D., pioneered the modern concept of stress and conducted groundbreaking research in the field. He knew more about stress than anyone else in the world.

As a young physician who emigrated from Central Europe to Canada, Selye first borrowed the English word *stress* from physics to describe the body's responses to everything from viruses and cold temperatures, to emotions such as fear and anger. Dr. Selye's definition of stress, nearly sixty years old, is still the best explanation of what it really is: "Stress is the body's nonspecific response to any demand placed on it, whether that demand is pleasant or not".

More than anything else, Hans Selye believed that "it's not what happens to us in life that counts, so much, as how we *take* it," and that we can transform stressful change into a positive force by altering our attitude. He often quoted the German proverb: "Imitate the sundial's ways; count only the pleasant days." I believe that Selye's ideas are more relevant than ever in today's fast-paced, frantic world, where there is more change in one of our days than there was in an entire decade of our grandparents' lives.

Hans Selye had a way of being able to explain complex scientific data by the use of easy-to-understand illustrations and examples. My colleague, Erik Olesen, also has this rare ability and demonstrates it brilliantly in this important book.

Many books implore readers to think and live positively, but few describe *how* to do it. *12 Steps to Mastering the Winds of Change* is refreshingly, substantively different.

In this book, Erik Olesen provides step-by-step instructions for responding exactly as Dr. Selye recommended so often. Olesen has distilled the essence of his interviews with forty peak performers in a wide variety of professions, as well as the results of his survey of many individuals from all walks of life. He introduces a comprehensive conditioning program that each of us can use to master the pressure of change as we accelerate through the remaining years of this decade and into the twenty-first century.

Were he alive today, I believe Hans Selye would like this book very much. I know I do.

—DENIS WAITLEY, Ph.D., author
The New Dynamics of Winning

Acknowledgments

My heartfelt thanks to the following people, who helped and supported me in many ways as I researched and wrote this book:

Bud Gardner, for his words of inspiration at the beginning of this project. Some things you never forget.

My wife, Mary Lee, for her patience, love, and encouragement when the going got tough, and also when it was easy.

My father, mother, and sister, Kristi, for their love, support, and amazement.

My sons, Ryan and Nathan, who kept me from getting too serious.

George and Mary Keating, for patience and understanding when I seemed to disappear into my office for days.

My wonderful agent, Maureen Walters, who copes with stress and change amazingly well.

Grace Shaw, who helped edit and focus this book, and showed as much poise under pressure as anyone I've ever met.

Eleanor Rawson, whose insight, experience, and great ideas made this book much better.

Duane Newcomb, for his patience, insight, and keen editorial eye.

Ellen Roberts, for convincing me to go on when I thought of giving up.

John Kohls and Marvin Todd, for hearing my bi-weekly progress notes on this book for years, and for still listening.

T. George Harris, for looking at life with love and excitement, and teaching me something about doing that myself.

Mary Cunningham, for reminding me about the importance of spirit.

Joe Vitale, for focusing on the positive, and gently pointing out the negative.

Barbara Chisholm and Mary Paulsen, for their support and patience throughout this project, and Edie Kuik, for the extra energy she provided in the latter stages.

Katie Ostrander, Bob Chope, and Craig Smith, for their inspiration, and for helping me reach higher.

Evan Sundby, for his invaluable help in creating and analyzing the survey for this book.

Dru Bagwell, for her support, insight, and frequent "Isn't that book done yet?" questions.

Special thanks to Bo, Dawn Dwyer, Richard Lui, Kris McNutt, Joanna McNutt, Bill W. and his friends, and Vivian Todhunter.

And finally, thanks to all the peak performers I interviewed. You taught me how to master the winds of change for myself.

1

Solving the Puzzle

Here be dragons. These words, written on the margins of ancient maps, warned mariners to steer clear of the unexplored realms beyond the known world. Only a fool, or a hero, would risk battle with dragons.

Today, thoroughly explored and mapped, the earth holds few secrets. Perched on the edge of the twenty-first century, we know that no mythical monsters lurk beyond the margins of our modern lives. But the dragons of change prowl everywhere.

In my work as a corporate consultant and professional speaker I see, hear about, and experience the severe problems caused by change and stress in organizations. As a licensed therapist and biofeedback trainer, I counsel people suffering from anxiety and tension as they scramble to deal with transitions in their lives. And as a business owner, parent, and overly busy person, I often struggle with change and pressure myself.

Yet there are people who seem to *thrive* on change. They face the dragons and master them. How do they do it? It would be important, I thought, to discover how these people, immersed like the rest of us in pressure-packed lives, transform change into a positive force. Is there a secret to their success? Can others learn it? I decided to find out.

First, I explored the answers others had found. After searching through professional journals and books, participating in seminars, and reading research studies, I assembled a long list of theories and strategies recommended by the experts. But I still had questions. Which approaches worked in the real world? Were some more effective than others?

Armed with the research findings, I continued my quest. I began interviewing a group of highly successful dragon tamers, striving to discover *exactly what they did to handle change and pressure.*

In selecting peak performers to interview, I looked for those who:

- Handle change and stress well
- Had been successful for a long time, or had become successful again after a challenging setback
- Appeared to lead balanced and happy lives

I avoided individuals who suffer from the success traps that Harvard Medical School psychologist Steven Berglas calls "the four A's":

- **Arrogance**
- A sense of **Aloneness**
- The need to seek **Adventure**
- **Adultery**

These four problems are, Berglas says, "the core attributes of people who achieve stellar success without the psychological bedrock to prevent disorder." Dr. Berglas, who has counseled and studied wealthy and successful people for more than ten years, says peak performers who lose their way suffer from at least three of the four A's.

A peak performer's downfall can come from developmental influences, the pressure of success itself, or a combination of the two. And, according to Berglas, "what's often missing in these people is deep community or religious activity that goes far beyond just writing a check to charity . . . it's the only antidote for narcissism. Be an Indian, not a chief. Lose your identity in a group. The healthiest people have that commitment."

Though I'm sure some suffer from an "A" or two themselves, the peak performers I interviewed are remarkably free from the pathology of success. Most are modest, work hard for charities, and have happy home lives. Many *do* like adventure, but they balance their escapades with an ability to step back when they get too close to the fire.

After choosing my subjects, I spent two years interviewing them. I spoke to forty peak performers, including:

- Walter Cronkite
- TV personality and cookbook author Julia Child
- Astronaut Edgar Mitchell
- Professional speaker and former IBM vice-president Buck Rodgers
- Entertainer, musician, and author Steve Allen
- Actors Jill Eikenberry and Michael Tucker of "L.A. Law"
- Notre Dame football coach Lou Holtz
- Weight-loss salon founder and executive Jenny Craig
- LeVar Burton, star of "Star Trek: The Next Generation"
- Prisoner of war turned professional speaker Gerry Coffee
- Top mail order catalog CEO Lillian Vernon
- CEO of Tootsie Roll, Inc., Ellen Gordon
- CEO and best-selling author Harvey Mackay

In the process of the interviews, I discovered that the key issue in my quest was *change*, although stress was part of the equation, too. Unfortunately, it was difficult to know whether my subjects handled stress well or not. Most appeared cool under pressure, but I could not tell if that impression was accurate. What *was* clear was their ability to manage change. They seemed to *thrive* on it—to invite change into their lives. This was a skill many others, I thought, could use.

Besides the interviews, I worked with a statistician, sending surveys to a random sample of peak performers picked from *Who's Who in America*. One hundred and twenty people, including most of those I interviewed, completed my questionnaires. The *Who's Who* group included a federal judge, a prize-winning physicist, a newspaper editor, two renowned artists, a nuclear engineer, an astronomer, and top corporate CEOs and presidents.

The surveys provided detailed information on the tools and strategies these peak performers use to handle change and pressure.

As my statistician and I analyzed the interviews and questionnaires, I felt excited about what we were finding. The data showed that the peak performers all used the same basic strategies to put pressure-packed change into perspective. We had found *the difference that makes a difference.*

Then, using experience gained in conducting seminars on change and stress for more than seventy organizations, many on the *Fortune* 500 list, I incorporated the data from the interviews and surveys into a workable change management method for the rest of us: *12 Steps to Mastering the Winds of Change.*

I strengthened the Steps further by including in them the most effective strategies garnered from my twelve years of clinical counseling practice with individuals and families undergoing profound change. Finally, I field-tested the 12 Steps in my seminars, counseling practice, and consulting work—fine-tuning the strategies and making certain that they worked effectively in the real world.

And that's what this book is about: how successful people, faced with tremendous problems and pressures, transform change into a positive force to advance their lives and goals. And how you can do the same. *12 Steps to Mastering the Winds of Change* provides a complete conditioning program for managing the pressure of nonstop change in the nineties and beyond.

THE PEAK PERFORMERS

My interviews with the peak performers ranged in length from thirty minutes to more than four hours. Most of those I spoke with were warm and supportive. They helped me feel welcome in their offices, homes, and hotel rooms. And, generally, they confirmed the adage "The bigger they are, the nicer they are."

The men and women I interviewed hadn't led easy lives, nor has life handed them success on a silver platter. They've dealt with plenty of change, much of it stressful. Entertainer Art Linkletter was an orphan. Top speaker Zig Ziglar's father died when Zig was a child. Pilots Bob Hoover and Gerry Coffee were both prisoners of war. John Johnson, founder and CEO of the highly successful Johnson Publishing Company, grew up in poverty and lost his father at an early age. And when she was growing up, mail order catalog executive Lillian Vernon's family fled Germany to escape the Nazis.

Yet, in spite of tough times, these peak performers enjoy life. They love doing what they're doing, and it shows.

They don't, however, do all the things many experts recommend. Most don't meditate or eat health foods. They work a lot— an average of about fifty-three hours per week.

But love for what they do shows through again and again. In fact, a long-term study of top achievers among Harvard Business School graduates found that most successful people *do* tend to lead balanced lives. Psychiatrist George Vaillant, who directed the Harvard study, reports that despite their long work weeks, most of those he surveyed had good health, stable marriages, and happy lives.

That doesn't mean that working long hours makes people happy. But doing what you love may help.

So, after years of searching and researching, I found the answers to my original questions about handling pressure-packed transitions. I call these solutions the 12 Steps to Mastering Change. And, starting in the next chapter, we'll explore them together.

NOTES

Steven Berglas's quotes about successful people are from "The Bigger They Are, The Harder They Fall," an interview with Richard Behar, in *Time* magazine, November 4, 1991.

Study on high achievers was summarized in "The Myth of the Balanced Life," by George Gilder, in *Success*, July/August 1988.

2

Unlocking the Secrets of Mastering Change

Primitive people dealt with plenty of change and stress, but their lives and choices were simple—fight the saber-tooth tiger or run away. Wait for the glacier to come—or move.

Modern life, however, is pressure-packed and far from simple. Today many of us face more stressful change than ever before, massive shifts in all aspects of our lives—job, home, family, and society. Hundreds of thousands of workers receive layoff notices. Strong, successful companies fall victim to hostile takeovers. Life grows more complicated every day. And the changes just keep coming.

The dramatic changes in our world create tension. A recent Harris poll found that 89 percent of adult Americans report suffering from high stress levels. Almost twice as many high-income as low-income people report experiencing *extremely* high tension levels. Professionals and executives, Harris found, feel more stressed than others.

Another study, this one by Northwestern National Life Company, found that seven of ten workers in America claim that job stress causes them frequent health problems. Seventy percent also say that excess pressure on the job makes them less productive.

Whether you are a professional person juggling a high-pressure career and a hectic home life, a middle manager dreading a forthcoming merger, a single mother struggling to make ends meet, or just one of the millions alarmed by the ever-increasing pace of world change, you may wonder how long you can keep up with it all.

The answer is, *you can stay on top indefinitely. If you know how to survive and work through the tough times, you can use change to enter an even brighter, more productive future.* I interviewed many who have done that already:

- In 1973, when Gertrude Crain's beloved husband died, she inherited Crain Communications, the largest independent trade-magazine publisher in the country. Since then Crain, as chairman, has sparked the company's growth from five to twenty-six publications, and from 100 to more than 1000 employees. Today, in her early eighties, Crain still works full time, and says, "I'm very happy with my life."
- Diagnosed with breast cancer just before the first season of "L.A. Law," Jill Eikenberry was terrified. But with the support of family and friends, she found the courage to go on. After her surgery, while filming the first episodes of the new show, Eikenberry capped each day's work with a trip to UCLA Medical Center for radiation treatments. Eikenberry recovered; "L.A. Law" became a hit.
- Harvey Mackay *created* positive change, turning a failing envelope company into a multimillion-dollar corporation; successfully led the campaign to build the Metrodome in Minneapolis; and wrote two bestsellers.
- After starring in Alex Haley's impressive and highly successful TV drama *Roots* at age nineteen, LeVar Burton became deeply depressed and had trouble finding work. But through commitment, humor, and optimism, plus therapy, Burton turned his life around. He went on to star in the popular television series "Star Trek: The Next Generation." Today, Burton says, he is the happiest he's ever been.

MASTERING THE WINDS OF CHANGE : THE PROGRAM

For many of us, handling change isn't easy. We need guidelines and tools to help us cope. This book provides them. You've probably heard of or used some of these strategies. Others, though, are new.

I was surprised by some of the techniques the peak performers recommended. These tools didn't appear in the literature—most books and research studies ignored them. I analyzed these strategies carefully and tested them at my seminars and with individual clients. Thus, *preparation, perspective,* and *learning from mistakes* became part of the 12 Steps.

THE 12 STEPS TO MASTERING CHANGE

1. View change as a challenge.
2. Build your commitment through goals and passion.
3. Stay committed when the going gets tough.
4. Know when to control, when to let go.
5. Deal with setbacks and go forward.
6. Be optimistic.
7. Use humor.
8. Learn from mistakes.
9. Maintain perspective.
10. Tune the body.
11. Build self-confidence.
12. Communicate effectively and . . . love.

A tall order? Not really. While writing this book, I've showed many people the essence of what the peak performers taught me. And those who have learned the skills find that they work—beautifully.

We *can* make important, positive changes in our lives. As T. George Harris, former editor-in-chief of *Psychology Today* and *American Health*, told me, "Research done in the last ten years shows our personalities are not stable—we go through important changes. The researchers in cognitive psychology are showing us that we create ourselves fresh every year, if not each day."

This is, Harris says, an enormously heartening view of the human condition, provided we avoid beating ourselves up for not changing enough or fast enough. So, as you create yourself anew, remember that it doesn't have to happen overnight.

But happen it will. In the course of writing this book, I've noticed dramatic changes in myself. When I was a kid, I hated change. I wanted life to be predictable. It seldom was.

Fourteen years ago, when I began working as a counselor and consultant, I focused on the topics I myself needed to work on—change and stress.

By the time I started researching this book, I knew a lot about handling pressure. After all, I'd been talking and writing about it for years. But something was missing. I still cared too much about what people thought of me. I worried more than necessary. And I sometimes fought change, even when there was nothing I could do about it.

Today my life is very different. The change has been a gradual process, but by applying the 12 Steps to Mastering Change I've become more confident, optimistic, and committed. I have more fun and communicate better. I even exercise more—at least five times a week. And when the inevitable setbacks come, I take them in stride.

I still have changes to make in myself, but the principles in this book have improved my life in real and important ways. Most importantly, I've learned an essential lesson from the peak performers I came to know—*how to find the opportunity hidden within every change*. And you can do the same, using the 12 Steps I explain in subsequent chapters.

YOU'VE GOT THE POWER

Just reading about the 12 Steps can help you feel better and accomplish more. And if you practice what you've learned, you'll make even more rapid progress.

Three elements are working for you throughout the book. The power of *stories, modeling,* and *motivation.*

The Power of Stories

Stories have immense power. Since the dawn of time, human beings have used tales to teach, entertain, and transmit beliefs and values. The best-selling book of all time, the Bible, contains hundreds of stories. Religious leaders of all faiths use parables, or teaching stories, to spread the word.

Of course, we have modern myths and stories, too. But many are negative. This book presents positive stories that help and heal. Throughout it, you'll read uplifting tales of people handling change effectively and making pressure work *for* them.

Recent research shows that the unconscious mind is more important than many had believed. Because stories influence us both consciously *and* unconsciously, they hold particular power.

The Power of Modeling

Another source of this book's power comes from something related to stories—*modeling*. Modeling is not hero worship. But in writing this book, I've dissected the peak performer's behavior so you can replicate it, if you choose.

How does an apprentice learn a craft? By first imitating the master, then going on to personal mastery. When we attempt to improve our skills, it's helpful to find someone who has already accomplished what we want to do.

Harvey Mackay, CEO of his own company and author of the

best-sellers *Swim with the Sharks Without Being Eaten Alive* and *Beware the Naked Man Who Offers You His Shirt,* believes in modeling. "If you want to be successful at handling stress and change, the best way to do it is to study other people," he told me. "Read about people who are successful. Find out what they did to get where they are."

To try modeling yourself, search for people who have done or are doing what you want to do. These role models don't have to be perfect. They need only do something better than you can. Watch and listen to what they say. Notice what they do. In short, stick with the winners.

While reading this book, you might also choose one or more peak performers with whom you closely identify. Pay special attention to what they say *and* what they've done. With the power of modeling, it could rub off.

The Power of Motivation

Top speaker, salesman, and author Zig Ziglar is doing what he loves best—speaking to a group of turned-on, pumped-up people. Trim, graying, and dynamic, Zig is all over the stage. For a moment he crouches, whispering. Then his voice rises to a shout. His eyes shine with conviction. The audience is transfixed. You can see it in their faces—they believe.

Dr. Forest Tennant, M.D., wondered if audiences actually *change* when they're listening to a motivator like Zig. Tennant is former drug adviser to the NFL and a professor at UCLA. To discover more about motivation, he analyzed the blood of five volunteers before and after listening to one of Zig's speeches. He found positive biochemical changes in all the subjects.

"There is a biochemical basis for why people feel good after these talks," says Tennant. "Something in hearing about success gives us an emotional charge that releases these chemicals into the bloodstream, and that makes the body function better."

Reading about success helps, too. University of Iowa psychologist and motivational expert Margaret Clifford says, "If books and tapes are well done, with solid principles based on psychological knowledge, they can be very effective."

Because even the strongest get discouraged sometimes, a dose of motivation can provide new inspiration. John Johnson, CEO of the vast Johnson Publishing Company, devoured self-help books as a kid, reading Napoleon Hill's *Think and Grow Rich,* Dale Carnegie's *How to Win Friends and Influence People,* and many others. He says they changed his life, helped him become more confident, self-assured, and effective.

Harvey Mackay also uses books for motivation. "I like self-help books," he says. "I like them on marketing, I like them on selling. I like the kind of book you're writing, Erik. I love to read about winners, successful people."

Ah, you say, but this motivation stuff must wear off eventually. Zig Ziglar agrees—it does. But, he says, the effects of bathing wear off, too. "Does that mean you should stop bathing, or does it mean that you should bathe every day?"

Ziglar, Johnson, and Mackay are successful, relaxed, and happy. They've filled their minds with motivation so they can reap the rewards.

Reading this book puts the power of motivation to work. That power can be reinforced by attending seminars, reading other self-help books, and listening to inspiring tapes. And the final chapter of this book reveals even more ways to keep your motivation level high.

THESE TOOLS WORK

Many people have already benefitted from the principles in this book. While writing it, I began presenting elements of the 12 Steps to Mastering Change in my speeches and seminars.

Mary is a manager with a big high-tech firm in northern California.* When I led a two-day seminar there, I talked with her before beginning the first day.

Mary told me she'd had difficulty dealing with change for years. Sometimes she handled transitions well, but at other times she became anxious, especially when major changes took place at the company. Then her voice shook and her hands trembled. Mary hid her anxiety, so most didn't notice, but she believed her problems with change were preventing her promotion at work. Mary also worried a lot. And when things went wrong at the office, she sometimes yelled at her kids when she got home—and felt terrible about it.

I told Mary that she might notice a difference after the seminar, and asked her to let me know of any positive changes she experienced.

Five months later, Mary sent me a letter. She wrote that after the seminar, she had put what she learned to work. She began reading books by successful people, including Mary Kay Ash and Eleanor Roosevelt. She spent more time with positive people and listened to inspiring cassette tapes.

---

*Names of noncelebrities have been changed to protect their privacy.

Mary said she also used three of the 12 Steps on a regular basis: commitment, optimism, and humor. She boosted her commitment by setting new goals, the most important of which was to learn to handle change and stress more effectively. Mary became more optimistic by changing the way she interpreted negative events (you'll learn to do this for yourself in Step 6). And she began emphasizing the lighter side of life and looking for the humor in situations that used to upset her.

In her letter Mary said, "I can't believe it. I feel much better. Somehow things just don't bother me so much any more. When there's lots of change, I usually feel good and confident and I know I'll do well. . . . People at work have said they notice a big change in me. And I'm up for a promotion now. I think I'll get it."

JUST DO IT

Mary isn't alone. Others have done what she did. You can, too. This is the starting point.

Throughout the book, there may be times when you may not like what I have to say. That's okay. I encourage you to take what you like and leave the rest. And you don't need to implement everything to profit from your reading. But if you choose to use even one strategy, the differences you'll begin to note in yourself can be amazing. As you read, remember this: *The power of stories, modeling, and motivation are working for you.*

And if you get discouraged, Harvey Mackay has a suggestion that may help: "When nothing seems to go right, think of a stone-cutter. He hammers away at a rock a hundred times without making a dent. Then, on the one hundred and first blow, the rock will split in two. It's not that one blow that did it, but all that had gone before. You have to hang in there tough, because one day, if you're practicing the right concepts, the rock will split."

While waiting for your particular rock to split, remember this old saying: "Success is a journey, not a destination." That's also true about managing change. Enjoy the journey.

NOTES

The Harris poll on stress was featured in "The Loss of Leisure," by Louis Harris, special to the *Sacramento Bee*, 9/28/87.

Studies on the unconscious mind were summarized in "In Search of the Unconscious Mind," by Kevin McKean, in *Discover*, February 1985.

3

Before You Read This Book

Perhaps you're struggling with a significant change or crisis right now and you need help quickly. If so, let's pause before moving into the *12 Steps for Mastering the Winds of Change*. Right now we'll discuss in brief some common transitions and problems that people struggle with, and I'll offer some quick tips for dealing effectively with them.

The tips that follow in "The First-Aid Primer for Dealing with Successful Change" are presented in alphabetical order, with references to a particular step (or steps) that will be helpful in coping with the problem.

To use this chapter most effectively, read the sections that are relevant for you and then move on to Chapter 4. In the long run, it's important to read *all* the steps. That way you'll greatly increase your ability to deal with nonstop change, now and in the future.

MAKE USE OF SUPPORT GROUPS

Support groups provide a tremendous opportunity for emotional first aid and ongoing support. The sections below mention several support groups. For more information about support groups in general, see steps 5 and 6. And if you want information about specific groups, call the American Self-Help Clearinghouse, at

(201) 625-9053. Volunteers at the Clearinghouse provide callers with information and referral to support groups all over the United States. They can also provide names and addresses for similar centers throughout the world.

In addition, many states have their own self-help clearing-houses, often available through a 1-800 number. To find these state organizations, ask 800 directory assistance for the number for the (state name) Self-Help Center.

A GOOD COUNSELOR CAN OFTEN HELP

Finally, if you still feel stuck after reading and using this book, working with a good therapist can often help. You'll find information on counseling in the last chapter.

A FIRST AID PRIMER FOR DEALING WITH STRESSFUL CHANGE

Accidents

After a traumatic accident, many people go into a state of physical shock. But even after the physiological shock has been taken care of and passed, emotional and mental shock may remain, leaving you feeling numb and dead inside.

To address the psychological wounds that accidents may create, focus on the following:

- After an accident, many people go through the stages of grief (see Step 5). Anticipating, understanding, and dealing with these stages helps us feel better sooner.
- If you're experiencing low moods or reduced energy, see the section on depression that follows.
- If you've recently had an accident, you'll benefit from learning about staying committed when the going gets tough (Step 3), and knowing when to control and when to let go (Step 4).

Adult Children of Dysfunctional Families

Did you grow up in a family where a parent or other caregiver had a problem with alcohol, drugs, food, sex, gambling, mental illness, or any other kind of compulsion or addiction?

Adults who grew up in a dysfunctional family situation of this kind generally have more trouble dealing with change and stress than those whose families were more stable. Adult children of dysfunctional families are also at increased risk for depression, anxiety, and compulsive behavior. If you grew up in a dysfunctional family, and you feel you're having problems in coping, these tips will help:

- Learn about when to control and when to let go (Step 4).
- Focus on becoming more optimistic (Step 6).
- Build your self-confidence (Step 11).
- Try attending a support group, like Adult Children of Alcoholics (ACOA) or Al-Anon. Both groups have chapters in most towns and cities. Look in the white pages of the phone book for more information. (ACOA is also open to adults who grew up in families where there were compulsions other than alcoholism.)

Anxiety/Panic

In our counseling practice, my associates and I work frequently with people suffering from anxiety, panic, and stress. When these clients first come to see me, they're usually very frightened. They tell me that their anxiety seems to have a life of its own. Yet stress, anxiety, and panic are readily treatable.

To teach yourself to handle anxiety or panic more effectively, focus on:

- Learning a deep relaxation technique (Step 9). Then, once you've learned the technique, practice it regularly. You'll teach your body and mind to react differently during times of stress.
- Reading and practicing Key #1: "Change Your Focus," in Step 4.

Also, though the two issues may seem unrelated, people suffering from panic attacks often report difficulties in their relationship with a spouse or lover. (Panic attacks are recurrent, unpredictable episodes of extreme fear and anxiety.) The relationship problems often predate the panic. Resolving the relationship problems through the techniques in Step 12, and/or through counseling, can help resolve the panic as well.

Anxiety can also stem from unresolved experiences from childhood. Counseling can help here, as can the journal writing technique described in Step 4, Key #8.

Career Change or Loss of Job

These days more and more people are dealing with career change—loss of a job, change in career, or perhaps a loss of interest in the type of work they're doing.

If you've lost a job, you're probably experiencing some of the following emotions: anger, sadness, grief, relief, happiness, fear, confusion. The best strategies for dealing with this transition are:

- Get support from others (Step 12).
- Focus on setting or revamping your goals (Step 2, especially the section on careers and career counseling).
- If you made any mistakes, deal with and release them (Step 8).
- Focus on staying committed and working through the setback, even though life may seem very difficult now (steps 3 and 5).
- Work on renewing or increasing your self-confidence (Step 11).

If your job has recently changed, you might focus on:

- Goal-setting to help you do what you want in the new position (Step 2)
- Becoming or remaining optimistic (Step 6)
- Having fun on your new job (Step 7)
- Building self-confidence (Step 11)

If you're bored with your job, or would just like to do something else, concentrate on:

- Researching to discover what you really love (Step 2)
- Figuring out what you *can* control and what you *can't* control on the job (Step 4)
- Boosting your optimism so you'll be ready to make the change (Step 6)
- Learning from any mistakes you may have made in choosing your current job (Step 8)
- Becoming more confident in yourself and your abilities (Step 11)

Chemical Dependency

According to the most conservative estimates, at least 10 percent of all Americans are dependent upon alcohol, drugs, or both.

If you have even a small suspicion that you might have a problem with one of these substances, or if anyone has told you they thought you did, the following information will help you:

- Focus on the issue of control (Step 4).
- Learn about the difference between healthy optimism and denial (Step 6).
- Consider attending a support group meeting. If you go, you can just observe and gather information to see if you really have a problem. You can contact Alcoholics Anonymous by looking in the white pages of the phone book. Most towns also have Narcotics Anonymous meetings available, geared to people who have a problem with drugs.
- Get more information about alcohol abuse by reading *Under the Influence,* by James Milam and Katherine Ketcham (Bantam Books, 1988).

Codependency

If you're close to someone who has a problem with alcohol, drugs, or one of the compulsions listed in the section after this, you're a codependent. In the belief they are helping, codependents often struggle to control the addict's behavior. Because controlling someone else is impossible, the codependent often becomes frustrated, anxious, and depressed. If you're codependent, here are a few ideas that will help:

- Read about control and lack of control (Step 4).
- Focus on maintaining your perspective (Step 9).
- Rebuild your self confidence (Step 11).
- Consider a support group, like Al-Anon, Nar-Anon, or Codependents Anonymous. (For more information about these groups, read Step 4, or contact one of the groups by looking in the white pages of the phone book.)
- Get further information by reading *Codependent No More* by Melody Beattie (Harper/Hazelden, 1987).

Compulsions and Addictions

Compulsions other than alcohol and drugs also create stress and make negative change more painful and frequent. Common compulsions include: compulsive overeating, sexual addiction, compulsive gambling, workaholism, and compulsive spending. If you think you might have one of these compulsions, or if you love someone who does, focus on:

- Learning about when to control, when to let go (Step 4)
- The difference between denial and optimism (Step 6)
- Learning to handle stress without resorting to the compulsive behavior (Step 9)
- Building self-confidence (Step 11)
- Finding a support group that focuses on your particular compulsive behavior—some options: Overeaters Anonymous, Gamblers Anonymous, Sex and Love Addicts Anonymous, Workaholics Anonymous, and Debtors Anonymous

Conflicts with Other People

Conflicts with friends, family, loved ones, bosses, and coworkers often cause us great stress. When significant transitions take place in our lives, clashes with other people may also occur. If you're having trouble with interpersonal conflicts, try one or more of the following:

- Talking it over with a friend, a religious guide, or a counselor
- Determining your values and purpose (Step 2)
- Maintaining your commitment to what you believe is right (steps 2 and 3)
- Writing about what is bothering you, and knowing when to let go (Step 4)
- Maintaining and building optimism (Step 6)
- Using humor to bridge the gap (Step 7)
- Learning from mistakes you may have made (Step 8)
- Keeping a healthy perspective on the situation (Step 9)
- Building self-confidence (Step 11)
- *Perhaps most important:* communicating effectively, setting limits, and becoming more loving (Step 12)

For conflicts with a spouse or lover, see the section on Relationship Problems, which follows later in this chapter.

Crime Victimization

If you've been the victim of a crime, you're undoubtedly dealing with tremendous stress, emotional pain, and perhaps physical pain. And coping with a crime also means struggling with profound changes in your life. If the crime occurred recently, the pain is probably acute. But even if the crime happened long ago, you may still be struggling with the negative ramifications of it. For first aid, try focusing on:

- Dealing with the setback, and concentrating on the process of recovery (Step 5)
- Regaining your optimism (Step 6)
- Getting a sense of perspective on the problem (Step 9)
- Renewing and expanding your sense of confidence (Step 11)
- Gathering more information by contacting the National Organization for Victim Assistance, 1757 Park Road NW, Washington, DC 20010. Phone: (202) 232-6682.

Death of a Loved One

The death of a loved one is perhaps the most stressful change a human being can suffer. Step 5 addresses in depth the issue of dealing with this type of transition and provides a model for effective recovery. In addition, the following support groups can help:

- For those who have lost a child, Compassionate Friends is a national support group with more than 600 local chapters. They offer information, referral, and support. Address: P.O. Box 3696, Oak Brook, IL 60522-3696.
- For those who have lost a spouse, the Widowed Persons Service offers information and referral to more than 230 chapters nationally. Address: 1909 K Street NW, Washington, DC 20049.

I once worked with a client whose uncle told her that crying at her father's funeral meant she was "being selfish." Nothing could be farther from the truth. When we allow ourselves to experience the grief and sadness, recovery comes more quickly. I often suggest to my clients that they write a letter to the loved one who died. In the letter, they focus on their feelings, both negative and positive, writing whatever occurs to them at the moment. Those who do this writing say that it helps them to deal with their grief and loss, and it provides a greater sense of completion with the loved one.

Depression

Depression can be the by-product of many changes. It also develops in some people when they've been coping with too much stress for too long. Several approaches help specifically with depression. They're found in steps 5, 6, 7, 9, and 11. In addition, regular exercise often alleviates depression (Step 10).

If, however, your depression is longstanding and severe, seeing a mental health professional is essential (see the Therapy section in Chapter 16.).

Many times, working with a good therapist will significantly alleviate depression. Sometimes, though, people who have been depressed a long time need medication in addition to therapy. That's because chronic depression can cause a change in brain chemistry. Antidepressant medication shifts the brain back to normal functioning, so that the depressed individual can work through his or her problems more readily. And taking this kind of medication doesn't mean staying on it forever. Most people take antidepressant medication for just six to twelve months.

Many antidepressant medications are available, and new ones are coming out each year. If you feel you might be a candidate for antidepressant medication, you'll need to go to a physician for assessment. Generally, a psychiatrist will prescribe this kind of medication, but some family doctors also do so.

If you wonder whether you're depressed, you can give yourself a quick assessment. When an individual has major depression, she/he will exhibit five or more of the following symptoms most of the time for at least two weeks:

- Decreased (or increased) appetite, sleep, or physical or mental activity
- Loss of energy
- Loss of interest in usual activities
- Guilt feelings
- Imparied thinking or concentration
- Indecisiveness
- Suicidal thoughts

Disasters

Fires, earthquakes, floods, accidents, and other disasters introduce enormously stressful changes into our lives. If you're coping with this sort of disaster, concentrate on the following:

- Keeping your commitment level up during the difficult time after the disaster (Step 3).
- Dealing effectively with the setback. (Step 5 tells how several peak performers dealt with severe setbacks, including a devastating fire.)
- Maintaining your sense of perspective when things look their worst (Step 9).

Divorce or Breakup of a Relationship

If you're dealing with a divorce, separation, or breakup, you may feel many of the same emotions experienced by a person whose spouse has died. To help yourself deal with this transition, center on the following:

- Reevaluating your direction and goals (Step 2)
- Learning to let go and accept (Step 4)
- Dealing effectively with the pain of this setback (Step 5)
- Learning from your mistakes (Step 8)
- Rebuilding your self-confidence (Step 11)
- If you have children, Parents Without Partners has 735 groups in the United States, providing support, information, and social activities. Write: 8807 Colesville Road, Silver Spring, MD 20910. Phone: 1-800-637-7974 or (301) 588-9354.

Recent research shows that trying to put your ex-partner out of your mind often makes you think of him or her more. Instead, express your thoughts and feelings by talking to someone else, or by writing about them (see Step 4, Key #8). That way you'll help the feelings resolve themselves and pass.

Family Problems (Children)

Because the family can be such a potent source of pleasure and support, family problems are particularly difficult to deal with. If you're having difficulties with your children, try one or more of the following:

- Read a good book on parenting. Most bookstores have an entire parenting section. Pick a book that looks right for you, after asking your bookseller's advice about a selection.
- Attend a parenting class (your county mental health center may sponsor such a class, or can give you a referral).
- If a child has problems in school, particularly with reading, have him or her evaluated by a specialist in learning disabilities. Your child's school or a local university or college can recommend a specialist, or contact the Learning Disability Association of America, 4126 Library Road, Pittsburgh, PA 15234. Phone: (412) 341-1515.
- Tutoring can also help a child get back on track at school. Look in the Yellow Pages of the phone book, under Tutoring.
- Children often manifest problems when their parents aren't getting along or there are other problems in the family. Kids are like little weather vanes—they point whichever way the wind is blowing. As famed psychiatrist Carl Jung said, "If there is anything that we wish to change in the child, we

should first examine it to see whether it is not something that could better be changed in ourselves."

- Try spending more time with the child. Even five minutes a day of loving attention can make a world of difference in a child's behavior.

Graduation

This is a positive change, right? Yes, but it's also very stressful. Prior to graduation, students often realize that they're not totally prepared for what comes next in their transition to adulthood, whether that is a job, job search, or more school. Graduation means significant change. To help ease the transition, center on:

- Knowing your passions and your goals (Step 2)
- Building your self-confidence (Step 11)
- Getting support from friends and family (Step 12)

You can also make use of counselors provided free of charge by most schools. (Also see the section on "Career Change or Loss of Job" above.)

Illness

A chronic or acute illness often changes our outlook on life. If pain is also part of the package, the discomfort can affect our mood, too. If your illness is chronic, seek support from others like you through a self-help group. (See the introduction to this section for directions on how to find such a group.)

For acute illnesses, time and patience are required for healing to take place. Unfortunately, when you're sick, patience seems to be in short supply. To help yourself with both chronic *and* acute illnesses, focus on:

- What you *can* control, and what you can't (Step 4)
- Dealing with the feelings that go along with this kind of a setback (Step 5)
- Maintaining your perspective through the tough times (Step 9)

Moving

If you've recently moved, or are about to, remember that it takes time to adjust to a new location. Most people report that it takes them one to two years to build a support system in a new place. You can hasten that process by joining groups in the new location. Check the local newspaper for clubs and other organizations that meet regularly. Doing volunteer work is another great way to meet new people and help yourself feel good at the same time.

You might also focus on:

- Staying optimistic about the change (Step 6)
- Keeping your sense of humor, which will also help draw new people to you (Step 7)
- Building your self-confidence so that you can reach out to others (Step 11)

And remember, even if the move is only across town, it can be stressful. Be gentle with yourself, and try to allow plenty of time to rest and adjust to your new surroundings.

Phobias

A phobia is a persistent, abnormal, or illogical fear of a specific thing or situation. Some phobias are minor and don't interfere with our lives. But if the phobia significantly changes the way you live—if, for example, you're afraid to leave your house, to use public transportation, or ride on an elevator—it's important to seek professional help.

Look for a therapist, psychologist, or psychiatrist who's experienced in dealing with phobias. (See the section on Therapy in the last chapter of this book.) Also, for information and referral, call or write the Anxiety Disorder Association of America, 6000 Executive Boulevard #200, Rockville, MD 20852. Phone: (301) 231-9350.

And if you have a phobia, remember that you're not alone. Millions of people suffer from phobic reactions. Many recover and go on to lead normal lives.

Pregnancy and Childbirth

Birth is a "blessed event," but pregnancy, delivery, and the weeks after a baby is born are often very difficult. Of all the transitions human beings go through, birth is one of the most profound, not only for the mother, but for the father and any siblings. If you're about to have a birth in your family, the following information will help:

- Attend a birthing education class early in your pregnancy. These classes help prepare you for the birth and teach techniques for making the birth less difficult. Your obstetrician can give you the names of classes in your area.

And, if you're about to give birth, or you recently did, bear these tips in mind:

- Practice strategies to remain committed in stressful or difficult circumstances (Step 3).
- Practice strategies for building and maintaining optimism and confidence (steps 6 and 11).
- Learn and practice a deep relaxation technique (Step 9).
- Talk to your physician about how to apply the exercise prescription in Step 10, so that you'll be stronger and healthier when you deliver and afterward.
- If possible, arrange to have someone available to help you after the birth. In Japan, where new mothers receive a great deal of attention and help, postpartum depression is nonexistent.

Relationship Problems

If you're having problems with a lover or spouse, the heartache can be profound. A few suggestions:

- The book *Getting the Love You Want* by Harville Hendrix, Ph.D. (Henry Holt, 1988) provides a framework for getting intimate relationships back on the right track.
- Couples counseling can also be very helpful. But what if one member of the couple won't go to counseling? I often get calls from wives who say, "My husband won't come to therapy." I suggest that the wife come in by herself. Often the husband will come later. And, even if he doesn't, when one person changes, the other usually does, too.
- Boost your self-confidence by reading Step 11.
- Improve your communication skills by reading Step 12.

For information on relationship problems with people other than a spouse or lover, see the section on "Conflicts with Other People," above.

Sexual or Physical Abuse

In my counseling practice, I've worked with many people who were sexually or physically abused as children or young adults.

When these clients come to see me, they're usually concerned about some issue other than the abuse. Some people don't even remember that the abuse occurred. Others deny the significance or extent of the abuse.

If you even *suspect* that you were abused as a child, you'll feel much better if you deal with the issue. Though it seems painful to dig it up, doing so will help you resolve it. Working with a good therapist can be very helpful, but make certain the counselor is experienced in dealing with physical and sexual abuse issues.

For those who've been sexually abused, concentrate on:

- Reading about the issue. For women, *The Courage to Heal* by Ellen Bass and Laura Davis (Perennial Library, 1988) is excellent. For men, *Victims No Longer* by Mike Lew (Perennial Library, 1990) is a fine resource.
- Survivors of Incest Anonymous is a support group for those who've been sexually abused by a family member, or by anyone whom they trusted. The address for SIA is: P.O. Box 21817, Baltimore, MD 21222. Phone: (301) 282-3400. Many areas also have a support group called Adults Molested as Children. Check your phone book or a local mental health center for information.

If you've been a victim of either physical *or* sexual abuse, focus on:

- Reading about control and lack of control in Step 4 of this book
- Increasing your optimism (Step 6)
- Building self-confidence (Step 11)

If you yourself have ever abused someone else, either sexually or physically, you're probably carrying a great deal of guilt and remorse, even if you're not aware of it. It's also likely that you yourself were abused as a child.

If you've practiced abusive behavior in the past, it's very important to deal with what you did, as well as with any abuse you may have suffered yourself. The best way to do this is to find a therapist who's experienced in dealing with these issues. Of, if you're not ready for that, try reading about the topic or attending a support group. For physical abuse, try Parents Anonymous, a group of parents who are, or fear they may become, abusive to their children. Address: 6733 South Sepulveda Boulevard, #270, Los Angeles, CA 90045. Phone: 1-800-421-0353.

For sexual abuse, try Sex and Love Addicts Anonymous or Sexaholics Anonymous. Both groups have chapters meeting in many communities. Or for more information, contact their national headquarters office:

- SLAA: P.O. Box 119, New Town Branch, Boston, MA 02258
- SA: P.O. Box 300, Simi Valley, CA 93062. Phone: (818) 704-9854

Therapy

See the section on therapy and counseling in the final chapter of this book.

4 STEP ONE

Viewing Change as a Challenge

"Some men see things as they are and say 'Why?'
I dream things that never were, and say, 'Why not?'"
—ROBERT KENNEDY

November 20, 1974. The U.S. Department of Justice sues AT&T, charging the giant corporation with monopolizing phone service in America. The suit demands that AT&T spin off its component companies.

Though the case isn't finally settled for years, AT&T's top brass know that whatever happens, changes in their business will be dramatic. They decide to reorganize the company. Mighty components, like Illinois Bell, discover they'll soon be on their own, struggling without the financial cushion of high long distance rates—fighting in a transformed marketplace.

With the reorganization beginning, executives at Illinois Bell face the daunting task of coping with a pressure-packed transition they can't yet fully understand. Some managers become depressed, others fall ill. They have come to rely on the status quo, and now there is none. They are adrift on a sea of change.

In the midst of this confusion, a group of researchers arrives at Illinois Bell, led by Suzanne Kobasa, a psychologist at the City University of New York. The scientists begin studying a group of Illinois Bell executives, seeking to discover why, when times are tough, some thrive and others don't.

After analyzing many variables, including income, religion, and job prestige, Kobasa makes a key breakthrough. She discovers that the executives who thrive in the dramatically changing work environment have three characteristics their collapsing colleagues lack. They:

1. Are **challenged** by change. They feel stimulated by stress and change.
2. Have a sense of **control.** They believe they can influence events around them.
3. Are **committed** to and intensely involved in what they are doing.

Kobasa calls these factors "hardiness." Other researchers label them "the three C's." Whatever the name, Kobasa realized that these traits are essential elements in handling pressure-packed change.

The executives who didn't have the three C's were stumped by the changes occurring at Illinois Bell. They suffered more illness, higher blood pressure, greater anxiety, and depression.

After Kobasa's study, other researchers extended her findings. Dr. George Solomon, studying long-term AIDS survivors at the University of California in San Francisco, discovered that they tend to fit Kobasa's definition of hardiness.

Researchers at Ohio State University Medical College found that, during exam time, hardy medical students have better immunity and less illness than do their classmates. And in a study at Rutgers University, college men who have the Type A behavior pattern (rushed, aggressive, and highly competitive) were asked to complete a frustrating task: tracing a line they could see only in a mirror. When hardy Type A's tried this task, they experienced a smaller rise in blood pressure than did the less hardy Type A's.

The accumulated research is clear: *Hardiness helps people cope effectively with change.* And, as you might expect, the peak performers I interviewed and surveyed for this book rate high in hardiness.

Thus the three C's make up the first three steps of the 12 Steps to Mastering Change. In this chapter, the peak performers reveal how they use **Step 1: View change as a positive challenge.** But first, a few words about how change can lead to stress.

FIGHT ... OR FLIGHT

In dangerous situations, the human body goes into a kind of overdrive, and we prepare to fight or run away. The following changes (and many others) take place:

- Heart rate rises.
- Blood pressure increases.
- Hands and feet become colder.
- Muscles tighten.
- Digestion ceases.

In primitive times, the fight-or-flight response was essential for survival. In modern life, though, this physiological response is often unnecessary. While presenting a proposal at an important meeting, it helps to be "up." But a thudding heart, trembling hands, and tense muscles won't do much for your credibility. And during an argument with a friend, cold hands and high blood pressure won't help you cope.

The fight-or-flight response is triggered by the hypothalamus, buried deep in the subcortex area of the brain. The hypothalamus is small, about the size of the tip of your thumb, but it's powerful. The hypothalamus helps regulate emotions, sex drive, and the fight-or-flight response.

When we fight change, the hypothalamus doesn't understand what we're resisting, it just knows there's a battle going on. It triggers the fight-or-flight response, and we're suddenly responding to change as if it's a matter of life and death. It seldom is.

If, instead, we view change as a positive challenge, the hypothalamus is less likely to trigger the fight-or-flight response. Thus, we deal more effectively with pressure.

WHY WE RESIST CHANGE AND WHAT TO DO ABOUT IT

Change and Loss

Many times we fight change, rather than riding easily into it, because we're afraid of losing something we care about, something familiar that seems more comfortable and less threatening than something new. And if you grew up in an unsettled or unsettling environment, where love and discipline weren't predictable, it's more likely you'll resist change and handle it less effectively than someone who grew up in a more stable environment.

At a young age, the child with a stable family, where he or she is loved and where appropriate limits are set for behavior, learns that someone will take care of his or her needs. This experience leads to confidence and self-sufficiency. The child—and later the adult—can risk change, for he or she feels secure, whatever the circumstances.

But even people who grew up in an unsettled environment can learn to view change as a challenge.

Problems and Promises of Change

Jack Lewis, chairman and CEO of the Amdahl Corporation, a major manufacturer of mainframe computers, helps his employees discover the positive benefits of change. That's not easy in the fast-changing computer industry. Lewis's company was started by industry legend Gene Amdahl, once the top computer designer at IBM. From the start, Amdahl successfully made mainframes that computed faster and cost less.

After stints at Xerox and IBM, Lewis joined Amdahl as president in 1977. He became CEO in 1983 and chairman of the board in 1987. Today Amdahl continues to challenge IBM. And Jack Lewis steers the company through the turbulent seas of change and competition. In 1988, Lewis beat IBM to the punch with a new product line. The biggest model, the 5990, outran anything Big Blue produced. Amdahl's revenues shot up—reaching over $2.16 billion per year in 1991.

I interviewed Lewis in his office on the second floor of one of Amdahl's buildings in Sunnyvale, California, where the company occupies more than ten city blocks. Tall, trim, and relaxed, Lewis was reserved at first. But when he talked about working with Amdahl's employees, his face lit up.

"I often tell our people that change is one of the great challenges of running a company. People don't like change. They like predictability, because it's comfortable. Yet in a fast-moving industry like this, change happens all the time. You've got to learn to live in that environment or you're in the wrong business."

COPING WITH CHANGE

Every change, even those that are negative, *presents an opportunity*. Thus change can be an ally—but only if we know how to take advantage of it. Unfortunately, most of us aren't trained to deal with the ups and downs of life. This section covers eight specific strategies peak performers take to harness change as a positive force for success.

First, though, a word of warning. Be careful not to overdo. Some people become addicted to change and the adrenaline generated by struggling to meet a challenge. That, obviously, isn't healthy for mind and body.

The key is balance. We must view change as a challenge, without becoming addicted to it.

Remember the Three Phases of Change

My wife and I had just moved from San Francisco to Auburn, California, a small town in the foothills of the Sierras. After planning the move for years, we found a fine house surrounded by oaks and meadows. It was beautiful—trees, birds, quiet. But I felt sad and confused. And the sadness wouldn't go away.

What was wrong? Through getting what we wanted, we'd lost things, too. We missed walking down the street for ice cream, watching the symphony in the park, and riding the trolleys. As with any change, we had to let go of something to have a new beginning.

William Bridges, author of the book *Transitions: Making Sense of Life's Changes*, believes that there are three steps in dealing with change.

The first step is **letting go or ending.** In any change, something is lost. So, whether the change is positive or negative, we must make peace with the past. Often this involves a time of sadness or mourning as we let go of something we once had.

The second step is the **transition.** Author Bridges also calls transition the "neutral zone or wilderness." In this stage, we often feel the worst. Direction seems to be gone—we're lost and floundering.

In some societies, people spent the transition step in the wilderness. Native Americans would go to the forest to "cry for a vision" of what they were to do with their lives. Rather than fighting the transition, they used it.

But in our instant pill-for-every-ill society, many of us don't want to deal with the prolonged anxiety and confusion inherent in transition. We want everything to be neat, clean, and settled. This stage *can't* be. *To make a new beginning, we must travel through the wilderness of transition.*

But transitions may not be as chaotic as they seem. Scientists are discovering order in chaos. Over the past decade, a new discipline called "nonlinear dynamics" has developed, originally as a way to understand the unpredictability of the weather. Scientists in this field believe there is often an important pattern within seeming disorder. A systematic search can pinpoint the pattern.

Similarly, in the transition phase we search for the meaning in change.

That doesn't mean it is easy. Ann Spaller, an employee assistance representative for Pacific Bell, often counsels employees who are struggling with transitions in their lives. She reminds them that some negativity and anger are normal in this stage, and can be expected.

As Rosebeth Moss Kanter, author of the book *The Change Masters* (Simon & Schuster, 1983), says, "Every change looks like a failure in the middle." Because it's so confusing, we often experience the most pain during the transition stage. Yet the pain and confusion are leading, bit by bit, to a new beginning.

In taking the third step, we're finally able to **start something new.** This can be frightening, enlightening, or a mixture of both.

When dealing with change, most of us want to begin again immediately. But we must first release the old and spend time in the wilderness of transition. As a farmer friend of mine says, "It's in a fallow time that the field becomes fertile." And we only get to new beginnings at the end.

Lillian Vernon, founder and CEO of the world famous mail order catalog company that bears her name, has dealt with the three phases of change all her life. When Lillian was twelve, her parents left their home in Leipzig, Germany, hoping to escape the growing influence of the Nazi party. Their move triggered a painful *letting go* process, as they mourned the loss of friends and family back in Germany. "It was very difficult leaving our friends and moving to someplace where we didn't speak the language," Vernon says today.

Lillian's family moved first to Holland, undergoing a profound *transition* from 1933 until 1937, as they struggled to adapt to their rapidly changing world. "It was very difficult," she says. "The stress in the family, making a living in the new country."

Finally, when war broke out in Europe, the family made a *new beginning* by moving to New York City. I asked Vernon what that first day in America was like for her. She said she preferred not to talk about it. "It's not because I'm sad," she told me. "It's just that those are very poignant memories for me. It's nothing bad— it really is a lovely, sweet, warm memory that I think I'd like to keep to myself," Vernon said, obviously moved.

Later in our interview, Vernon summed up her perspective on change. "We all change," she said. "It is the natural progression of life and business."

And an essential key to handling that natural progression is understanding the three phases of change. As Vernon says, "I love my work and understand that there are times when it's tough, but they always pass. I never let setbacks defeat me. I don't view a problem as a problem, but as a challenge to my ingenuity and creativity."

STRATEGY 2

Remember—This Too Shall Pass

Paula Kent Meehan, founder chairman and CEO of the beauty products company Redken Laboratories, Inc., also knows that tough times eventually pass. Like Vernon, Meehan has dealt with profound life transitions, some of them painful, some not.

Originally a model and actress (she played the hatcheck girl in television's "77 Sunset Strip"), Meehan couldn't find beauty products that worked well with her fair hair and sensitive skin. Figuring that there were other women with similar problems, Meehan began studying hair and chemistry, reading everything she could find on the topics.

Then in 1960, Meehan took $3,000 that she'd earned from appearing in a Hamm's beer commercial and started Redken. Leasing a 3,000-square-foot warehouse in Los Angeles (the landlord later told her he didn't expect she'd last a year), Meehan hired a food-and-drug consultant and began making Redken's first shampoos.

From the beginning, the company sold beauty products only in professional salons, with Meehan traveling the country to promote Redken and her new scientific approach to hair care. The first year the company sold $90,000 worth of shampoo, the next year $300,000. Redken continued expanding rapidly, with annual sales going over $150 million in 1991.

But the growth wasn't always smooth. Meehan told me about what she calls "the most difficult" time in her life.

"Back in 1986, Redken had never known a difficult year. Year after year, we'd had huge sales increases. But at that time, we hadn't been aggressively marketing new products. And our administrative staff was too large."

Redken's sales volume stopped growing for the first time. Meehan wondered if the company had grown stagnant. Then the other shoe dropped. Doctors told Meehan's husband, John, chairman of Redken's board of directors, that he'd have to have triple bypass surgery. And business problems continued to multiply.

"We had to drop our largest distributor, someone I was very

close to, because he just wasn't doing the job. To top it all off, I had recently hired a new company president, and he didn't work out. So I had to let him go."

The combination of stressors made Meehan's life seem like purgatory. I asked her what she did to get through that time. "First, I worked a lot of hours, trying to get things back on track. Second, I quit smoking. I had to have all my energy, and couldn't let cigarettes drain me. And I had a belief that 'This, too, shall pass.' I had to believe that."

So Meehan repeated that key phrase to herself, striving to keep her thoughts positive as she struggled to handle the profound changes occurring around her.

And the bad times *did* pass, though Meehan also took action to make positive changes happen. "I took the company private," she says, "because I felt that was one of the solutions to getting the spirit, productivity, and achievement orientation of the staff back." As part of this process, Meehan made thirty-two key employees shareholders. That, she says, gave the company back its entrepreneurial spirit. Sales volume grew significantly. And thankfully, her husband's surgery was successful.

Today Redken and Meehan are more prosperous than ever. When I interviewed her, she and her husband were preparing to leave for a vacation in Cannes, France, where they planned to relax aboard their yacht.

STRATEGY 3

Ask—What Can I Change in Myself?

When stressful change occurs, we often blame outside circumstances for our feelings. We forget the importance of our reaction to the change. The way we interpret an event dictates how well we handle it in the long run.

Ellen Gordon is president of Tootsie Roll Industries, a company picked by both *Forbes* magazine and *CFO* magazine as one of the fifteen best small companies in America. Gordon says that when uncomfortable changes take place, we can benefit from them. "Yes, sometimes things don't go right," she told me. "But then I ask myself, 'What can I learn from this?' And usually I realize that the change has expanded me in some way."

Sometimes, though, the expansion hurts. In 1977, an unknown nineteen-year-old student from the University of Southern California starred in the hit television miniseries *Roots*. After playing the role of Kunta Kinte, a defiant African slave, actor LeVar Burton found his life changed overnight.

With his name suddenly a household word, young Burton told a reporter, "From now on, I don't think I'll have any problems in this business." He soon came to realize how wrong his statement was.

For several years, Burton did build on his *Roots* success, appearing on talk shows and acting in a few movies. He earned lots of money but spent most of it on friends, family, women, fast cars, and big houses.

"I was very impulsive," he now says. Eventually Burton's career cooled off, and he had trouble finding work consistently. At first he took it personally and wondered if it had to do with "the color of my skin." But whatever the outer causes, Burton was also in trouble inside. Though he'd made significant achievements, he was miserable.

"I was the picture of an unhappy guy. I forgot who I was, where I was, and what I was doing. There were so many distractions—fame, money, energy. I was out of balance with myself and my higher purpose."

That higher purpose had been very important to Burton earlier in his life, when he went into a Catholic seminary. Although he eventually decided not to become a priest, spirituality remained important to him. But in the gloomy days after *Roots* he lost touch with the spirit within him.

Then, in 1983, Burton found a new sense of purpose when he became host of "Reading Rainbow," the now highly successful PBS children's program. His love for kids and reading made it a natural move. But he still hadn't hit bottom.

"I was in a relationship with a woman who really loved me, but I sabotaged the relationship," he told me. "And then, when I had pushed her out of my life, it made me stop and think.

"I said to myself, 'I want to love and be loved in a relationship. And I've just blown a tremendous opportunity to experience exactly what I keep saying I want.'" Burton realized that he'd been running for a long time. "I ran from relationships, ran from intimacy, ran from myself."

The loss of his relationship became a catalyst for the actor to examine himself and his life. He began seeing a therapist to try to unravel the knot of his life. And he focused on his body, too, undergoing the intense muscle manipulations of Rolfing, a type of body work that emphasizes aligning the body and releasing emotional blockages.

Burton's transformation didn't come easily—it required years of effort. But over time, he began feeling better about himself and his life.

"At first I beat myself up for the mistakes I'd made. But eventually I got a larger perspective. I learned that everything happens for my greater good, no matter what it feels like at the time. Now I remember that *whatever happens is an opportunity for me to grow*. That makes everything easier to handle."

As Burton grew happier inside, his outer life became better, too. In 1986, he landed a starring role on "Star Trek: The Next Generation," playing Geordi LaForge, the blind engineer of the starship *Enterprise*. Burton was ecstatic—it was just the kind of role and the type of series he'd wanted. The critics praised his work on the show.

Today "Star Trek: The Next Generation" is a success, "Reading Rainbow" continues to delight both children and adults, and Burton is very different from the scared kid who ran from the world after *Roots*.

When I finally met the new, improved LeVar Burton, he had just finished shooting a "Star Trek" scene with Whoopi Goldberg. We're inside the huge building on the Paramount Studios lot that houses the "Star Trek" sets. Actors clad in Federation uniforms rehearse a scene in the background.

An assistant helps Burton out of his "Star Trek" tunic and into a brightly patterned silk shirt. The actor and I walk to his trailer just outside the building. As we begin our interview, Burton leans toward me, intense and full of energy. "I'm really happy these days," he says with a grin, his eyes flashing. "I'm pleased with the work I have done. I know who I am. And I've learned to love this person," he says, pointing to himself.

Burton tells me he now understands that courage is an essential element in handling change. "There have been many times I've been afraid of change. But I've learned not to let my fear paralyze me. In fact, I've discovered that when I'm fearful of something, that's an area I need to pay attention to," he says, spreading his arms wide and smiling.

"When I was younger, I took fear as a sign that it was time to get out of the kitchen—it was too hot. Today I experience fear as an ally, creating a tremendous opportunity to grow."

As I listen to Burton, I realize that this is a man who has made peace with himself. Not that he's always peaceful—his energy level is too high for that. But through pain, hard work, and courage, he has come to accept himself and the changes in his life.

LeVar Burton discovered that running away doesn't make transitions any easier. He learned to stop running and face himself and examine and learn from his fears. In so doing he transformed his life, and made his inside experience match the material blessings he enjoys in his life and work.

STRATEGY 4

Turn the Challenge Positive

Comedian, writer, and musician Steve Allen is a striking example of someone who knows how to weather change by making problems positive. In the late 1940s, Allen hosted a popular music-talk show on radio station KNX in Los Angeles.

Allen told me about the time Doris Day was scheduled for a twenty-five-minute segment on his show. She never arrived. But Allen turned potential disaster into a crowd pleaser.

"I was new in the business then," he said, "so it was a serious problem. I had nothing planned. I was in big trouble. These days I would welcome that happening, because now I know how to work with disasters. But then I was uncomfortable and disappointed. Doris Day was a very important figure and a marvelous singer. It turned out later she had never known she was booked on the show, so it wasn't her fault.

"In any event, I couldn't sit there and indulge my emotions. I had no announcer. There was no one but myself to take over, so I just kept talking. The only other thing I might have done was play the piano for half an hour."

Then Allen had a brainstorm. To turn the challenge positive, he moved out into the audience for spontaneous chats.

"I grabbed the old-fashioned heavy stand-up 'mike,' the kind you see in old pictures, and carried it around talking to people in the audience. There were smaller hand mikes available, but I didn't have one. Fortunately, that big heavy mike looked so dumb that I got some side laughs and funny comments."

Allen's solution was a hit and became a regular part of his radio and, later, television shows. Steve Allen transformed an embarrassing moment into what became one of his trademarks. He did it by thinking fast and taking a risk. Today Jay Leno, Oprah Winfrey, Phil Donahue, Arsenio Hall, and other talk show hosts frequently go out into the audience, a successful adaptation of Steve Allen's original idea.

Something unexpected also happened to another of the peak performers I interviewed—entertainer Art Linkletter—when he was on live television. Years ago, Linkletter spoke at the Emmy

Awards, before a nationwide audience. As he began, "Good evening, ladies and gentlemen," the master light switch blew up, creating total darkness in the auditorium. Frantic stage hands began trying to repair the problem. In the process the great Grecian stage set was knocked over. Columns, facades, and walls toppled into the orchestra. Part of the orchestra's string section was buried under a huge cardboard pillar.

When the lights came back on, Linkletter looked over the mound of debris and said, "For an encore, ladies and gentlemen, we will now set fire to Lucille Ball."

The audience laughed, the crew relaxed, and a potentially disastrous moment passed.

Art Linkletter and Steve Allen are alchemists. They transform problems into opportunities. And though they're especially good at working this kind of magic, it's an approach any of us can use.

STRATEGY 5

Convert Fear to Energy

The Ferrari roared into view, drifting perfectly into the turn, then accelerating to over 180 miles per hour. The driver passed one car after another. Her polka dot helmet bobbing, she took the checkered flag and won the race grinning.

The Ferrari's driver? Denise McCluggage—race car driver, journalist, skier, and lover of challenges. McCluggage has a unique way of dealing with change and fear it generates. "I use fear for energy," she told me. "There's nothing like a good dose of it to clear the cobwebs and organize your directions."

McCluggage has been creating energy for years. In 1947, she began working as a reporter for the *San Francisco Chronicle*, the only woman on staff. Because of the then strong prejudice against women reporters, her editor had to hide her when the boss came through the newsroom.

Later McCluggage worked for the *New York Herald Tribune*. While in New York, she met Briggs Cunningham, renowned car builder and racer. He helped her get started in her first race, driving a Jaguar convertible.

"Were you scared?" I asked McCluggage. "I sure was," she said. "But I really wanted to race, so I practiced turning the fear into energy. I had a *lot* of energy that first race," she said, laughing.

I asked McCluggage how she converts fear to energy. "You use body thinking," she said. "First, of course, you have to study hard and practice the sport, or whatever skill you wish to use. Then, once your body knows how, you, the mind, must get out of the way and allow it to operate."

"How do you do that?" I asked.

"It is a centering process," McCluggage said. "When something faces me that is dangerous or needs an immediate response, I've learned to center automatically. I push my breath deeper into my gut, and I think of centering my energy in my stomach."

The centering served McCluggage well. Ferrari builder Luigi Chinetti saw the journalist drive and offered to support her new career.

McCluggage quickly became one of the finest women drivers in the world—some called her the best in the nation. And McCluggage didn't just race with women. Many of her races were against the finest male drivers—racing legends like Juan Manuel Fangio, Stirling Moss, and Phil Hill, among others.

Today, McCluggage edits, writes, and consults for several magazines and pens a syndicated newspaper column called "Drive, She Said." She still drives in vintage car races and travels the world, covering automobiles and racing.

Now gray-haired but feistier than ever, McCluggage continues transmuting fear to energy, whether she's in her cozy office or driving the globe. "Instead of walling off your energy, let it flow," she says. "People who wall off their fears dissipate energy. I use the word *excitement* instead of fear. It's a more positive word."

Professional speaker and former NFL referee Jim Tunney agrees, but he puts it another way. "Back in 1960, when I first began working as an NFL referee, I got pretty nervous. But soon I realized that I could look at my feelings differently. I began to see the anxiety as excitement. I'd say to myself, 'This is going to be an exciting football game.' For me, anxiety is excitement. And making that mental shift has helped me handle pressure much better."

Tunney's excitement also helped him become successful. In 1989, the *Detroit Free Press* surveyed five hundred pro sports players, coaches, general managers, and media personalities. They name Tunney the best official in pro football. And this was after he had already achieved success as a school superintendent earlier in his life.

Everyone feels anxious when coping with change. But some allow that fear to defeat them. Denise McCluggage, Jim Tunney, and other peak performers have a different perspective. They think of the fear as energy and excitement and use it as fuel to do what they most desire.

And many times, fears and worries aren't a big deal anyway. Researchers at the University of Michigan studied "what people worry about." They found that of these worries:

- 60 percent were unwarranted (there was really nothing to worry about).
- 20 percent were already resolved.
- 10 percent were petty.
- 10 percent were legitimate concerns, but only 2 percent were about significant issues.

Gertrude Crain makes short work of worries. As chairman of the board of prestigious Crain Communications, Inc., she is one of the world's premier business periodical publishers, issuing twenty-six business periodicals, including *Advertising Age* and *Automotive News*. Crain deals with plenty of pressure, but she doesn't let it get to her.

"I don't worry unnecessarily," she told me. "I look at the brighter things of life and don't worry about what bad things are going to happen." Avoiding worry helps Gertrude Crain stay healthy and master change. In her early eighties now, she looks years younger. So much so that, in 1984, *Forbes* magazine reported that Crain was "in her sixties," when she was really seventy-three.

Next time *you* feel frightened about a challenge, avoid wallowing in worry. Instead, ask yourself, "Am I scared or excited?" You may call it fear but, if you're like most people, the fright has a large amount of excitement within it. Put that energy to work.

―――――――――――――― **STRATEGY 6** ――――――――――――――

Analyze the Situation

The store telephone rings . . . again. The young clerk answers, "Good afternoon, Waldenbooks, may I help you?"

Crackling over the phone line, a voice growls, "A bomb is planted in your store. It will go off at exactly 2:00 P.M. Get that devil Rushdie's book out." Then the line goes dead. Her face a mask of fear, the clerk relays the message to her store manager, who calls the district manager immediately. Soon the phone rings at the Stamford, Connecticut, office of Waldenbooks' then president and CEO Harry Hoffman. "We've got another bomb threat, Harry," his secretary says quietly.

The date is February 12, 1989. Days earlier the Ayatollah Khomeini, spiritual leader of Iran, offered a $5-million reward for the death of Salman Rushdie, author of the book *Satanic Verses*. Much of the Moslem world believes the book is blasphemous, that it defiles the name of Mohammed.

Throughout the United States, bookstores are picketed, employees threatened, bomb threats received. In Berkeley, California, a fire bomb is thrown through the front window of a Waldenbooks store. And a bomb blast partially destroys another bookstore on the same street.

Harry Hoffman faces a challenge. As CEO, he has helped make Waldenbooks one of the top book sellers in the nation. Now his stores, employees, and customers are threatened. An ex-FBI agent, Hoffman knows the power of terrorism. Thus, on February 16 he orders *Satanic Verses* taken from the shelves. Managers hold the books in the back of the stores. They're available by request.

Immediately publishers and writers pressure Hoffman to display the book. He's caught in the middle, torn between his desire to protect the safety of employees and customers and his belief in the First Amendment. When I interviewed him, Hoffman told me how he made a challenging decision.

"Late that afternoon, I said, 'The first thing we've got to do is take it off the shelf until we find out what this is all about.' We continued selling it, but held the books in the storerooms. Then, after the newspapers reported our action, we got a lot of flak. I sent a message to the stores, telling them they had the option of displaying the book if they chose to.

"I agonized over this, but think in retrospect that we handled it correctly. I carefully weighed all the information that had come in, yet part of my action was intuitive. And being able to relax under pressure, in the midst of change, was a big part of solving this, and other problems.

"We ran a full-page newspaper ad the next Monday in many major papers. We stated our position explicitly: (1) We have never stopped selling *Satanic Verses*. (2) If the books are not in our stores now, it's because the publisher is out of stock. (3) We will display the book with the safety of our staff and customers in mind. (4) We support the First Amendment. And (5) we admire our brave young people who are exposed to this kind of threat."

Reactions to Hoffman's decision varied. Some of the early letters sent to his office were attacks, occasionally vicious. Then the nature of the mail changed. Most later letters were supportive—

some from employees, grateful that they were protected and given a choice about their own welfare.

Harry Hoffman faced a critical decision in the face of a crisis. He analyzed the factors involved and made a decision, one which in hindsight appears correct. And Waldenbooks emerged stronger than ever from a stressful situation.

Stanley Marcus, former chairman of the board of Neiman-Marcus, told me, "I frequently reappraise situations. I say to myself, 'Is this something where I can effect change by any reasonable action?' If I can, then I try to do it. I figure out what the odds are, and act accordingly."

The Serenity Prayer, used often by members of Alcoholics Anonymous, says much the same thing:

> God grant me the serenity,
> To accept the things I cannot change,
> Courage to change the things I can,
> And the wisdom to know the difference.

When you're in the midst of change and transition, follow the example of Marcus and Hoffman and analyze the situation. Determine the direction you'd like to take. Is it possible and realistic? If it's not, let go. If you believe in God, release the problem to the God of your understanding. If you don't have that kind of spiritual belief, release it symbolically, perhaps by writing it on a piece of paper. Then tear up the paper, letting the problem go.

If you decide your direction or goal *is* possible, you may also want to ask for spiritual help. Or, if that's not your way, ask your unconscious mind for help in marshalling your resources. Then— *go for it.*

───────────────── **S T R A T E G Y   7** ─────────────────

Think Clearly, Act Calmly

Famed flyer Chuck Yeager has little faith in most pilots. He believes only a few have the "right stuff." But Bob Hoover gets Yeager's approval. The two worked together as test pilots in the Air Force, and later flew in air shows all over the world.

Today Hoover is an aviation company executive, and he's still a frequent flyer at air shows. His office, located on the south side of Los Angeles International Airport, features a big map of the United States studded with pins. Each marker shows the site of an upcoming air show. As we talked, he sometimes looked out at airplanes taking off from LAX.

Tall and lanky, Hoover seems as relaxed as Jimmy Stewart. He speaks with a Tennessee drawl, pausing between thoughts, always polite and straightforward. If you don't know, you'd never guess he's one of the hottest pilots in the world. Hoover told me how he calmly handled a crisis situation.

"About three years ago, I was performing in an air show in Columbus, Ohio. Right in the middle of the performance, I lost my air speed indicator. That didn't bother me much, except that I had a strong cross wind, and I thought, 'I'll have to be on my toes to handle this.'

"About that time I started smelling wires burning. I saw some smoke and looked outside. The whole airplane was on fire behind me. I made it around the traffic pattern and picked up the downwind leg and realized that the fuel tank had ruptured."

"When I dropped the landing gear, that pumped in all kinds of air. So the flames moved up the fuel stream and the whole wing became a blowtorch. I could feel the heat on my face when I turned to land."

Hoover knew he was in trouble, but he planned his actions and kept his cool under fire. "I landed and took the plane off the runway. It was burning like you can't believe. But the fire trucks had been called, and they had that fire out in a minute and forty-two seconds. It seemed to me like about three hours.

"I had fifty gallons of 100 octane fuel that was in another tank, right next to the one that was burning, plus three high-pressure oxygen bottles. That's the biggest bomb you could ever think about, oxygen and gasoline. The tanks expanded and when they put them in the lab they quickly exploded. So time had truly been of the essence."

In his autobiography, Chuck Yeager tells of another opportunity for clear thinking—the time Hoover's engine failed during a flight. Hoover landed the plane by bouncing it off the roof of an automobile so he'd make it over a fence and back to the airfield. With characteristic modesty, Hoover told me the story was true, but that the car just happened to be along his flight path—he had no choice but to nudge it.

"I didn't bounce off anything really. The nose gear hit the top of the car right above the windshield. It didn't hurt the fella that was driving it."

Hoover got the airplane onto the landing field, though it hit hard enough to break up. The firemen had to chop him out.

How can you master clear thinking and calm action for yourself? One way, obviously, is to learn to fly. Each of the pilots I interviewed insisted flying was an excellent way to boost self-confidence and the ability to handle change. But if you'd rather keep your feet on the ground, what else is available?

- Purposely put yourself in situations that require quick thinking under pressure. These might include a sport (skiing, basketball, tennis); challenging volunteer work; learning a new skill (playing a musical instrument, dancing); or even playing a difficult board game.

  Many business executives now attend outdoor "challenge" courses where they learn to survive in the wilderness, or practice demanding activities like rock climbing or canoeing through river rapids.
- Practice deep relaxation or meditation. These activities improve concentration, clarify thinking, and promote a balanced response to change and pressure. Step 9 explains a simple, effective relaxation strategy.
- Mentally rehearse an upcoming challenge. Experienced truck drivers often plan their potential response to danger. As they approach an intersection, they imagine what they'd do if a car ran the red light. This helps the driver act quickly if needed.

  To try your own mental rehearsal, close your eyes and imagine yourself performing well under pressure.
- *Respond positively*, rather than just reacting. When change is taking place, avoid a knee-jerk response. Instead, *pause* (unless, of course, you're in a situation that requires instant action). Ask yourself, "What can I do here that will be most effective?" Then act. Even if there's no time to pause, talk yourself through the situation, mentioning each step you must take, so that you act calmly and avoid overreacting.

As you practice these strategies, remember that a cool reaction to change stems partly from experience. Gain that experience, then aid it with imagination. By so doing, you'll build your ability to convert change to success.

STRATEGY 8

Seize the Opportunity

George Bernard Shaw once said, *"The people who get on in this world are the people who get up and look for the circumstances they want, and, if they can't find them, make them."*

Change brings with it tremendous opportunity—*if* we're able and willing to take advantage of the opening. Hockey superstar Wayne Gretsky says, "I skate to where the puck *is going to be*, not to where it has been."

The will to win is fierce in those I interviewed. As I talked to two of them, Gene Perret, a top television producer, speaker, and comedian, and Harry Hoffman, whom you met earlier in this chapter, I realized they've taken risks that helped them have richer, happier lives. In the process, they learned to handle change more effectively, too. Here are their stories.

Harry Hoffman

Consultant and author Harry Hoffman, former president and CEO of Waldenbooks, has been successful partly because he looks for challenges and then seizes the opportunity a challenge carries. His ability to handle change has grown as he has.

Hoffman is in his mid-sixties but looks younger (as do many of my interviewees who have learned to master change). He has an athletic build, due to years of aerobic exercise and weight-lifting. He's friendly, outgoing, and thoughtful. After graduating from college, Hoffman took a job with the FBI. For three years he did criminal investigations and domestic security work. But the pay was low and the hours long.

To earn more and have more time with his family, Hoffman took a risk. He went to work for Proctor & Gamble, selling cleanser and Crisco.

"In sixty days I had gone from carrying a gun to carrying soap. I started making calls on small grocery stores in upper Manhattan, part of Harlem, and it was a tough experience. I had trouble coming off the clouds after the FBI, thinking, 'I'm really a big shot.' And then here I am going down into terrible rat-infested places, carrying a box of soap and dealing with people who weren't very happy to see me in the first place. It started to gnaw at me, and I got an ulcer. But I stayed with it for four years, and got promoted in the meantime.

"Wanting to get out of that situation was a powerful motivator. I tried to improve myself constantly so I didn't have to keep going out to stores and pounding on the doors."

When he left the pressure of P&G, Hoffman's ulcer cleared up. In the years that followed, the risk he'd taken paid off. He learned to handle change more effectively as he worked at several other companies. But Hoffman wanted to run his own outfit.

In 1968, he joined the Tennessee Book Company, now called

Ingram. The company was a small, struggling wholesaler of library and school books. Soon promoted to VP and general manager, Hoffman began expanding Ingram's market by selling to bookstores. Sales went to $1 million that year.

The company was doing well, but in 1972, Hoffman took another chance and seized an opportunity no one else saw.

"I was visiting publishers and I saw a guy using microfiche for accounts payable. I thought, 'It would be wonderful if we could provide our wholesale customers with a weekly microfiche of our inventory. We could provide them with a microfiche reader, and they could call us and order books.

"I met with a lot of opposition. Over the years, any time that I had a new idea, most people didn't want to do anything with it. We had to buy two hundred machines and, being a small company, that was a big investment.

"But we did the program. Six weeks elapsed from the time I had the idea to its introduction in the stores. I took the first machine out on the road myself and showed it to a few retailers. They had to pay $125 a year for the service, which was unique at that time.

"By the time we were through we had ten thousand retailers subscribing. It led to a lot of wonderful things. But initially it was tough convincing people it was going to be a good move."

When Hoffman left Ingram in 1978, it had grown a hundredfold, becoming a $100-million company. Today it's the biggest wholesaler in book publishing. Ingram is successful because Hoffman took risks, even when the conventional wisdom might have said to play it safe. Rather than avoiding challenge, he looked for it and searched for ways to make *positive* changes.

"Sometimes I didn't know as much as I thought I did. But I remained positive about things and kept trying new approaches. I'm not hesitant to take risks. I think it's exciting to try something new to see if it works.

"If something does fail, I don't feel badly about it. I may regret it, but I just say, 'Well, you learn from it and you go on and do something else.' I think that it's important for young people to take risks. So many people, of any age, are afraid to."

In 1991, Harry Hoffman retired from Waldenbooks to start what he calls his "second career"—sailing. Though he still works part-time as a consultant in the publishing and bookselling industries, Hoffman devotes much of his time to sailing his fifty-four-foot ketch.

Nor has Hoffman become frightened of change and risks. He plans to sail around the world sometime in the next few years.

Until that time, he's writing a "how-to" book on thriving in the corporate world.

Gene Perret

Another peak performer, Gene Perret, has produced hit television shows like "Three's Company," "Welcome Back Kotter," and the "Tim Conway Show." He's won three Emmy awards and is Bob Hope's head writer. Perret is also a hilarious speaker and comedian. But at one time he didn't do any of these things. Perret was an engineer at General Electric.

After one of his recent speeches, Perret and I took time out for an interview in the lounge of the Sacramento Hyatt, where he'd been speaking to the local chapter of the National Speakers Association. He told me how he took risks at GE and elsewhere.

"When I was at GE, they offered me a supervisor's position. I didn't feel qualified and asked myself, 'What if I fail? What if I don't know how to do it?'

"Then it dawned on me that I didn't offer myself the job. *They* offered it to me. And the new job could go in two different directions. I could do a good job, which meant I was qualified, or I could do a bad job, which meant they weren't qualified for asking me to it in the first place. So then I didn't worry about the change."

Perret was successful in his new job as a supervisor. And he tried something new—emceeing and writing for GE's retirement dinners and roasts. His humor was so popular, management asked him to do it again and again. "I got to be the Bob Hope of General Electric," Perret says with a laugh.

Then one night Perret and his wife were watching television. He turned to her and said, "I can write better than that."

"Why don't you?" she said.

So Perret began sending jokes to comedians, including Phyllis Diller. Diller liked his work and hired him to write for her. Perret was on his way to a new career.

Then, while writing for Diller, Perret had a chance to help *her* handle change. The comedienne suffered a shoulder injury that put her in a cast for several weeks. She called Perret, asking if he could provide a joke to explain the cast. He obliged.

Opening night in Las Vegas, Diller walked onstage, sporting her cast and said, "If there is someone in the audience who has just bought the new book *The Joy of Sex*, there's a misprint on page 206."

When the audience stopped laughing, Diller said, "It'll break your arm, but it's worth a try."

"I think most people can do more than they think they can," Perret told me. "If you fear change, you're stuck where you are for the rest of your life. And that's no way to live."

When starting the supervisor's job, and later when he decided to become a comedy writer, Gene Perret faced the self-doubt that often accompanies major life changes. In each case he faced his fears, seized the opportunity, and captured a dream.

SUMMARY: ALLOW CHANGE TO BE A CHALLENGE

Successful people don't necessarily like painful or drastic change. But they realize it may provide opportunity. They take advantage of the opening by:

1. Recognizing the three phases of change: letting go, transition, and a new beginning
2. Remembering, This too shall pass
3. Asking, What can I change in myself?
4. Turning the challenge positive
5. Converting fear into energy
6. Analyzing the situation
7. Thinking clearly and acting calmly
8. Seizing the opportunity

NOTES

Information on Solomon's study is from "Why Do Some People Survive AIDS?" in *Parade* magazine, 9/18/88.

The study on hardy medical school students is summarized in "Be Upbeat and Beat Illness, Stress," in *USA Today*, 8/26/85.

The Rutgers experiment with Type A's is summarized in "The Hardy Heart," by Clive Wood, in *Psychology Today*, January 1987.

5

STEP TWO

Building Commitment Through Goals and Passion

Whatever you can do or dream you can, begin it.
Boldness has genius, power and magic in it. Begin it
now.

—GOETHE

It's 9:45 and the painter hasn't arrived. When I first spoke with him on the telephone he said he'd be here today at 9:00 A.M. He hasn't arrived. He hasn't called. I never hear from him.

Later I walk into the convenience store to buy milk and eggs. The teenager at the register is engrossed in a phone conversation with a friend. Finally, after I've waited several minutes, she hangs us and begins slowly ringing up my purchases. She never even greets me or makes eye contact.

Sound familiar? In 1983 the Public Agenda Forum surveyed nonmanagerial workers in the United States and discovered that:

- Less than one out of every four workers say they work at their full potential.
- Half of those surveyed put no more effort into their job than what's required to keep it.
- Almost six out of ten say they "do not work as hard" as they used to.
- The majority, 75 percent, said they could be significantly more effective than they now are on the job.

And work isn't the only place where commitment is fading. Teachers report that each year fewer parents attend parent–teacher conferences. They say some parents won't even return their calls. And, though marriage is fashionable again, many people don't stick with it very long.

Whatever happened to commitment? Fortunately, it's alive and well, but not with everyone. Most successful people, however, are highly committed to job, family, and ideals. They become successful by doing what they say they will when they say they'll do it.

The peak performers who responded to our survey have high levels of commitment. Replying to the statement "I am committed to my work," 82 percent said they strongly agreed, 18 percent simply agreed. None disagreed. When asked how they felt about the statement "When I believe something is important, I say it," 95 percent agreed or strongly agreed.

Psychologist Suzanne Kobasa, the researcher who developed the "Three C's" (the qualities—Challenge, Commitment, and Control—that help people remain strong during stressful change), says commitment makes people more productive and healthy. It also helps them handle change effectively.

"People strong in commitment find it easy to be interested in whatever they are doing," Kobasa says, "and can involve themselves in it wholeheartedly. They are rarely at a loss for things to do. They seem to make the maximum effort cheerfully and zestfully."

THE IMPORTANCE OF COMMITMENT

Buck Rodgers spent thirty-four years at IBM, ten of them as vice-president of marketing. There he directed Big Blue's worldwide marketing efforts. His motto? "I keep my commitments."

Rodgers became a legend at IBM. In fact, Peters and Waterman, in their highly successful book *In Search of Excellence*, called him "the modern incarnation of IBM founder Thomas J. Watson, Sr., insisting on the Golden Rule of service."

When Rodgers retired from Big Blue, the legend followed him to his present office in Darien, Connecticut. From there he manages a career as one of the highest paid professional speakers in the country. His best-selling books also stress the value of commitment. In our interview, I discovered that Rodgers's commitment extends beyond his work—to people.

Rodgers is warm, articulate, and accessible. When we talked, he used my name frequently—not as a hyped-up salesman would, but in a way that made me feel comfortable and relaxed with him.

Rodgers talked about *Lonesome Dove*, the book and TV miniseries. "It really got to me because of the sense of commitment. Before he died, one of the characters had asked his long-time friend to bury him in a special place. To do this meant a three-thousand-mile trip, with the man carrying his friend's body the whole way. "I could relate to that, because when I tell somebody I'm going to be somewhere or do something, they can count on that being the case. That to me is the most important thing of all. As Ralph Waldo Emerson says, 'What you are thunders so that I cannot hear what you say to the contrary.' It's what you do that makes the difference."

Commitment isn't dead. It lives in Buck Rodgers and people like him. It helps them to stay on top, even when pressure-packed change takes place—just as it can help you.

COMMITMENT CHANGES LIVES

Zig Ziglar is one of the most sought-after speakers in the world. He's also written eight books. But, as a young man, Zig had difficulty getting on track.

Just after marrying his wife, Jean, Ziglar took a door-to-door sales job for a cookware manufacturer. Ziglar's sales record wasn't awe-inspiring. "For two and a half years we nearly starved to death," he told me. Then Ziglar got to test his commitment.

"I had promised the company that I would be there for every sales meeting and every training session. In the years I'd been with them, I had not only never missed a meeting, I had never been late for a meeting.

"Once I had been at an all-day training session on a Monday and hadn't learned anything. Then the baby kept us up most of the night. So at 5:30 the next morning, when the alarm rang for me to get out of bed, I rolled out of bed from force of habit and looked out the window at ten inches of snow on the ground. In those days I was driving a Crosley automobile without a heater. Man, I got right back in bed.

"But the words of my mother came back to me, 'You made a promise, you said you were going to be there. If you are in something, get in it. If you are not, get out.' I stumbled out of bed and made that long, cold drive from Columbia, South Carolina, to Charlotte, North Carolina. It was a tough drive, but I made my meeting—and on time."

It was at that meeting that sales trainer P. C. Merrell, who worked for the company, told Ziglar he had what it took to go straight to the top. Merrill's words inspired Ziglar deeply, and he shifted into overdrive. By the end of the year, Zig was the second best salesman in a company with a sales force of more than seven thousand.

"If I hadn't gone to that meeting, I have no idea where I would be today," he says. "Going to the meeting that day had to do with commitment and integrity. It was the turning point in my life."

DETERMINE YOUR VALUES AND PURPOSE

Commitment gives us energy, strength, and direction. Those qualities are essential when change is in the wind. But a mission doesn't just pop up. It emerges from our values and desires.

What Do You Love?

Do what you love. It's a radical thought. Most successful people work at what they care about . . . passionately. Their love provides energy and motivation to persevere, especially when they suffer setbacks and problems.

Many people, however, are taught to do whatever they fall into, or whatever pays well, whether it suits them or not. Jenny Craig, president of the weight-loss company that bears her name, told me how she observed this phenomenon when she spoke recently at Harvard University.

"In talking to some of the students, I asked how they chose the kind of work they were planning to do when they finished school. And they'd say, 'That's where the money is,' or 'That's what my dad does.'

"To me," Craig continued, "that's approaching a career from the wrong direction. I've never worked primarily for material gains, though I certainly appreciate what I have. First decide what it is you really love to do. If you love something you will be good at doing it and you'll be successful."

Top entertainer Bob Hope enjoys one of the longest careers in show business. He earns lots of money, but Hope's top writer, Gene Perret, let me in on a secret.

"Hope told me," Perret says, "'You know, I'd do this for free, just don't let it get around.'"

Comedian, musician, composer, and writer Steve Allen says much the same thing. When our interview started, he was reserved and a bit shy, very different from the zany man on TV. Later, though, when I mentioned my background as a professional musician, he seemed excited about our common interest. From then on he warmed considerably.

I asked Allen how he writes so many songs.

"Since I can't read music," he said, "I just put all my own songs on tape, and after I have maybe twenty melodies on a cassette, then we send it out to somebody who writes down whatever he hears. So that's how all my songs end up on paper and get published.

Allen has written more than four thousand songs. Hundreds of musicians have recorded or performed his tunes, including Louis Armstrong, Count Basie, Sammy Davis, Jr., Ringo Starr, and Ella Fitzgerald, among others.

From his headquarters in Van Nuys, California, Allen runs Meadowlane Music, Rosemeadow Publishing, and several other businesses. Wherever he goes, he carries a small tape recorder. Into it he dictates song ideas, books, comedy bits, and a host of other creative flashes.

In addition to his songs, Allen has written thirty-one books and many articles for national magazines. "I don't write so I'll be more respected," he says. "My next book is my thirty-second and I couldn't be any more respected for that than I was for my nineteenth or whatever. By the time I'm up to my thirty-seventh, I'll get no more respect than I have now as a writer, because eventually they judge you on quality anyway.

"So it's not to prove anything or show off or make a bigger reputation. A reputation, such as it is, is already there. I just love to do it."

Put Your Love to Work

Most people don't spend enough time doing the things they love. Psychologist John Reich, at Arizona State University, asked a group of students to note their favorite activities. Reich instructed half the students to do these things more often. The other half did not change their activity level. The group that did more of what they enjoyed reported greater happiness than the other group.

To harness the power of love, know where your passion lies. If you're unsure, or just curious, take the following steps:

1. Make a list of twenty things you love to do most, whether they're work or play or both. The list can include anything—from skiing, to sales, to sex.
2. Rank each item on your list according to how much you

enjoy it. If there are fifteen items, you'll number them one through fifteen.

3. Figure how often you do the things you love. Next to each item, note how many times you do it in an average month.

Pick one or two activites on your list, and commit yourself to do them more often. Doing so will also help you handle change more effectively, because you'll feel more positive and happy.

Next, think about the kind of work you've always wanted to do. It doesn't need to be practical. Just allow yourself to dream. What have you always wanted to do, whether you've tried it or not? Again, make a list of the things you think of.

Does your current job appear on the list? If so, great. If it doesn't, spend some time thinking about the items you've written. Is there any way you can begin to include one in your life? It could even be through volunteer work or moonlighting.

You could also talk to a career counselor about making a shift to work you love. Career counselors specialize in helping people discover and land the right job. Sessions with a career counselor typically involve:

- Discussion of your work history
- Testing to discover what kinds of jobs you'd enjoy and be good at
- Tips on how to get the job you want
- Help with resumés, interviewing techniques, and job search strategies

You'll find these counselors listed under "Career and Vocational Counselors" in the Yellow Pages of the phone book. Many community colleges (and some universities) also offer career counseling for people in the communities they serve.

What Do You Believe In?

Passion is important, but so are beliefs. What ideas, causes, and things are important to you? Successful people have strong values. Yet they're also flexible in their beliefs, and will change them if presented with the right evidence.

During his walk on the moon, *Apollo 14* astronaut Edgar Mitchell experienced a profound shift in his beliefs and perspective. When I interviewed him in his home in Palm Beach, Florida, we talked about that transformation.

Mitchell doesn't look much like the stereotypical astronaut. Not the John Glenn type—staunch and upright. More like a business-man, which is what he is these days.

But Mitchell has something too many business people don't—commitment. He feels *it's essential to remember that we choose our belief system.* As part of his quest to do this for himself, he founded the Institute for Noetic Sciences. The Institute is a nonprofit foundation "organized to sponsor research programs in the nature of human consciousness and human potential."

Mitchell told me about his work and beliefs. "What I have been doing since the *Apollo* flight was reorganizing a belief system.

"Our belief system determines personal reality. Reality out there doesn't matter, it's how you perceive it in here," he said, pointing to his head. "So we can create a belief system just about any way we want to. It's shaped by our environmental factors, it's shaped by our early training, it's shaped by the media."

Edgar Mitchell insists that *we can rewrite our beliefs.* Why is that important? Because a negative (or ineffective) belief system can interfere greatly with our ability to handle change. For instance, if you believe that things always turn out badly in your life, it's likely that they will.

Think about your own belief system for a minute. When is the last time you thought about what you believe? When did you last challenge some of those beliefs, to see if they still hold true for you?

- Take a few minutes now to pinpoint where you stand.
- In your mind or on paper, list things you think are important, whatever the area. It could be work, family, recreation, politics, religion, or anything else.
- Re-examine any beliefs you've listed. Ask yourself if they're relevant for your life today.
- If some of your beliefs are no longer relevant, be flexible. Make the changes that will help the flame of your convictions burn hot and true.

What Do You Want for the World?

Another aspect of our values lies in what we want for the world. Peak performers gain strength and serenity from helping make the world a better place.

Stanley Marcus began working at Neiman-Marcus in 1926, becoming company president in 1950. From 1972 to 1977, he served as chairman, guiding the large retailer to year after year of record profits.

Marcus is retired now from the business that carries his family name. Today, the balding, white-bearded Marcus is a consultant, helping other retailers serve customers as he did. He's written three books, owns a publishing company, and pens a popular column for the *Dallas Morning News*.

When we spoke, I was surprised by Marcus's low-key manner, especially as he is such a powerful man. Marcus is articulate, intellectually curious, and above all, committed to what he believes.

"I felt strongly about the integration of blacks in Dallas thirty-five years ago," Marcus told me. "I felt that school children shouldn't be the ones required to do the integration, but that adults needed to do it before children were put to the test. And I integrated the lunchroom facilities in the store, before the rest of the community did."

Marcus's executives pressured him, saying his decision would destroy the business. Marcus responded, "If it'll collapse over this, let it collapse. I don't think you're right."

Three charge accounts closed the day Marcus ordered the restaurant integrated. The next day two of them were reopened.

"Of course, I never underestimated the value of any customer, but I never would permit a customer or group of customers to dictate how I live my life."

CAN YOU BE OVERCOMMITTED?

Throughout this chapter we've covered the benefits of commitment. But it's possible to overdo it. Some people declare a mission and plow toward it regardless of the consequences. Perhaps you know someone like that—a person who's so sure of a mission that he or she refuses to see, hear, or feel anything else. That kind of devotion can lead to workaholism or worse. It can cost people their friends, family, and health.

I consulted once with a successful building contractor. Raised in a poor family, Jim became an alcoholic in his teens. Finally, in his late twenties he got sober. Trying to make up for lost time, he put every ounce of energy into learning a trade. Then he started a construction business and struggled to make it fly. Jim was smart, committed, and good at sales. Within a year his company had twenty-five on the payroll. Though cash-flow was still a problem, the business was off to a great start.

Unfortunately, Jim put all his commitment in one area. His family suffered. Most days Jim left home at 6:00 A.M. and didn't return until 7:00 in the evening. His kids got in trouble at school and home, and his wife felt resentful. The more successful the business became, the more the family fell apart.

Jim couldn't understand what was happening. He was sober and successful—shouldn't life be getting better? The problem was a lack of balance.

Fortunately, Jim made important changes before it was too late. After we talked, he brought in a manager to help share the load. He created a business plan, with realistic steps for growth carefully noted. And he promised his family he'd moderate his work time and spend no more than sixty hours a week on the job. Jim followed these steps and kept the agreement he'd made with his family.

It took time, but his life became more balanced. Today his kids are back on track, his wife is content, and Jim reports he's much happier. His business is doing better, too.

- Take a moment to examine your life honestly. Are you guilty of overcommitting in one or more areas? Have people mentioned that you work too much, or that you're putting all (or most) of your energy into one area and ignoring other important aspects of your life? If so, in the goal-setting section that follows, take care to build flexibility into your mission. That doesn't mean forgetting your beliefs. Instead, it means being open to ideas that might help you get what you want without hurting yourself or others.

SET GOALS TO MAKE COMMITMENTS REAL

Realistic, effective goals help people cope with change more effectively because they fuel commitment, even when life is stressful. Goals can be set in many different areas: professional, financial, emotional, spiritual, or family. Notre Dame football coach Lou Holtz has goals in all these areas, and more.

Holtz grew up in West Virginia, a skinny kid with a passion for football. In elementary school, he was usually the last person picked for teams. But when his uncle started a football team at Holtz's school, young Lou studied all the positions and pored over the playbook. "He would try to tell me what play I should call," his uncle recalls. Holtz was fascinated, and told his family he'd coach the Fighting Irish of Notre Dame someday.

Holtz went on to play college football at Kent State. After college he took a series of assistant coaching jobs, finally accepting one at the University of South Carolina. His wife was eight months pregnant with their third child. The young couple spent everything they had on the down payment for a new home. Then, a month after arriving at South Carolina, a new head coach was hired. Holtz's job was eliminated. They kept him on as a scout, at 60 percent of his original salary.

Holtz knew then he'd have to set goals to reach his dreams. So he made a list of 107 aspirations. They included coaching at Notre Dame, achieving coach of the year honors, meeting the Pope, and scoring a hole in one.

Two years later, Holtz was at Ohio State with the team that won the national championship. A year after that, he became head coach at William and Mary. He took the school to its first bowl game.

Holtz went on to become one of the most winning college coaches in history. And in 1985 he achieved one of his top goals. Holtz became the football coach at Notre Dame. He took the school to its first national ranking since 1980. And his 1988 team finished the season with a perfect 12–0 record and the national championship. Holtz garnered coach-of-the-year honors from the Football Writers Association of America.

Today, twenty-plus years after he set them, Holtz has accomplished 89 of his original 107 goals. Notre Dame continues as a perennial college football powerhouse. And on the wall of his Notre Dame office, across from a picture of Knute Rockne, rests a plaque commemorating the completion of another goal—a hole in one.

At five feet ten inches and 148 pounds, Holtz disappears from view when his players gather around. But under the baseball cap, behind the wire-rimmed glasses, burn a pair of forceful blue eyes. "He's not the biggest guy in the world, but he seems to possess a lot of power," says former Notre Dame tackle Jeff Alm.

A good chunk of Holtz's power and success stem from his goal-setting. Today, in addition to coaching, he's a popular speaker, earning more than $10,000 per talk. And he's still working on the last eighteen of his original goals. He's also set a few more.

"There are many things I wish to do professionally," he told me. "Some are intermediate goals, some are long-range. Obviously, we'd like to win the national championship at Notre Dame every year, be in the top ten, and go to a bowl game.

"There are things I wish to do as a husband, and as a father. One is to see our children graduate from college.

"Then there are financial goals. And things I'd like to do just for excitement, like jumping out of an airplane, or going down the Snake River, or going on a safari. I'd like to own my own business someday. That's been a goal I've had for years. It hasn't come to fruition yet, but it will."

Holtz aso has goals for helping others. He gives speeches and raises money for groups he believes in. "It's important to have goals in different areas. You need to look at your obligation to society, to self-improvement, your ambitions financially and professionally, your ambitions excitement-wise, and your goals for your family."

When you set concrete goals, the results can be almost magical. You'll find that outcomes arrive faster and more easily. And, because you're looking toward the goal, you, like Lou Holtz, will tailor your life and work to reach it.

How to Set Effective Goals

Goals provide a strong stabilizing influence in times of turmoil. Good goals grow from following these five points:

1. Make your goal realistic.
2. Be specific and write it down.
3. Imagine yourself attaining the goal.
4. Ask yourself key questions.
5. List the action steps needed.

Let's discuss each of these five points.

1. Make your goal realistic.
Realism in goal-setting is a two-edged sword. Some people set goals that are too high. Others don't make their aspirations fly far enough.

Several years ago, I was called in to consult with the very frustrated CEO of a manufacturing company. The executive, whom I'll call Leon, set sales goals that his people couldn't seem to attain. So he got angry at himself, and at them. I suggested that the original goals might be the problem. "But I'm a committed person," he said, "and attaining those goals is part of my commitment."

Yet when we analyzed the goals, Leon saw that they weren't realistic for the current market. He realized that battling windmills was not commitment but wasted energy. He reset the sales goals at a more reasonable level. Lo and behold, the salespeople came through. Success! From there Leon jacked up the goals bit by bit. The success continued, because the targets had now become practical.

Leon set his original goals too high. But some people set their goals too low. Others don't bother to have any at all.

The key is balance. Pick goals that stretch you, but make them realistic.

2. Be specific and write it down.

Decide exactly what you want to do, how you want to do it, and when you'll achieve it. Next, write your goal, noting the specifics of time and place. I worked with one manager, Diane, whose goal was to become executive vice-president of the bank for which she worked. She noted the goal, along with the time frame in which she wished to attain it.

Diane's goal: "To become executive vice-president of _____ Bank by September 1, 1991."

To begin the process for yourself, think of something you have a strong desire to attain. Next, to clarify and commit yourself to your goal, write it down. Be specific and concrete, as Diane was.

3. Imagine yourself attaining the goal.

Visualization is an effective way to practice and achieve new behaviors. Step 11 reveals some of the proof of how well visualization works.

For now though, take a few minutes to visualize yourself after you've achieved the outcome you want.

Imagine yourself after you've reached your goal.

- What do you look like?
- How do things around you look?
- How do you sound?
- How does the environment around you sound?
- How do you feel?

Diane, the woman I've just mentioned, answered these questions as follows:

- I *look* self-assured, happy, strong, and attractive.
- I *see* my new office at the bank; my secretary at her desk outside the office; other employees greeting me, the executive v.p.; myself at a meeting.
- I *sound* confident, happy, calm, energetic. My voice is just the right pitch, and I speak clearly and concisely.
- I *hear* my boss congratulating me on my new job; myself dictating a letter as executive v.p.; myself answering the phone in my new office; myself talking at a meeting—making a well-received suggestion for the bank's growth.
- I *feel* happy in my new job; full of energy and ideas; able to handle the changes that come my way; excitement as I look

out the window of my new office. I also feel the surface of my new desk; my new telephone as I pick it up; the texture of a letter with my name and title on it.

Now, if *you'd* like to attract your goal in a particularly powerful way, write the answers to the five questions previously stated. But first, visualize the steps, as Diane did.

4. Ask yourself key questions.

- Does your goal fit with other plans you have? For instance, if you want to work in politics, a home in an isolated small town won't help.
- Does reaching your goal create a win/win situation? If you want to go on the road as a salesperson, a spouse who hates it when you travel will be a problem.
- What obstacles will you have to surmount to reach your goal?

5. List the action steps needed.

Attaining goals usually requires gaining new knowledge and/or information. To promote progress in these areas, management consultant Charles Shepard, of The Leadership Project, recommends a unique projecting and tracking system.

For each step toward your goal, determine the following elements. (I've listed four of Diane's items.)

Ideally, you'll have a minimum of eight to ten action items on

PROJECTING AND TRACKING YOUR GOALS

Action Item	Person Responsible	Due Date	Estimated Time
1. Ask my boss for advice on preparing myself for an executive position	Myself	Within two weeks	One hour
2. Take a class on executive communication skills	Myself	Fall Semester	Approx. 100 hours
3. Find a mentor	Myself	Within two months	Variable
4. Read five books on leadership	Myself	Within six months	100 hours

the list. This is one way to convert a goal to reality. Otherwise it's just a dream.

But what if you have problems carrying out one or more action items? Say, for instance, that your boss agrees to give you advice but never does. Knowing when to adjust your approach is an essential element of handling change *and* achieving success. First, study your boss's habits to determine the best time to approach her. Then, at such a time, gently remind her of her promise to help you. Then, if she still doesn't come through, choose someone else who can help you.

When you've tackled this process with one goal, you might do it with others. It's amazing how effectively aspirations become reality. But there's another step.

Keep Your Goals in Mind

Don't just set 'em and forget 'em. Reemphasize your goals on a regular basis, preferably every day, so commitment doesn't wane.

Try keeping your written goal and the action steps in a convenient location. At least once a day, read the goal (to yourself or out loud). Then imagine having attained it. You'll condition yourself to reach the outcome you've set.

It also helps to make a list of daily goals. Mary Kay Ashe, founder of Mary Kay Cosmetics, believes that one of the keys to her success is making a daily "to do" list.

Keep your list realistic. Don't overburden yourself—that will just add to your stress level. Instead, make a realistic assessment of what you'd like to accomplish that day and *what is reasonable to accomplish*. Then make your list. You'll gain a feeling of energy as you cross off each item completed.

Set New Goals When Necessary

Some goals change. This happens through shifts in circumstances, resources, or your desires. Goals also change when you achieve what you've been going for. Top pilot and Evergreen International Aviation vice-president Bob Hoover told me how that worked for him.

"I was absolutely convinced the thing I wanted to do was to become a fighter pilot, and I never changed my outlook until I got there. When I became a fighter pilot, my next goal was to become a test pilot. I always kept setting new goals.

"Today, every time I go out and fly, my challenge is to do it a little better than I did the last time around."

Hoover still flies in air shows almost every weekend. Though he's now in his late sixties, his skills are better than ever.

"[Famed test pilot] Chuck Yeager and I were talking about this the other day. We agreed that we haven't lost our skills at all. Every now and then, some young person half my age will challenge me to a dog fight, and I've always managed to come out on top. It's because I keep my skills up; I'm constantly thinking about doing the best job possible and getting the most out of the airplane.

Enjoy the Trip

It is possible, though, to take goals too seriously. Goals become negative when we forget to enjoy the process of attaining them. True commitment doesn't require that we become grim and self-righteous.

"There's a great saying I learned in Japan," writer and consultant Ken Blanchard told me. "If you run your life only for profits or for outcomes, it's like playing tennis with your eye on the scoreboard and not on the ball.'"

If you're bogged down in the present, stuck in one of those inevitable periods when everything seems like drudge work, focus on the goal. This will energize you and provide inspiration to continue.

WHAT TO DO WHEN YOUR GOALS ARE BLOCKED

You've pinpointed your desires and beliefs, written out your goals, and are hotly pursuing a few outrageously good outcomes. Suddenly, a roadblock appears. What next?

I asked this question of many of the peak performers in my interviews. When I did, most got a gleam in their eyes. Some even admitted they get a charge out of dealing with roadblocks.

In our discussions, I discovered a three-part strategy successful people use to deal with roadblocks.

Analyze the Situation

When a roadblock appears, peak performers don't despair. Instead they analyze the situation and use intuition to discover a course of action.

Maureen DiMarco, California's Secretary of Child Development and Education, asks herself two questions when reassessing a goal. She told me she uses this strategy whenever an important project seems to be bogging down.

"The first question is, 'Is it still worth it?'" she said. "The second is, 'Are you making any progress?' If you aren't making progress, then either you change what you're doing or decide whether or not you have the means to make it."

DiMarco asked herself these questions many times after Governor Pete Wilson appointed her to a cabinet post in 1990. When she took office, DiMarco set the goal of improving education and well-being for the more than 5 million school children in California. But the somewhat tarnished Golden State faced severe school funding cuts because of a $14-billion deficit. During the inevitable periods when she became discouraged by this financial Catch 22, DiMarco asked herself the two questions again:

- Is it still worth it?
- Are you making any progress?

Her answer to the questions was always "yes," so DiMarco continued working toward her goals, discovering ways to improve the schools in spite of the deficit.

In addition to DiMarco's questions, you might ask yourself these:

- Can I take another path to the goal?
- Do I need to alter the goal somewhat?
- Is the goal itself inappropriate?

Sometimes we set a goal that, in the long run, isn't correct. If your analysis reveals you'd be better off doing something else, don't despair. Millions have changed or substituted goals. It's certainly better than forging ahead into something you know isn't right for you.

Use Intuition

Intuition can also help to clarify direction and the means to get where you want to go. To tune in to your own intuition, try one or more of these strategies:

- Find a quiet place where you won't be disturbed for at least fifteen minutes. Spend a few minutes relaxing your body and mind (see Step 9 for guidelines on how to do this). When you feel relaxed, ask (in your mind) for an answer to whatever it is you're struggling with. Perhaps the answer to your dilemma will come immediately. But often it arrives after you've gone back to whatever you were doing previously. At that point, the answer to your problem may just pop into your mind.

- Write about the issue that is bothering you (see Step 4 for more information).
- Talk to a friend. When something is bothering me, I often get new perspectives (and solutions) by discussing the problem with someone I trust and respect. Afterward I almost always feel more optimistic and committed.

Change Gears

"L.A. Law" star Michael Tucker told me about a time when a major goal of his was blocked. In the early 1970s, Tucker, his wife, Jill Eikenberry, and their young daughter, Alison, moved to New York City. Tucker and Eikenberry were to perform in a Broadway play called *Moonchildren*. Unfortunately, the play closed in two weeks. Though he'd worked as an actor for years, Tucker couldn't find further work in his chosen field.

"It was an enormously frustrating time in my life. I couldn't get an agent, and we were financially strapped," he said. So Tucker shifted gears. He got a job with a company that produced sales meetings and trade shows for businesses. At first he did voice-over work for them. But soon he began writing, too.

"That saved me," he said. "I would meet with the vice-presidents and presidents of various corporations, and then write speeches for them. They loved it, because I had a dramatic sense that they didn't have. I was very successful at this and earned a lot of money. That helped carry us through the year or two when we were first in New York. It was actually a very interesting time in my life.

"And then, Jill's career got to the place where she was earning more money, which enabled me to stop doing that and go back to acting."

The German philosopher Friederich Nietzsche once said, "Many are stubborn in pursuit of the path they have chosen, few in pursuit of the goal." But peak performers are different. When confronted by a broadblock, they try a new path. Michael Tucker continued to work toward his ultimate goal of making a living through acting. In the meantime, he shifted gears and used his talents in a new way.

SUMMARY: GOALS AND PASSION

Though we may eventually change a goal, the first step, obviously, is to set it. But many people never do that.

If you haven't done so already, you might devote a few minutes now to take some of the steps that peak performers use to advance their missions.

First, determine your values and purpose. Where does your passion lie? What do you believe in? What do you want for the world?

Then, use these questions to help focus your power.

- Are you doing what you want in your life?
- Are you over- or undercommitted?
- Are you focusing your energy in the right areas?

Sometimes people fight the wrong wars or take on too many battles. Are you wasting your time and power sweating the small stuff or the wrong stuff?

Ask yourself also if you're committing yourself to someone else's mission. That can be fine, *if it's also right for you.* But if you feel obligated to follow another's path, resentment will overtake commitment before long.

After answering these questions, write out your goals to make commitments concrete. Set long-term goals and imagine yourself having achieved them. Then create an action list of strategies to keep your mission alive. Use daily goals to keep yourself on track. And remember to update goals when your desires or circumstances change. You'll avoid ending up someplace you don't want to be.

As Zig Ziglar's mother said, "If you are in something, get in it. If you are not, get out."

NOTES

The Public Agenda Forum study was done by Daniel Yankelovich and Associates in 1983.

The Hardy Executive: Health Under Stress, by Suzanne Kobasa and Salvatore Maddi, Dow Jones-Irwin, 1984.

Garfield is quoted in *The Wall Street Journal,* January 21, 1983.

The happiness study was reported in "The Paradox of Happiness," *Psychology Today,* July/August 1989.

Charles Sheppard's Leadership Group is located at 204 E. 2nd Avenue, Suite 514, San Mateo, CA 94401. Phone: (800) 788-9877 or (415) 348-8941.

6 STEP THREE

Staying Committed When the Going Gets Tough

You gain strength, experience, and confidence by every experience where you really stop to look fear in the face . . . You must do the thing you think you cannot do.

—ELEANOR ROOSEVELT

How can you keep committed when grappling with change? Start by getting **POWERFUL**. In my interviews, I discovered eight strategies peak performers use to keep committed. These tactics form the acronym **POWERFUL**. The strategies are:

1. **P**ersist.
2. **O**pen your mind.
3. **W**ork.
4. **E**njoy.
5. **R**emember your mission.
6. **F**eel it happen.
7. **U**nderstand resistance.
8. **L**et others help.

─────────── **STRATEGY 1** ───────────

Persistence: How It Helps Us Keep Going

When I interviewed author and speaker Ken Blanchard, he and the Reverend Norman Vincent Peale had recently completed their book *The Power of Ethical Management*. In it they present a concept called "the five principles of ethical power." The fourth principle is *persistence*.

Blanchard's success story illustrates this principle. In the early 1980s, Blanchard, then a university professor of management, had an idea for a book called *The One-Minute Manager*. At first no publishing company would handle the book, so he persisted and published it himself. In spite of the nay-sayers, the book was soon picked up by a major publisher and became a huge success. Today, business people listen closely to Blanchard's ideas. *The One-Minute Manager* and his subsequent books have become perennial best-sellers.

Executive Harvey Mackay demonstrates persistence in a different realm. At age twenty-six, he bought a failing envelope company and struggled to make it go. Today, the Mackay Envelope Corporation is a multimillion-dollar operation, producing over 10 million envelopes per day.

Now in his late fifties, Mackay is the epitome of the successful executive—lean, well-groomed, and hard-charging. But the dynamism is tempered by warmth.

I caught up with Mackay at his home near Minneapolis. He'd been on the road the previous week, promoting his latest best-selling book. Now he was taking time for rest and relaxation. The deck of his house overlooks beautiful Christmas Lake. Only a thirty-minute drive from the clamor of downtown Minneapolis, the lake seems light years from city stress.

Mackay told me how his father, Jack, provided a model of commitment for him.

"In 1932, during a Minneapolis bank robbery, a man was murdered. A small-time thief named Leonard Hankins was arrested and convicted of the crime. He was sentenced to life imprisonment. Later, through the testimony of others, it became clear that Hankins was innocent. And my father, who was the Associated Press correspondent in St. Paul, worked on the case, trying to get him free, for nineteen years."

The elder Mackay wrote about the case again and again, drawing attention to the injustice of Hankins's imprisonment.

"My father hung in here," Mackay said. "He was Hankins's only advocate." In fact, Jack Mackay was often Hankins's sole visitor on Christmas and Thanksgiving.

Finally, in 1951, Governor C. Elmer Anderson convened the state pardon board in a special session. They ordered Hankins freed from prison and agreed he'd never committed the crime.

Mackay remembers his father's commitment, especially when the chips are down in his own life. Two years after the younger Mackay bought his envelope company, he was ready to build a new manufacturing plant.

"In order to be a success I had to move out of the rat trap that I had initially purchased. It was a broken down building in the red light district. It wasn't safe to stay there at night.

"I went out to try to find a mortgage and got thirteen no's— one from every bank and mortgage company in the Twin Cities. No one would give me a cent, because I was in my twenties and I needed a quarter of a million dollars, which was a lot of money back in '62. But knowing my father worked on a case for nineteen years gave me the persistence to hang in there."

Mackay got a map and a dime store drafting compass. Using Minneapolis as the center, he drew a three-inch circle. Then he contacted the banks and mortgage companies that fell within that circle. No luck. So he drew a bigger circle.

"I finally found my money 325 miles from Minneapolis, in Milwaukee," Mackay said.

How to Build Your Tenacity

Remember that your energy will vary in intensity, says Ellen Gordon, president of Tootsie Roll Industries, Inc. "Energy comes in waves," she told me. "At times it hardly seems worth the effort. But at those low times, the next wave of energy is already on its way."

And Gordon *is* persistent. Since 1972, her company has acquired other candy makers like the Mason Company (makers of Dots), Bonomo (Turkish Taffy), Cella's Confections, and the Charms Company, while maintaining what *Forbes* magazine calls "exceptional profitability." As Gordon's husband, Tootsie Roll CEO Melvin Gordon, once said, "Ellen's persistence in telephoning possible acquisitions was instrumental. She's probably the most persistent person I've ever seen in business. She will go over, around, under, or through a problem, but she won't stop until she has the answer."

To build your tenacity, think of a time when you've been persistent. Imagine yourself back in that situation. Do you notice a certain strength in your body? Many people report they feel a sense of power in their chest and/or stomach area that can be called upon when needed.

Then, next time you want to marshall your persistence, remember the earlier tenacious time. Feel the point of power in your body. The memory, and the feeling, will help you forge ahead today.

Barbara Boxer, U.S. senator from California, told me, "If you stick in there, somebody is going to take a swing at you. It isn't easy. There are days when you say, 'What am I doing?' But you have to persist. I say to myself, 'If you don't do this, somebody else is going to.' I remind myself how important it is to get out there and fight for the things I think are important."

During her first term in the U.S. Congress, Boxer fought for what she thought was important, investigating and exposing the military's infamous $7,600 coffee pots, $400 hammers, and $300 no-smoking signs. Though she ran into flak from the military, Boxer persisted, introducing legislation mandating competitive bidding for military parts and equipment. Because of Boxer's determination and hard work, the bill passed.

------------------------------ STRATEGY 2 ------------------------------

Open Your Mind to What You Can Do

Use what you have. Open your mind to what you can do. Professional speaker and former NFL referee Jim Tunney told me how one young man did just that.

"I go to the California State Special Olympics every year," Tunney said. "One year, I saw a kid with cerebral palsy who couldn't use either hand and one of his legs. He was entered in a wheelchair race, but all he could use to push himself was his one leg. And that wouldn't make the chair go forward.

So, Tunney says, the kid turned his wheelchair around and pushed it backwards. He won the race.

"So whenever I have a goal that didn't make it," Tunney says, "I think to myself, 'How can I approach it differently?' There's always an alternative way. So often we get stymied. We think, 'That's the only way I know to solve that problem, and it's not working. I'm frustrated.'

"Instead of thinking that way, stop a minute. Take a deep

breath. Leave it alone for an hour, a day, two days, and then come back and take a fresh look at it."

----------------------------------- STRATEGY 3 -----------------------------------

Work Is Required

Author and television personality Julia Child worked hard to gain her goals and success. After training at the famed Cordon Bleu school in Paris, Child and two French women, Simone Beck and Louisette Bertholle, opened their own cooking school in Paris.

Then, in 1953, Child and her two collaborators signed a publishing contract for a book with the working title *French Cooking for the American Kitchen.* The three cooking writers worked for five years, finally completing the manuscript for the book—all 850 pages of it. The publisher turned the manuscript down.

Child and her friends went back to work, totally revising the book over the next year. With the manuscript now totaling 684 pages, they called the book *French Recipes for American Cooks.* Again the publisher rejected the manuscript, saying in part, ". . . It is a big, expensive cookbook of elaborate information and might well prove formidable to the American housewife. She might easily clip one of these recipes out of a magazine but be frightened by the book as a whole."

But Julia Child didn't give up. She and her collaborators went back to work again, finally landing a publishing contract with Knopf, which published the book in 1961 with the title *Mastering the Art of French Cooking.* Though the book was big and expensive, as the earlier publisher had observed, it sold well.

Then, when Child began appearing on "The French Chef" show on public television, the book's sales really took off. On November 25, 1966, *Time* magazine featured Julia Child on its cover. Today, *Mastering the Art of French Cooking* has sold more than a million copies, and brisk sales continue. But Child still works hard to stay at the top of her field, partly through perusing the hundreds of cookbooks that line the floor-to-ceiling bookshelves in her Cambridge, Massachusetts, office.

Writer, venerated editor, and health researcher the late Norman Cousins also worked hard for his commitments. In our interview, shortly before his death in 1991, he told me how he had learned to play Bach on the piano, even though he couldn't read music.

Earlier in his life, Cousins had gone to a music teacher in New

York City who was known for her expertise in teaching musicians to play the compositions of Bach. Cousins told her he wanted to play the great composer's works.

"How long have you been studying?" the teacher asked.

"I haven't studied," Cousins replied.

When the teacher asked if he had been playing Bach, Cousins said, "Yes, but not acceptably." He told her he wanted to learn more about technique and about the nuances of playing.

"So she spread some music in front of me," Cousins told me, "and she said, 'Play this.'"

"'I don't read music.' I said.

"Well, she said that was the most absurd thing she had ever heard of. She said, 'You mean that you want to play Bach without reading music?'

"I said, 'I play by ear and I would like it if you could give me some pointers on playing what I know.'

"So I played some Bach, and she said, 'This is outrageous, no one is able to play Bach by ear. You have studied music. You are trying to deceive me. The interview is over.'"

I asked Cousins how he did learn to play Bach by ear.

"I got all the recordings I could find of a single piece," he said. "Let's say the Toccata and Fugue in D Minor. I listened to E. Power Biggs on the organ. Then I would listen to several other recordings, and I could feel the music in my fingers when I listened. I just worked on it, over and over until I could do it. Now I play just for my own pleasure."

The bottom line is this: Anything that's worth accomplishing will require work, and lots of it. If you make the necessary sacrifices—and inject some fun into your work—you'll find your goals rushing to meet you.

STRATEGY 4

Enjoy—Do What You Do with Enthusiasm

The work involved in commitment isn't always drudgery. It can be fun. In fact, the pleasure of the task can make working a delight. Many I interviewed insist that enjoying your work is the *key* to commitment.

In the 1988 Winter Olympics, Debbie Thomas of the United States competed against Katarina Witt of East Germany. The media called the figure skaters the "dueling Carmens," as they both performed to music from the famous opera.

Many people expected Thomas, then a twenty-year-old pre-med student, to win the gold medal. She didn't. In her last routine, she missed three jumps and finished with a bronze.

"I just wasn't having fun," she said afterward. "It has been eating on me. I'm glad it's over, so I can get on with my life."

Katarina Witt skated well enough to earn the gold medal, though her routine was conservative. But a relatively obscure Canadian skater, Elizabeth Manley, won the hearts of the audience. She gained the highest marks of the night from the nine judges, and won the long program. This boosted her to the silver medal.

Manley's feat was amazing, especially since she'd suffered a nervous breakdown earlier in her career. In rebounding from her disability, Manley made an essential shift. She decided that she would skate to enjoy herself, rather than to win. And her pursuit of pleasure led her to triumph over Debbie Thomas, who had forgotten how to have fun.

The peak performers say, don't try *too* hard. Years of research show that increased motivation improves performance on simple chores. But when the task is complex, trying too hard actually diminishes effectiveness. Struggling leads to tension. Tension chokes performance. Do what you do with gusto, but allow yourself to remain relaxed by having fun.

--- **STRATEGY 5** ---

Remember Your Mission

Jenny Craig, founder and president of the Jenny Craig International Weight Loss Centres, has a mission. In 1969, after the birth of her second daughter, Craig couldn't lose the forty-five pounds she'd gained.

"I looked at myself in the mirror and just cried. None of my clothes fit. I had been a model prior to getting married, and I always enjoyed dressing up."

So Craig, then a dental assistant, began carefully planning her diet and doing calisthenics at a local New Orleans gym. After several months she had lost the excess weight—and gained a mission.

"I began noticing what happened to women as a result of weight loss. I became fascinated with the whole topic. Once I'd lost the excess weight, the manager of the gym asked me to become manager of a studio, and I did."

Craig went on to hold several executive positions with Body Contour, Inc., Figure Salons. Finally, in 1983, she and her husband, Sid, started Jenny Craig International, eventually opening more than five hundred Weight Loss Centres worldwide.

Today, from her office overlooking the ocean in Del Mar, California, Craig keeps her motivation up by sharing her clients' joy in their successes. In her late fifties now, Craig still weighs just 122 pounds. Her infectious smile and enthusiasm help other people believe that they, too, can change their lives.

Gertrude Crain's mission is equally powerful. In 1973, Crain suffered a devastating setback, one that required all her commitment to overcome. Her beloved husband, G. D. Crain, Jr., founder and president of the business publishing company Crain Communications passed away. Within four months, Gertrude Crain went from a job as secretary/treasurer to company chairman.

Today Crain describes the loss of her husband as the toughest time in her life. "We were very happily married for thirty-seven years. I still miss him every day," she says.

But Gertrude Crain had a mission, and that mission sustained her during her adjustment to the greatest change in her life. "My husband founded the business, and it meant a great deal to him," she told me. "It was a tremendous help for me to go in there and try to carry on and uphold the things that he started."

And carry on she did. Crain put her energy into running Crain Communications and promoting the principles her husband had worked for, especially his concern for the company's employees. Working with her two sons, vice-chairman Keith and president Rance, Gertrude Crain has guided Crain Communications from five to twenty-six publications, and from one hundred to more than one thousand employees. Gross revenues have risen more than twelvefold, and the company has gone from regional to international status. Two of Crain's publications, *Advertising Age* and *Automotive News*, are the most important trade publications for their respective industries.

By committing herself to keeping her husband's memory alive through their company, Gertrude Crain survived one of life's most difficult transitions. Her mission kept her going.

- Remind yourself of your mission by referring to it frequently. If you wrote down your goals in the previous step, look at them again. Recommit yourself to what you believe in. Your mission will rejuvenate and inspire you, especially when the winds of change are blowing strong.

─────────────── **STRATEGY 6** ───────────────

Feel It Happen

In the last chapter, you discovered the power of visualization in attaining a goal. Imagination can also help you stay on track and maintain your commitment.

If you find your commitment weakening, practice visualizing two situations:

- First, imagine what will happen if you don't attain your goal. What will the negative *and* the positive features be? Do you want that outcome for yourself and your mission?
- Second, imagine again what it will be like when you attain your goal. What will you look like? What will your environment look like? How will you sound, and how will those around you sound? How will you feel?
- Visualize the positive and the negative side of the issue. That way you'll keep your mission on track . . . if that's where you still want it to be.

─────────────── **STRATEGY 7** ───────────────

Understand Resistance

One of the prime lessons of commitment is that obstacles do not prove you're wrong. Instead, they may be an indicator of just how right you are.

In our interview, Ann Rudin, then the popular two-term mayor of Sacramento, California, told me how she dealt with resistance. Before becoming mayor, Rudin served on the Sacramento City Council, the first woman to do so since the 1950s.

I first met the mayor in her office, located in the renovated turn-of-the-century city hall. As we began to talk, Rudin leaned slightly toward me, as if trying to reduce the distance between us. She didn't look high-powered, yet I sensed strength and determination in her.

I asked the mayor about something I'd seen on television—an incident when she'd spoken to an arena full of sports fans, many of them hostile. Back then Sacramento had just landed its first National Basketball Association team and was angling for professional football and baseball teams.

Rudin took a strong stand in favor of regulating growth in the area where the stadium was planned. Some said she was anti-sports. Untrue, Rudin insists. But she did want future growth well planned. I asked her how she handled the stadium situation.

"Every time I went to a sporting event they would boo me. When I was asked to go and present the championship trophy for the playoffs between Oakland [Warriors] and Sacramento [Kings], I wasn't sure I wanted to.

"I said to myself, 'Why should I subject myself to that kind of abuse?'" Rudin thought about it for a few days and decided it was her job to present the trophy, and she'd do it.

"When I walked out onto the arena floor, I was surrounded by deputy sheriffs. I think they thought that I would be mobbed if I went out alone. I went and sat in Greg Luckenbill's [the owner's] box."

Luckenbill began speaking, and the crowd booed him. Mayor Rudin took his arm and whispered, "Let's just keep quiet until they quiet down." And soon they heard some cheers mixed with the boos. She decided to ignore the boos and go ahead. Rudin stepped to the microphone and began to speak.

"By the time I finished speaking," she said, "there were more cheers than boos. They have this huge applause-meter there, and I could see the volume of cheers rising, and I knew that the crowd, at least a majority of them, were mine. They were angry with the ones that were booing because they felt it was rude.

"I, too, thought it was rude of them to boo the mayor, but I cannot personalize and internalize these things. I felt that they were booing me as a symbol."

When Rudin left that night, people from all over the arena came over, congratulating and thanking her for coming. "That made me see that I had some guts," she says, "and that I could hold my own, that I could fight back.

"So, the event at the arena was painful. I dreaded it. But in the end, I was glad I decided to go and just take the pain, which was only momentary.

"People have told me that I earned a lot of respect on that occasion, and that that's what turned around their attitude toward me. After that the sportscasters were less abusive, and more positive things began happening with the arena, too. It was a turning point in my career."

Ann Rudin took a risk, confronted the resistance, and turned it around. Shortly after our interview, Rudin decided not to run for a third term as mayor. But today, as a private citizen, she still works for the issues she believes in, and she understands how to confront and deal with resistance.

If you're committed, you will definitely encounter resistance. That's great! If you never shake anyone up, you'll never get anything done. Expect the resistance. Then, when it comes, reassess your position. If you still believe in your mission, do what your convictions tell you to do. You may even win a few detractors over to your point of view.

STRATEGY 8

Let Others Help

Just as some will oppose you, others may help. Sometimes you can't achieve your goal alone. One of the major reasons people fail is that they don't enlist, or allow the support of others.

To enlist the support of others, try recruiting a team from your own circle of friends, business associates, or neighbors. The composition of the group you gather will be dictated by your particular goal. Choose individuals who are willing *and able* to lend their support and strength to your quest.

Then ask your group to meet with you regularly (every week or biweekly) to support each other in going for the goals. It's a very powerful system.

This book is partially a product of just such a support group. I had the idea for *12 Steps to Mastering the Winds of Change* years before I began to write it. Something always seemed to happen to prevent me from beginning.

Finally I asked a friend and fellow consultant, Craig Smith, if we could support each other in committing to our dreams. He agreed, saying that *he* wanted to work on expanding his consulting business. After that, we met regularly, in person or on the telephone for several months. Each time Craig and I spoke, we reminded each other of our goals and discussed ways to reach them. My talks with Craig helped me keep going.

You can utilize the support of others through a formal group or just by enlisting friends. You'll find that your supporters will help keep you on track to your goal, even when your own commitment wanes.

SUMMARY: STAYING COMMITTED

Remember to stay **POWERFUL** in pursuit of your mission.

1. **P**ersist.
2. **O**pen your mind.
3. **W**ork.
4. **E**njoy.
5. **R**emember your mission.
6. **F**eel it happen.
7. **U**nderstand resistance.
8. **L**et others help.

If you follow these steps, you'll be well on your way to achieving your goals, keeping your commitments, and handling change more effectively.

NOTES

Research on motivation is summarized in "Trading Up," *Psychology Today*, October 1988.

7
STEP FOUR

Knowing When to Control, When to Let Go

The young woman looked lost as she walked slowly toward me. The rest of the group was out on a break during one of my public seminars. Hesitantly the woman introduced herself. "Hi, my name is Jackie . . . I'd like to talk to you . . . I just don't know what to do anymore."

Jackie and I sat down to talk. She told me that she was facing tremendous change and felt she had lost control of her life. Her husband had recently filed for divorce and moved to another state, leaving Jackie with their four children, aged three to ten. Jackie worked for a large bank, in a job that required her to travel two days a week. On those days she often didn't get home until after 7:00 P.M.

Jackie felt great anxiety about the changes in her life. She knew she needed to spend more time with her kids, but she had to continue earning enough money to support them, especially since her ex-husband's new job paid poorly. Jackie and I explored her options and came up with a solution—asking for a transfer to another department. She knew her boss might be upset, and there weren't many other positions available, but Jackie decided to try anyway.

A week later Jackie called to update me on her situation. After several days of phone calls and inquiries, she had discovered a job in another department. The new position would allow her to be home by 5:30 P.M. every day. She applied and was hired. Jackie was ecstatic and so were her kids. She had found a way to reestablish control over her life.

HOW LACK OF CONTROL AFFECTS US

Unfortunately, control is sometimes farther out of reach than it was for Jackie. When that happens, change may seem utterly overwhelming.

Control is the second of the three elements of *hardiness* we discussed in Step 1. Suzanne Kobasa, the City University of New York psychologist who conducted the original hardiness research, says, "People in control believe and act as if they can influence the events taking place around them. They reflect on how to turn situations to advantage and never take things at face value."

In contrast, Kobasa says, "People who feel powerless believe and act as if they are the passive victims of forces beyond their control. They have little sense of resource or initiative and prepare themselves for the worst."

Author Tom Peters tells of researchers who asked two groups of adults to proofread a document and solve complex puzzles. While they did, researchers broadcast "a combination of two people speaking Spanish, one speaking Armenian, a mimeograph machine running, a desk calculator, a typewriter, and street noise— producing a composite, nondistinguishable roar."

The researchers showed those in one group a button they could use to turn off the noise.

The group that had the off switch was much more productive. They made many fewer proofreading errors and unraveled five times as many puzzles as their control-less cohorts. And, according to the researchers, ". . . none of the subjects in the off switch group ever used the switch. The mere knowledge that one can exert control made the difference."

Helpless and Hopeless

Arthur Schmale, director of Psycho-Social Medicine at the University of Rochester Cancer Center, pinpointed two components of loss of control. One is *helplessness*, "a feeling of being deprived, let down, or left out, which was perceived as coming from a change in relationship about which the individual felt powerless to do anything," according to Schmale.

The other component is *hopelessness*, where the individual begins to feel that the situation is impossible and nothing can be done to change it.

Lack of control causes tension, and that reduces our ability to manage change effectively. Yet we can learn to establish more control over the elements in our lives. The peak performers I interviewed and surveyed are experts at doing just that. When surveyed, 89 percent of them agree or strongly agree with the statement "I exert an important influence on my surroundings." These peak performers rarely feel helpless and hopeless. And even when they must deal with the uncontrollable, they're able to bounce back.

But peak performers also know when to take it easy.

OUT OF CONTROL?

Each of us has a tendency either to undercontrol or overcontrol. Undercontrollers become helpless and hopeless when pressure-packed change strikes. They feel there's nothing they can do, and they often give up.

But overcontrolling can be hazardous, too. Trying too hard to command a situation, particularly one that isn't controllable, breeds tension. Rather than letting the situation unfold and helping where necessary, the overcontroller tries to do it all.

The most common manifestation of this behavior is in chemical dependency and codependency. A codependent, someone who is in relationship with an addicted or compulsive person, often becomes very controlling. Because the addict is making a mess of his or her life, the codependent thinks, "I'll help, to make certain nothing bad happens."

So the codependent begins taking over the addict's responsibilities: calling into work when she or he's hung over, covering up for him or her with family and friends, and cleaning up the mess-ups. This behavior is intended to help, but it actually hurts. The addict resents losing his or her control. And there's no way to clean up completely after an alcoholic or addict. The problems continue. And the codependent becomes more and more frustrated.

What's the solution? Balance. Whether we're codependent or not, we need to balance control and acceptance. When control isn't possible, acceptance is essential. For the codependent that may mean a choice between accepting things as they are or leaving the situation.

ACCEPTANCE—AN IMPORTANT COPING TOOL

London, England—World War II. Residents of London experienced devastating change and stress as the German Luftwaffe bombed the city night after night. Six months after the blitz ended, the incidence of peptic ulcers in residents of Greater London had increased by 300 percent. (Peptic ulcers are most frequently caused by stress.)

Interestingly, residents of various parts of the city reacted differently to the stress of the bombing. In London's core area, where the bombs had fallen every night, residents showed a 50 percent increase in ulcers. Where bombing was unpredictable, in the outskirts of town, citizens had a 500 percent increase in ulcers. Residents who *knew* they were going to be bombed each night were able to plan for and accept it, thereby reducing their stress level. The increased uncertainty for residents in the outskirts led to an increase in their stress, and in their ulcer levels.

Some situations cannot be changed, and acceptance helps us cope more effectively with them. Gene Perret, Bob Hope's head comedy writer, told me how Hope learned an important lesson on acceptance.

"Bob Hope was going to Vietnam to do a show, and the gentleman who had the cue cards was an hour late, so the plane was delayed. Finally they took off. While they were in the air, a bomb went off in the hotel they were going to check into.

"Hope later did jokes about it. He said, 'It's the first time I ever had a hotel check out before I checked in.'

"But he said, 'If we had forced that guy to be on time, we would have been in the hotel when it blew up. His being late saved our lives. So, I'm not going to worry about things anymore. If someone's late, he's late."

Acceptance doesn't necessitate giving up on your goal. Instead, it means accepting the way things are, even as you work to get what you want. It can also mean accepting a situation that cannot be changed and deciding to make the best of it.

Maureen DiMarco, California's Secretary of Child Development and Education, told me about dealing with potentially overwhelming change when she began her current job.

"When I first came to this office, within a week, I was 400 phone calls behind. You cannot physically return over 400 phone calls. I was so worried about it I was making myself sick.

"A friend of mine actually had beaten our record and had over 500 phone calls on his computer. 'What did you do?' I asked him. He said, 'I figured if it was really important they were going to call back.'

"I thought about that and realized, 'He's right.' So I just accepted that I wouldn't be able to return most of the calls. It felt like a sin, but the bolt of lightning didn't come from above. And you know what? They *do* call back if it's really important."

FINDING BALANCE

Especially in the midst of change, the key to control is balance. All his life, Nobel Peace Prize winner Archbishop Desmond Tutu has balanced action with acceptance. He's probably better at doing that than anyone else I interviewed.

Until recently, most South Africans had little control over their lives. Twenty-five million blacks were forced to bend to the will of 5 million whites. The system of apartheid did not allow citizenship for blacks. They couldn't travel outside certain areas, and they earned as little as one-sixth of what white South Africans did. From 1948 until the late 1980s, nearly 4 million blacks were taken from their homes and forced to move to barren wastelands the government called "homelands."

In high school, Desmond Tutu earned money selling peanuts in suburban railway stations and caddying at an elite white Johannesburg golf course. Eventually he became a teacher. But when the government introduced a program of inferior education for blacks, Tutu and many other teachers resigned in protest.

Tutu went on to become an Anglican minister, rising quickly through the church ranks and becoming increasingly active in the anti-apartheid movement. Government officials responded by confiscating his passport, so he could not travel abroad to gather support for the anti-apartheid movement.

Then, in 1984, Tutu received the Nobel Peace Prize. The Nobel committee said, in part, "This year's award should be seen as a renewed recognition of the courage and heroism shown by black South Africans in their use of peaceful methods in the struggle against apartheid."

Today Desmond Tutu is archbishop of Capetown. He maintains a travel schedule that would exhaust most people. I asked the archbishop how he deals with the uncertainty of the struggle for freedom.

"I believe in offering God the best that you are able to do, then leaving the consequences in his hands. Committing everything to him and saying, 'God, I know that you want the very best for all of us. We have done our part, it's over to you.'

"I have to keep saying to myself that, in the end, there isn't much else that I can do. Having done what I can, I can't now influence the outcome. I have to wait, patiently."

This balance is essential for mastering change—it requires doing what we can, then letting go. There are several ways to accomplish this. If you believe in God, turn the results over to your Higher Power or the Universe.

If, however, you don't have spiritual beliefs, there are other ways to master acceptance. Positive self-talk can help. You might, for instance, say, "It's out of my hands now," or "I've done what I can, now I'll wait to see what happens."

DON'T PANIC

Sometimes we can't control *or* accept a new situation. It happens so fast that we must act immediately, with no time to ponder. That can lead to panic, perhaps the most common loss of control. And panic diminishes control even further.

Rushing Causes Mistakes

Rushing is a type of panic. When we rush, we've convinced ourselves that the situation is potentially out of control. That puts *us* out of control.

Some people say that rushing makes them more productive. Actually, the opposite is true, because we make mistakes when rushing. Try dialing a telephone number ten times—first doing it as fast as you can. Then try it again at a measured pace. You'll probably find that the errors you made while rushing made you less productive.

Many successful leaders have refused to rush—Abraham Lincoln, Harry Truman, and Winston Churchill, among others. Certainly, no one can argue about their productivity.

Beyond that, slowing down will help you enjoy life more. All my life I've had a tendency to rush. Once, when a number of projects were all due at once, I made a decision. I would complete the tasks at a measured pace, without rushing. Later that day, I drove home on a winding road through an oak forest. Many times in the past I had driven fast on that road, intent on my destination.

That afternoon, though, I drove slowly, enjoying the surroundings. I rolled the window down and listened to the birds. Then, around a bend in the road, a deer appeared at the side of the road. Because I was going slowly, the sound of the car hadn't frightened her. I stopped and we looked at each other for a few moments. Then, as she continued to watch, I drove slowly by. The next day was the most productive I'd had in weeks.

How to Beat Rushing and Panic

Rushing and panic help no one, says speaker, author, and minister Norman Vincent Peale. Peale wrote to tell me his tips for handling change and pressure. The first?

"I follow an old-time Chinese proverb, 'Always take an emergency leisurely.'"

Sometimes we panic and forget that advice. One way to get back in control is to do what comes naturally . . . breathe. I asked professional speaker and former NFL referee Jim Tunney how he uses breathing to handle pressure-packed change.

"Stop a minute," he said, taking a deep breath. "When you take a breath like that, you absorb oxygen. Oxygen is a supplier to the blood. That allows you to relax.

"Watch athletes, and you can see how they use breathing to help them succeed. Greg Louganis [Olympic gold medal–winning diver] is on the three-meter springboard, and he's waiting to start his approach step. The first thing he does: take a deep breath. Watch quarterback Joe Montana. Just before he goes into the huddle, he takes a deep breath, because it gives him the kind of energy he needs. Oxygen is an incredible source of energy."

When you feel panicked by pressure and change, slow your breathing to clear the mind and relax the body. You might also use this quick breathing exercise:

1. Imagine smiling to yourself with mouth and eyes.
2. Breathe in to the count of three.
3. Breathe out to the count of three. As you exhale, let your jaw drop and your shoulders drop.

I often teach this exercise at my seminars. Attendees report it helps them cope with change and stress.

In addition, remember the tips from Step 1: Think Clearly, Act Calmly.

1. Purposely put yourself in nonthreatening situations that require quick thinking under pressure.
2. Practice deep relaxation or meditation (Step 9 tells you how).
3. Mentally rehearse an upcoming challenge.
4. Respond rather than react.

CONCENTRATE ON CONCENTRATION

Thinking clearly in both crisis and noncrisis situations requires concentration. Without it, control is impossible and change seems overwhelming. The top achievers I interviewed have formidable focus to help them gain mastery.

Concentration is mind control—the ability to focus on one issue, ignoring extraneous influences. Unfortunately, in our age of high technology, the ability to concentrate is becoming rare. We're surrounded by innumerable influences and conflicting messages, all vying for attention. But peak performers are still able to focus on what's important.

Walter Cronkite is renowned for his relaxed demeanor. Nicholas von Hoffman, former journalist and author of several political books, called Cronkite a "national security blanket."

It's been more than a decade since Cronkite left the helm of the "CBS Evening News." Cronkite hasn't changed much in twelve-plus years. He still has the relaxed manner that reassured America each night for nineteen years. A recent Gallup poll found that 92 percent of adults still believe what Cronkite tells them.

Cronkite is not an introspective man. Like a few others I interviewed, he seems genuinely unsure of why he is the way he is. But on the topic of concentration, he's clear. I asked him how he stayed calm and focused on the air, even when things went wrong in the studio.

"It was just a question of doing my job. When you're on the air, you simply can't permit a show of temper or displeasure. Your job is to deliver the news. I concentrated on doing that."

Cronkite always believed his own viewpoints didn't belong in the news. He strove for unbiased reporting.

"You learn to put your personal prejudices aside and to recognize them if they appear in your copy, so that you can edit them out. That's part of the skill of the craft, and it takes concentration. I think it's a matter of training and constant vigilance."

How to Concentrate Better: Mindfulness

Have you ever watched the absolute concentration of a child at play? Children do it naturally, but most people lose this ability over time. You can relearn concentration, but it takes some play to do so.

Years ago I counseled a man, John, who managed a successful winery in northern California. Bored with his job, he'd gone back to school to become an attorney. John had a large family, and I asked him how he handled the conflicting demands on his time.

"I'm just going all the time," he said. "I can't recall the last time I just concentrated on what I was doing. I'm always thinking about what's coming next."

John had forgotten how to live in the present. He had to learn to do it again. To begin that process, I taught him how to relax his body (see Step 9 for instructions). Next, we began training his mind to focus on one thing at a time through mindfulness. Zen Buddhists say that the key to self-realization is: "When you eat, just eat. When you walk, just walk." They call this kind of awareness "mindfulness."

I suggested that John practice mindfulness. One mindfulness exercise I taught him is summarized below. You might try it, too. As John practiced it, he breathed calmly and easily to sharpen his concentration.

- Pick a nice, ripe piece of fruit. Start by putting it before you. Just look at it. Notice the color, the shape, the curves. Pick it up and feel the weight and texture.
- Slowly begin to peel it. Carefully notice each sensation. Feel the tensing of your muscles as your fingers pierce the rind. Remember to continue breathing slowly and easily.
- As you separate the segments, or cut up a fruit that is not segmented, feel the release as the pieces move apart, see the little spurts of juice. Then put a piece of the fruit in your mouth, and move it around. What does it feel like?
- As you begin eating, stay focused on what you're doing. Notice each motion, every sensation. You might close your eyes to focus better.
- If your mind wanders, gently bring it back to what you're doing.

After John practiced with fruit, he expanded his exercises to new areas: eating other foods, walking slowly, making love, and, finally, working and studying. Soon he was often able to immerse himself in what he was doing. He reported enjoying what he did much more. His was not an overnight improvement, but John kept at it, and he got better and felt better.

"It's the same thing with sex," one of my interviewees said. "When you're making love, you focus on the present rather than thinking about the end result. That attitude makes sex quite extraordinary. And the lesson applies to all of life."

HOW TO LOSE CONTROL

It's easy to lose control. Abuse alcohol, drugs, or food. Get trapped in other compulsive behaviors. Allow a substance or a behavior to take control of your life.

For people caught in negative behaviors, help is available. Facing those behaviors alone is seldom successful. Luckily, for most compulsions, there are self-help groups that aid people in bouncing back. Alcoholics Anonymous (with almost 2 million members worldwide), Narcotics Anonymous, Cocaine Anonymous, Sex and

Love Addicts Anonymous, Gamblers Anonymous, and Debtors Anonymous can help, as can other similar groups. You can find all these groups through your telephone book or a social service agency in your locality.

Trying to control others is another compulsion. We discussed it earlier in the context of codependency—the attempt by a loved one or friend to control someone who is manifesting compulsive behavior. Codependency is a compulsion in itself. I've worked with people who were as addicted to their codependency as the alcoholic is to booze.

There are self-help groups for codependents, too. One is Al-Anon, the organization for the friends and family of alcoholics. Nar-Anon is for loved ones of drug dependents. And Codependents Anonymous is for any codependent.

Many years ago I began working in a counseling agency, treating alcoholics and drug dependents. Though I liked the job, I became overinvolved in my clients' problems, sometimes worrying about them when I was at home. My supervisor suggested I attend Al-Anon. Grudgingly, I went. At first, I felt out of place in the meetings. But over time, I found support and perspective from the people there. It helped me to be a better, less controlling counselor.

If you wonder whether you have a compulsion, don't rely on your own assessment. Denial is one of the chief characteristics of an addiction. To get a more realistic assessment, ask someone else. But pick a person who will tell you the truth, not one who will say what they think you want to hear.

THE EIGHT KEYS TO GAINING CONTROL

All of us sometimes feel a lack of control during times of change. I've devised the Eight Keys to Gaining Control through interviewing and surveying peak performers. One or more of these strategies will work in almost any situation.

––––––––––––––––––––– K E Y   1 –––––––––––––––––––––

Change Your Focus

Focus on What You *Can* Control

Many of us make an error when we meet obstacles. Faced with a negative situation, we focus on it. A more effective strategy is to focus instead on something positive, something you *can* control. This was the most frequently mentioned "control" strategy during my interviews with peak performers.

As Eileen Ford, cofounder and vice-president of Ford Models, Inc., told me, "There's no point in getting upset about change, because it won't do you one darn bit of good."

But how can we avoid getting upset? It's easier to shift your focus if you believe, as consultant, author, and former Waldenbooks CEO Harry Hoffman does, that another part of your brain is still working on a solution to your problem.

"I've been able to build a talent for putting everything out of my mind," Hoffman told me. "That's where the idea of living life in day-tight compartments comes in. I work for ten or twelve hours, but as soon as I leave I'm on to something else. I know that I have done everything I could do for that day.

"I also know that my subconscious mind is at work on a constant basis. So if I've got a problem that I've articulated during the day, I can forget about it, because I know there are forces working toward solving the problem subconsciously.

"It took me a long time to get to this point. Eventually, I realized you just do the best you can and then leave it alone. Things will work out because your subconscious mind is working on it for you."

Focus on What You *Can't* Control

There is *one* area where shifting your focus will fail. Psychologist Daniel Wegner of Trinity University in San Antonio, Texas, discovered that when people obsess on a thought, suppression doesn't work. The harder they try to put the thought out of mind, the stronger it becomes.

You can test this for yourself. **DON'T THINK ABOUT AN ELEPHANT.** What happened? Did a picture or thought of an elephant come to mind? It does for most people. When we tell ourselves to "stop thinking about _____," the forbidden thought or image sometimes takes center stage.

Fortunately, there's an effective cure for this kind of out-of-control thinking. Consciously focus on the thought you've been trying to banish. Researchers at Trinity University told a group of worriers to devote half an hour a day to thinking about their concerns. If they worried at other times, the psychologists instructed them to avoid suppression, but to refocus on the thoughts during their upcoming half-hour stewing session.

Within one month, the group who had a worry period improved significantly when compared to a control group. They fretted much less, and sometimes found themselves with nothing to worry about when the time came to fuss.

Does this work? Absolutely. I've used it with over one hundred of my clients. Try it yourself: *Set aside half an hour (or more) per day to think and worry about the issue bothering you.* Be certain that you *devote the entire period to worrying.* Even if it feels uncomfortable, stick with it. The results can be amazing.

KEY 2

Think Objectively

The way you think can take you to heaven or to hell. The myth is that circumstances lead directly to emotions. For instance, if your boss harshly criticizes you for a report you wrote, that event leads directly to your feeling angry and depressed. Right? Wrong. In reality there's an intermediate step—your thoughts.

A   **B**   **C**

Events lead to **Thoughts,** which lead to **Emotions.**

Differing thoughts lead to different emotions. When I first began giving seminars ten years ago, I felt upset when someone in the audience got up to leave. I'd think to myself, "That person doesn't like the seminar." Having that thought made me feel anxious and unsure of myself.

Over the years I've learned to think differently. Now when someone walks out of a seminar, I think, "She must be leaving for an appointment," or "Perhaps he has to go back to work." Because my thoughts have changed, my emotions are more positive. I continue to feel strong and confident.

Step 11 provides an excellent system for changing negative thoughts. But for now, experiment with this concept. Next time you feel a negative emotion, chart it. Write down *A—the event, B—your thoughts,* and *C—your emotions.* Then experiment with substituting positive thoughts for your negative ones. You may find that your emotions change, too.

Remember, though, that analyzing the roots of your emotions doesn't mean you have to suppress them. Expressing feelings is important too.

KEY 3

Get Real

Control over everyday emotional ups and downs *is* important. But it's also essential, when truly important things happen, to feel and appropriately express your emotions. That shows humanity and maturity.

KEY 4

Say "No"

There's another time to say what you feel. People hesitate to say "no" for fear of offending others. Negative people who say it all the time *are* offensive. But those who rarely or never say "no" alienate people, too. They may not do what they originally promised, because they took on too much to begin with.

Professional speaker and former NFL ref Jim Tunney told me how he coaches kids to say "no."

"Kids will say to me, 'Well, my friend made me do that.' And I say, 'Wait a minute, nobody makes you do anything you don't want to do.'

"'Well, they persuaded me.'

"Then you agreed with them," I say, "and you did what you wanted to do from their words and their peruasion, but don't blame them. They didn't do it to you. You did it to yourself."

- If you regularly say "yes" when you don't want to, experiment with exercising the opposite approach. Start with small things, just to practice. Saying "no" sometimes will help you gain essential control you've been missing. And, as psychologist Suzanne Kobasa found in her hardiness research, an increased sense of control will help you handle change and stress more effectively.

KEY 5

Make a Plan

Norman Vincent Peale wrote to me, "My method of handling a volume of work is to plan my day and work my plan." This is particularly true when he's confronted with stress and change.

- To do this for yourself, try taking a few minutes in the morning (or the night before) to write out a plan for the upcoming day. You'll gain feelings of mastery and serenity. And, even if abrupt change derails your plans, you can get back on track when the disturbance subsides.

As cookbook author and television personality Julia Child told me, "Sometimes you wake up in the middle of the night thinking of all the terrible things you have to do the next day. It really helps if you make a list, seeing which items are most essential."

KEY 6

Keep Trying

Just as persistence enhances commitment, it often delivers increased control. Bob Hoover, the famed test pilot, discovered this at age sixteen, when he was learning to fly. Hoover had a big problem—he became airsick whenever he went up in a plane. But he kept trying.

"I had motion sickness even on a swing in the park. But I wanted to be an aviator so badly that I thought, 'You've got to learn to live with this.'" Hoover kept at it, going up day after day in a small, single-engine plane. He flew his yellow Taylor Cub in the very maneuvers that made him feel worst. I asked Hoover how he gained control.

"It was a matter of gritting my teeth and doing whatever it was that made me nauseated and continuing that until I could tolerate it," he said. "Then I would go on to something else that bothered me and keep after that until once more I had conquered it."

Hoover continued to work on his problem. Time after time he went up, battling airsickness as he worked for control so he could do what he loved. By the time he beat the nausea, he'd become a fine flyer.

Control doesn't come easily. It requires commitment, courage, and even stubbornness.

KEY 7

Change Face

When we're dealing with a tough situation, our faces show it. We may grimace, frown, or tighten the jaw. And that actually creates negative emotions.

In 1984, psychologists at the University of California Medical School in San Francisco hooked up a group of subjects to biofeedback equipment. The instruments measured their heart and breath rate and other physiological reactions.

Then researchers asked the subjects to adopt certain facial expressions. Some looked angry, others sad, and still others happy. And these facial emotions were reflected in their bodies. Researchers could tell the expression on a subject's face just by looking at the readout from the biofeedback machines.

Since that time, several other studies have replicated these findings. And more and more scientists believe that our expressions *do* partially dictate emotions. This doesn't mean, of course, that smiling will heal a deep depression. But if you're feeling a bit down, angry, or anxious, changing your expression can help you feel better. It's a useful tool for regaining control.

KEY 8

Write It Down

Many people tell themselves, "I can't tell anyone about it," or "It's too terrible to talk about." They may *have to* keep quiet when they are with others, or *choose to*, for fear of judgment by others.

But we do need to release these feelings and thoughts. How? By writing, talking to someone else, or speaking into a tape recorder. Psychologist James Pennebaker, of Southern Methodist University, discovered that expressing emotions this way can lead to better health.

In one experiment, he divided fifty college students into two groups. He asked the first to write about superficial topics, twenty minutes a day, for four days. The second group wrote about problems or unresolved painful events, using the same writing schedule.

Researchers took blood samples from both groups before and after they began writing, and again six weeks later. The results were fascinating.

"At the end of the experiment," Pennebaker says, "students who wrote about experiences that weighed heavily on them showed an increase in lymphocyte response, which indicates an enhanced ability to fight infection." But the group that wrote about trivial topics displayed no immune system improvement.

Six weeks later, the group who had written about problems still had enhanced immune response. And another study found that the benefits lasted. Six *months* later, students who wrote about traumatic events had been to the doctor far less frequently than those in the other group.

Former congresswoman and U.S. vice-presidential candidate Geraldine Ferraro experienced the power of writing firsthand. In 1986, her twenty-two-year-old son was arrested in Vermont for selling a small amount of cocaine to an undercover policeman.

I asked Ferraro why her son's arrest was so tough to deal with.

"I do not excuse what he did—neither does he," she answered quickly. "It was wrong. But he was treated differently because he was my kid. Plus I was totally helpless. There was nothing we could do. If there's something I can do, I'll deal with any problem. But once I give control over that problem to somebody else, I become terribly frustrated."

The pressure was so severe that Ferraro got a duodenal ulcer. She had thrived and survived through tremendous changes during most of her life. It was only when she lost control of a key event in her life that the stress manifested itself physically.

Ferraro used the power of writing to help herself bounce back. "During the course of my son's legal case, I sat down every night and wrote about it on my word processor. There were things I couldn't tell my husband, there were things I couldn't tell my son, there were things I couldn't tell the lawyers. I had feelings and emotions and there was nobody else I could talk to.

"So I talked to the word processor. It was like a confession on a daily basis. It was great. And it really helped me to feel stronger again."

Research shows people can also attain excellent results by telling someone else, or even talking into a tape recorder about what's bothering them.

- Give your immune system and your spirits a boost. Take a few minutes a day, or even a few per week, to write or talk about unresolved issues or problems that bother you. You'll benefit from doing it now, and for many months to come.

SUMMARY: CONTROL STRATEGIES

Acceptance, deep breathing, concentration, living one day at a time—it will take awhile to integrate these and the other control strategies into your life. That's okay. Just reading the stories you've found in this chapter can reprogram your subconscious mind to help you handle change more effectively.

Remember to use the Eight Keys to Gaining Control:

1. Change your focus.
2. Think objectively.
3. Get real.
4. Say "no."
5. Make a plan.
6. Keep trying.
7. Change face.
8. Write it down.

President Dwight D. Eisenhower knew the secret of letting go. He often told the story of an old Quaker farmer who would never use the name of the Lord in vain. But one day, when he slapped his mule's reins to get the animal moving, it wouldn't budge an inch.

The farmer tried everything: coaxing, cajoling, even pleading, but without success. Finally he reached the end of his rope.

"Mule," he said in a quiet voice, "thee knows that because of my religion I cannot beat thee, or curse thee, or abuse thee in any way. But, mule," he contiued, "what thee doesn't know is that I can sell thee to an Episcopalian."

NOTES

Kobasa's quotes about control appeared in "Hardiness: Why Some Executives Thrive Under Stress," in *The Rodale Report*, October 1984.

In Search of Excellence, by Tom Peters and Robert Waterman, Warner Books, 1982.

Schmale's thoughts on helplessness, and Kobasa's observations on reacting to changes at the office, are summarized in *The Healer Within: The New Medicine of Mind and Body*, by Steven Locke and Douglas Colligan, E.P. Dutton, 1987.

Gallup poll that included impressions on Cronkite appeared in "The Way It Was, The Way It Should Be," by Maureen Orth, in *Vogue*, April 1986.

Information on obsessions is drawn from *White Bears and Other Unwanted Thoughts*, by Daniel M. Wegner, Viking Press, 1989.

Research on facial expressions is from "Facial Expressions May Cause the Emotions They Depict," by Daniel Goleman, the *New York Times*, July 30, 1989.

Pennebaker's research is summarized in the *Journal of Consulting and Clinical Psychology*, Vol. 56, pp. 239–245.

STEP FIVE

Dealing with Setbacks

Sometimes our fate resembles a fruit tree in winter.
Who would think that those branches would turn
green again and blossom, but we hope it, we know it.
— G O E T H E

When I first wrote this chapter, my wife and I had suffered a setback. During Mary Lee's fourth month of pregnancy we lost the baby. We'd been planning the birth for months. Suddenly life was tenuous and frightening. Everything seemed risky, especially raising a family. We wondered if we had enough strength to pick up the pieces.

Over time, using the principles I'll discuss in this chapter, we worked through the loss. We found that we were stronger than we'd known. And, though we still felt sad about losing our baby, we discovered greater inner strength than we'd previously known. Since then both of us find that we have less fear and more confidence and more ability to survive the hard knocks and the big changes.

How do some people convince themselves to keep on when the odds seem too great, the opposing voices too loud? In surveying and interviewing peak performers for this book, I discovered

seven ways they use to bounce back from setbacks and catas-
trophes.

FIVE WAYS TO BOUNCE BACK WHEN YOU'RE FEELING DOWN AND OUT

─────── **S T R A T E G Y   1** ───────

Have Faith in a Positive Outcome

The high achievers I interviewed have one important trait in
common. Whatever the change or setback, they maintain a stubborn faith in a positive outcome to the problem or crisis.

Many of our peak performers who have been through cata-
strophic experiences have a strong belief in God. They say, "It's
God's will, and God wants the best for me." But those I interviewed who *don't* believe in God have the same stubborn faith in
positive results.

Navy pilot Captain Gerry Coffee experienced a catastrophe he
eventually transformed into a positive outcome. On February 3,
1966, while flying a mission over North Vietnam, Coffee's Vigi-
lante fighter was hit by antiaircraft fire. The pilot and his crew-
man ejected from the aircraft as it went down.

The men found themselves floating in the ocean just off the
Vietnamese coast. Coffee had a broken arm, dislocated shoulder,
and a shattered elbow.

"The Vietnamese were coming toward us," Coffee told me, "with
six or seven army militia men in each boat shooting automatic
weapons and rifles. The bullets were zinging over our heads,
splatting in the water around us. No chance to escape. The first
boat pulled alongside, and they dragged me roughly aboard."

Coffee was taken to the infamous Wah Lo prison in downtown
Hanoi. He told me about his initial feelings of confusion and helplessness. "I found myself thrust into a foreign and hostile environment, with no one to turn to for advice or help or sympathy, no
other source of strength except what I brought in with me.

"My cell was about three feet wide, six and a half feet long.
Along one wall was a concrete slab, eighteen inches wide . . . that
was my bed. There was a small window high in the back wall
with a double row of iron bars, through which all I could see were

the shards of filthy broken glass embedded in the concrete on the top. A small tin can in one corner of the cell was supposed to take care of all my physical requirements.

"In those earliest weeks and months," Coffee says, "the interrogations, the extortion, the pressure were the most intense."

Sometimes guards handcuffed Coffee's hands behind him and locked his ankles in stocks at the foot of his "bed." Left in that position for three weeks or more, Coffee said, "You didn't know how you were going to go on to the next day. So you'd take a day at a time and try to get to the next day, which would probably be better in some respects. And, sure enough, soon the better day would come."

For almost eight years Gerry Coffee was held captive. His captors tortured him four times while he was imprisoned. Sometimes he wondered if the United States had forgotten him. Yet Coffee found a strong faith that sustained him.

"Initially I couldn't believe it was happening. There was the period of wondering, 'Why me, God?' But that didn't last long. Ultimately it changed from 'Why me, God?' to 'Show me, God.' By that I mean, 'Okay, I accept the circumstances. Now show me, please, what I'm supposed to do with them. I know that this is for a purpose. I know that I'm here to learn something and that I'm supposed to use it in some way.'"

It took many years for Coffee to discover the positive result in which he had such faith. But the pilot also sustained himself in other ways.

"You always have control of your mind," he told me. "It's like the lines from the old poem, 'Stone walls do not a prison make, Nor iron bars a cage.' You are always free to think the way you want to. The only thing I could control there was the perspective in which I placed the experience. Maintaining faith was the same as maintaining control. So I emphasized my faith—in myself, in my wife and family, in my country, and in God."

Coffee also relied on the support he received from his fellow prisoners, even though they could only communicate by tapping out messages on the walls of their cells. (More about that in Step 12.)

In January 1973, after almost eight years of imprisonment, Gerry Coffee was released. He came home to his family, and a son who hadn't yet been born when Coffee was shot down.

"When I came home," he said, "I was asked to speak at various places. It became apparent that there was great value in sharing the insights that came from my prisoner of war experience. I realized I was helping people. It became clear to me that this was my mission, this was what God had showed me."

Today, Coffee is a professional speaker and writer. He speaks to organizations all over the world, telling others what he went through and what he learned.

Coffee believes anyone can benefit from the sources of strength he applied. "Every person, whatever their role in life, whether they're dealing with professional setbacks or personal disappointments, can draw on the same sources of strength.

"We're all 'imprisoned' by certain circumstances at various points in our lives—and we're all more capable of dealing with these things than we give ourselves credit for."

Many of us focus on the negative during setbacks. Yet Coffee's faith led him in a positive direction. When experiencing a crisis or major change, focus on the reality of a positive outcome. Having faith that it will be there helps it to occur.

Many people report benefits from repeating a positive statement over and over when circumstances seem bleak. Sometimes, during the tough times, I tell myself, "I know that this is leading to something good."

You might take a moment now and find a simple phrase that makes sense for you to use when life gets tough. Here are a few possibilities:

- This, too, shall pass.
- I know this is leading to something good.

Or, if you believe in God:

- Thank you, God, for what's happening and the good that's coming from it.

STRATEGY 2

Recognize That Bad Things Happen

Painful changes and unpredictable events happen to everyone.

Abraham Lincoln failed twice in business, suffered the death of his beloved, had a nervous breakdown, and lost eight elections. Yet, at age sixty he was elected president of the United States and became one of the most respected chief executives in U.S. history.

In experiencing setbacks, though, we often feel alone and unlucky. Ken Blanchard, coauthor of the *One Minute Manager* series, told me a meaningful story about setbacks. Ken had just finished his sixth book, *The Power of Ethical Management*, written with motivational master the Reverend Norman Vincent Peale, whose change management tips also appear in this book. Blanchard told me one of Dr. Peale's favorite stories.

"Peale was walking down the street in New York. He saw an old friend coming toward him. From his face and the way he was walking, he could tell that George wasn't into the ecstasy of life. And Norman said, 'How ya doing, George?'

"George took this as an invitation, and thirty minutes later he had finished dumping his last problem.

"At the end he said, 'Norman, I'm fed up . . . nothing but problems, problems, problems. I'd give you a $5,000 check right now for your shirt if you could get rid of all my problems.'

"And Norman thought, 'I've never been anybody to turn my back on such an offer.' So he ruminated and cogitated and contemplated. And he said, 'George, just yesterday I was in a place where there were a lot of people. And I don't think anybody there has any problems. Would you like to go?'

"George said, 'Norman, that's where I want to be. When can we go?'

"Norman answered, 'Tomorrow afternoon. I'll take you to the Westchester Cemetery. The only people who don't have stress and problems are people who are dead.'"

As long as we're alive, problems appear. Accepting that fact helps us cope more effectively with setbacks. And yes, negative emotions rise during setbacks, but self pity doesn't help. Instead, allow yourself to experience the emotions, but deal with them, and move on.

STRATEGY 3

Understand that Setbacks Can Make You Stronger

In 1986 actress Jill Eikenberry completed the pilot for a new television show, "L.A. Law." She and her husband, actor Michael Tucker, felt excited about the prospects for the show. They planned to leave their home in New York and move to L.A. if NBC accepted the pilot.

Suddenly their rosy future turned dark. In May, Eikenberry's doctor told her she had breast cancer.

"The news came completely out of the blue," Eikenberry told me. "At first I thought I was going to die and that was it. I spent some time just lying on the bed and crying, unable to imagine how my family was going to get along without me."

Husband Michael Tucker was scared too. "I remember the moment when the doctor said, 'It's malignant.' I've never been so scared in my life. I thought I was going to lose her." But Tucker and Eikenberry gave each other strength. "Michael and I just held each other for a long time. That helped," Eikenberry says.

Then, several days after learning of the diagnosis, Eikenberry went to the screening of a film she'd recently done. One of the other actresses from the film was there, and when the young woman saw Eikenberry she asked if something was wrong.

"I spilled it all out to her," Eikenberry says. "And she took me over to her mother who was there too. When her mother heard the story she grabbed me and dragged me into the ladies' room. She hiked up her blouse and said, 'Look, this is eleven years ago, I have a scar here and that's all I have to remind me of the breast cancer. This too can happen to you.'

"It was the first time I ever had any sense that there was hope, that I might not die," Eikenberry says. "Her words gave me the courage to seek a second opinion. The first doctor had told me a mastectomy was the best idea, but the second physician said no, I was a good candidate for a lumpectomy."

So Eikenberry opted to have the lumpectomy, a less radical procedure. The operation was successful. But treatment wasn't finished. When Eikenberry began filming the regular episodes of "L.A. Law," she left the set every day at 3:30 P.M. to go to UCLA Medical Center for radiation treatment.

"She was exhausted," Tucker says. "After she got home, she'd rest for the rest of the night, and then go back to work the next day. And this is how we did the first three or four episodes of 'L.A. Law.'"

Eikenberry told me how it was for her. "I just had to keep on keeping on," she said. "And today everybody says, 'Oh, that must have been so hard for you.' And it was. But if you have something else you have to do, it helps. Continuing to work was very therapeutic. I was also playing the Ann Kelsey role which was so strong and aggressive and confident. I think that really helped me make it through. Today I'm celebrating my fifth anniversary cancer-free.

"Once you've fought something like cancer and won, there's not much that's scary. I used to be scared of flying, but I'm not anymore. After cancer you've seen the thing that we all spend a lot of time denying. You've looked death in the face. So fear plays much less of a role in my life than it used to."

Jill Eikenberry kept on keeping on and discovered that change and setbacks really *can* make you stronger.

STRATEGY 4

Change Direction When Necessary

Sometimes "toughing it out" isn't enough. Our culture puts a premium on forging ahead, whatever the obstacles. At times, though, the best way to deal with a setback is to try something different. We can handle a roadblock many ways: imitate Rambo and go through it, go around it, stop and wait for it to disappear, or turn around and go back.

In 1951, Lillian Vernon, then a pregnant twenty-four-year-old housewife, invited change into her life. Vernon took the money she'd received from wedding gifts and bought a supply of belts and purses. She placed a $495 ad in *Seventeen* magazine, offering to personalize the items with the customer's initials. Hoping to earn $50 a week with her new business, Vernon was surprised when the ad brought in orders totaling over $32,000.

Over the next few years, Vernon continued to run small magazine ads, expanding her product line to include personalized combs, blazer buttons, and collar pins. Within a few years, she'd built a mailing list of more than 125,000 customers. Then Vernon published and mailed her first catalog to that list—sixteen black-and-white pages—and the business began to grow even faster.

In the 1970s though, the good times came to an abrupt halt. "We had a period of much too rapid growth," Vernon told me. "It taxed all of our resources. We overexpanded and ran out of cash. We couldn't get the orders out."

I asked Vernon how she handled the setback. "Sometimes there are just so many demands on you that it is very, very tough. You must prioritize what is most important. I had two choices. I could file for bankruptcy. Or I could put my shoulder to the wheel and get the business back on track."

Vernon decided she'd change direction and try a new approach. "We tightened our belts. The principals, including myself, went off salary. We'd get paid when cash flow improved. We trimmed the staff to only essential people. We cut expenses throughout the company dramatically."

Vernon's customers got their orders. They remained loyal to the company, and eventually things *did* turn around.

"I learned an important lesson from this," Vernon says. "It's easy to build fat in a company. You really have to pay attention to make certain that doesn't happen."

Today the Lillian Vernon Corporation ships more than 4.2 million orders each year and employs more than 1,400 workers. By changing the company to overcome a setback, Vernon enabled it to survive.

And Vernon continues to remember the lesson she learned about keeping the company lean. Several years ago, *USA Today* published a story comparing the offices of various top executives. Vernon's office was the smallest and least flashy—understated but elegant. She doesn't need a big power office to boost her ego. Lillian Vernon knows where her company's real power lies—in pleasing her customers.

Often the key to weathering setbacks and severe change is to change direction. But first you have to decide which direction to go. To do that, try the following system:

1. Talk to other people about the problem at hand. Use them as a sounding board, and get their suggestions for solutions. One of those suggestions just might be the one you need.
2. Spend at least half an hour, preferably more, alone. Take time to become relaxed (for instructions on deep relaxation, see Step 9). Ask yourself, "What can be done to make this situation better?" Then just focus on your breathing and allow your unconscious mind to come up with options for new directions.
3. When you've found one or more new options, make a plan for putting it/them into action. Which seems most feasible? Which would be most fun? Which has the best chance of success?
4. Choose one option and use it to change your direction.

STRATEGY 5

Know and Use the Stages of Recovery

October 20, 1991. A firestorm sweeps through the beautiful wooded hills above Oakland, California, destroying over 2,300 upscale homes. Fire officials call the blaze one of the worst urban fires in U.S. history.

My friend and colleague, Leslie Koved, then regional administrator for the Employee Assistance Program at First Interstate Bank, witnessed the fire first-hand. On that Sunday afternoon, Leslie was at her hillside home with Andrew, her four-month-old baby. Leslie's husband was jogging in the hills with their three-year-old son.

"I was listening to the radio," Leslie told me, "and they said there was a big fire. I saw some smoke in the air, but the fire still sounded far away. But then I started hearing explosions and sirens. The smoke was getting thicker. I put the baby and a few things into the car, wrote a note for my husband, and left."

Leslie got out unharmed. Fortunately, her husband and young son escaped the fire, too. Some were not so lucky. Twenty-five were killed by the blaze, and many more were injured. Leslie and her family spent that night at the home of friends, anxiously watching the inferno's progress on television.

When they were finally allowed to return to their home, "The area looked like a battlefield—blackened ruins. We walked around and cried for a long time," she said.

As part of her job, Leslie works with company employees who are dealing with setbacks. Now she had one of her own to deal with. Leslie helped herself and her family through a difficult time by using her knowledge about coping with loss. For one thing, they went back to look at the remains of the house every few days.

"That helped us get through the denial," she said. "We had so much to do—taking care of two little kids, full-time jobs, insurance. For the first week and a half both my husband and I were very task focused."

Elizabeth Kubler-Ross, M.D., the renowned authority on death and dying, found that we experience five stages in grieving over the death of someone close to us, or in preparing for our own death. These same emotions may arise following other changes and setbacks like losses of relationships, jobs, or important material possessions.

The five stages of grieving are:

- Denial
- Anger
- Bargaining
- Depression
- Acceptance

The emotions don't always appear in order. Many people move back and forth between them, as Leslie did.

In the *denial* stage, we say to ourselves and others, "This cannot be true." We pretend that the problem isn't real or serious. Denial can be positive, at least at first, because it helps us avoid feeling overwhelmed by the event. But eventually we must go beyond the denial. Leslie made the frequent trips back to the site of her house to help ease through the denial phase.

During *anger,* we may complain bitterly and feel rage.

Bargaining takes place when we ask for "one more chance" or we promise to stop a negative activity if only things can be as they were. In some cases, the bargaining stage may be passed over.

Depression is almost always experienced after major setbacks. It is difficult to cheer or reassure someone who is in this stage. They need to experience it fully in order to move on. If, however, the depression is severe, and lasts longer than a few months, it is best to seek professional help.

Eventually *acceptance* arrives, as it did for Leslie Koved. We still feel badly about the setback or loss, but acceptance signals a willingness and ability to move beyond it.

Art Linkletter also experienced these emotional stages after the tragic death of his youngest daughter, Diane, in 1969. Diane died by falling or jumping from the sixth-floor balcony of a Hollywood apartment above Sunset Strip. The coroner found no drugs in her system. Yet in talking to her friends, Linkletter came to believe her death may have resulted from a flashback to a previous negative experience with psychedelics.

When I asked him how he handled the death of his daughter, Linkletter paused before answering. Finally he spoke, his voice carrying the sound of old hurt.

"When you have a major tragedy in your life, you're not going to be left unchanged," Linkletter said. "You're going to be changed. You have two choices. You can change for the worse— or you can change for the better.

"If you are going to hug the loss to your heart and make yourself angry, cynical, disbelieving, and suspicious, then you're going to be a lesser person."

Instead, Linkletter says, you can think of the good things and the wonderful memories.

"You can confront this question," he continues. "'What if I had had a choice when the child was born?' What if you had known that he or she was going to die at the age of twenty? Knowing what had happened in those twenty years, would you have said no?

"You finally come to the realization that you lived part of your life that you would never give up. You try to find out if there's some way you can make things better for other people, which I did."

Denial, bargaining, depression, and anger are part of recovery from a setback. But to avoid remaining bitter and negative, we must learn what we can, from the pain, experience our grief fully and move on to acceptance.

STRATEGY 6

Help Others

Many of the peak performers I interviewed help other people by using the knowledge gained in coping with painful changes in their own lives. They channel their experience, strength, and hope to others who are in pain.

Since the death of his daughter, one of Art Linkletter's chief interests has been fighting drug abuse, a topic on which he writes, speaks, and broadcasts.

Jill Eikenberry works hard to educate the public about breast cancer and its prevention.

Gerry Coffee speaks all over the world, recounting what he learned as a prisoner of war, to help others handle adversity.

After losing her home in the Oakland fire, Leslie Koved discovered that helping others, through her job as an employee assistance counselor, enabled her to deal more effectively with the loss she and her family had suffered.

Some Ways to Help Others Survive a Bad Time

If you've survived a setback or catastrophe, you, too, can help others. There are countless ways. You might:

- Volunteer at a hospital.
- Give speeches about your experience.
- Counsel people who've suffered similar problems.
- Write an article.
- Volunteer to work on a telephone crisis line or help line.
- Join SCORE (the Service Corps of Retired Executives).
- Work with other people in a support group.

Put your pain and knowledge to work helping others. You'll feel better and they will, too.

SUMMARY: YOU CAN BOUNCE BACK

We've all suffered setbacks and painful changes. The five recovery strategies enable us to bounce back and go on. To sum up, they are:

1. *Have faith in a positive outcome.* The foregoing survivors did.

2. *Recognize that bad things happen to everyone.* Self-pity won't help. Use the tools we've discussed, deal with the setback as best you can, and move on.

3. *Change direction when necessary.* Recovering from a setback may mean changing direction or trying something new.

4. *Know and use the stages of recovery.* Be willing to acknowledge and experience denial, bargaining, anger, and depression. Only then can you finally accept the setback and get back on track.

5. *Help others.* Helping others makes you feel better about yourself and those you help. Your ability to handle current and future setbacks blossoms.

Finally, remember what the old proverb says: "The harder you fall, the higher you bounce."

9
STEP SIX

Being Optimistic

A happy person is not a person in a certain set of circumstances, but rather a person with a certain set of attitudes.

—HUGH DOWNS

The dogs cower, motionless in small black boxes. Benches and instruments clutter the laboratory around them. Though the barrier in each enclosure is low, the dogs avoid it. They passively absorb the mild electric shock that jolts them through the floor of the box. The dogs could easily leap out, but they do not. They're trapped . . . not by the barrier, but by their past.

The year is 1966. The dogs are conditioned. Before this experiment, they were exposed to electric shocks from which they could not escape. The dogs learned they couldn't get away and gave up, though now freedom from the discomfort is just a jump away.

Psychologist Martin Seligman first wrote about experiments like these when he was a young graduate student at the University of Pennsylvania. He called the behavior of the dogs "learned helplessness," and speculated that it was related to the earlier situation where they couldn't escape electric shocks. Seligman wondered if human beings might also give up after being exposed to severe "shocks" in their lives.

Over the years, Seligman and his associates refined and expanded this theory. They found that human beings can interpret events, so helplessness and depression don't always result from negative incidents. Instead, people "explain" unfavorable occurrences in different ways. Seligman calls this the "explanatory" style. He says that the explanation we use dictates our mood— and our ability to manage pressure-packed change.

Explanatory style also relates to optimism and pessimism. According to one old saying, "The pessimist sees the difficulty in every opportunity and the optimist sees the opportunity in every difficulty."

And optimism helps, not just in times of crisis but in everyday life. Research shows that a positive explanatory style leads to improved health, increased happiness, and greater success in career pursuits.

Our top achievers are an optimistic group. Their positive explanatory style helps them handle change and achieve success.

"I look at the brighter things of life, and don't worry about what bad things are going to happen," says Gertrude Crain, chairman of the board of Crain Communications, Inc.

For Crain and the others I interviewed, optimism makes change easier to handle. They expect something good eventually will happen if they work for it, even during adversity. It often does.

SUCCESSFUL PEOPLE DON'T ALWAYS FACE REALITY

Perhaps you're saying, "Sure. Optimism may help *you* succeed, but it's not real. The real world is a place that invites pessimism. It's the only honest approach."

Reality is kinder than that. A recent *Los Angeles Times* poll found that people say they become happier as they grow older. Only about 50 percent of people between the ages of eighteen and forty-nine rate their lives as very satisfying. Yet nearly 75 percent of those over age sixty-five say they find great satisfaction in their lives.

The poll reported that older people are also less likely to be depressed or lonely, less likely to have money worries, and less fearful about disease or death. For many, life improves as we get older. So perhaps optimism isn't ridiculous. Maybe pessimism is the unreal approach.

And a prejudice toward the positive can help us cope more effectively, even with problems. In 1988, the *Psychological Bulletin* published a review of several hundred studies of optimism and pessimism.

Shelly Taylor, the UCLA psychologist who cowrote the review, said, "People negotiate their days by drawing strength from positive illusions. If you woke up knowing in advance how little you'd accomplish, about the awful times you'd have with people, about the rejections you'd get, how would you get out of bed? Positive illusions spawn optimism."

As Eileen Ford, cofounder and vice-president of the highly successful Ford Models, Inc., told me, "God gave us the ability to forget, and that's the shield you have to use. You can't dwell on the negative things in life."

HOLDING ON TO HOPE

Norman Cousins beat the odds time and again. He faced challenges greater than most of us will ever experience.

I interviewed Cousins shortly before his death in 1991. He was slender, boyish-looking, with thinning gray hair, and his brown eyes jumped and sparkled. Color photographs lined the deep green walls of his office at UCLA. Cousins had photographed Albert Schweitzer, Nikita Kruschchev, Dwight Eisenhower, Pope John, and Hubert Humphrey, among others. Each photograph had a poignancy and optimism to it. And in his life, Cousins needed every ounce of that optimistic spirit. In our interview, he described the central role optimism played in helping him cope with his complex life.

In 1964, Cousins was the highly respected editor of the *Saturday Review*, having brought the magazine from near bankruptcy to robust circulation. He had just returned from a trip to the Soviet Union as cochairman of a U.S. delegation on cultural exchange.

A few days after his return, Cousins began having difficulty moving his limbs and was hospitalized. Doctors said he was suffering from a collagen disease—a weakening of the connective tissue. Soon much of his body was paralyzed.

According to one specialist, Cousins's chances of recovery were one in five hundred. Until then, Cousins had let the doctors call the shots. But when he found that he would have to beat such odds, he decided to take a more active role in his healing.

Cousins remained optimistic. With the help of his personal physician, he researched the disease. He'd previously read studies showing that negative emotions can have negative effects on body chemistry. Cousins wondered if positive emotions could induce positive changes.

"During my trip to the Soviet Union I encountered many frustrating situations," he told me. "I think the illness was partially the result of the effect of stress on my immune system. The opposite of exasperation or frustration is laughter. So I went ahead very systematically and began my own program of recovery."

First, Cousins arranged to have Allen Funt, the producer of "Candid Camera," send him films of some of the funniest of those classic television shows. Cousins watched the films in his hospital room, hoping that laughter would help his condition.

As he watched and chortled, Cousins made a delightful discovery. If he laughed, a real belly laugh for at least ten minutes his pain diminished, and he could sleep for at least two hours. Medical readings corroborated his discovery. The nurse took readings just before and several hours after his bouts of laughter. Sedimentation dropped by at least five points each time. He had discovered that laughter was indeed good medicine.

The specialists regarded Cousins's self-healing ideas with amusement. Only his own doctor supported him. But he continued. Next, Cousins also decided that a hospital wasn't a good place to be sick. He moved to a hotel room because, he said, it was quieter, cheaper, and a better environment in which to recover.

Cousins also drew on other research he'd found. He asked for massive doses of vitamin C, instead of the aspirin and phenylbutazone the doctors had prescribed. The vitamin C also contributed to significant drops in his sedimentation level.

Within a few weeks, Cousins could move his thumbs without pain. The sedimentation rate continued to drop, and bit by bit he was able to move more of his body. His connective tissue was regenerating itself, something the specialists had said couldn't happen.

After a trip to Puerto Rico with his wife and friends, Cousins felt even better. Healing was still a long, laborious process. But Cousins completely recovered. He beat the odds through optimism, laughter, and a belief in himself.

FACING CHALLENGES

Though Norman Cousins met his illness with optimism, his positive attitude didn't begin there. "When I was nine years old," he told me, "I was sent away to a tuberculosis sanitarium. If the doctors at that time had been asked to make predictions about my longevity, I doubt that any of them would say that at the age of seventy-six I'd be fully active, playing tennis and golf, and having a hell of a good time."

And the challenges continued. In 1940, he became editor of the *Saturday Review of Literature*. "I got the job because no one else would take it," he said. The magazine was in severe financial trouble, with a circulation of 20,000.

"My predecessors and associates said that no quality magazine in this country has a circulation more than 30,000. I really enjoyed having people say that, because we sailed through that 30,000 barrier as though it never even existed and eventually got to 650,000.

"To achieve the impossible, you must believe in the possible. To believe something is possible creates energy. To believe that something is impossible depletes it."

While Cousins was at the *Saturday Review*, the United States dropped the atomic bomb on Hiroshima. The editor began a "moral adoption" program with his readers, where they supported four hundred children orphaned by the blast. This success encouraged him to start another program—one the experts were sure would fail.

Cousins told me what happened: "I had a project to bring to the United States some of the young women disfigured and crippled by the atomic bombing of Hiroshima. I arranged for plastic surgeons to provide their service and helped find homes where the young women could stay. The State Department opposed the project. They said that the experts in cultural anthropology believed the project would fail.

"I said, 'Did the anthropologists say anything about the power of love to close all those gaps? What happens when these girls meet with doctors and people who have an outstretched hand and are willing to help them and to take them into their homes?

"We didn't have a single girl who couldn't make the adjustment," Cousins told me.

Time and again people told Cousins that what he was doing was impossible. Each time he was optimistic about his chances. And each time his beliefs and hard work carried him through to success.

Norman Cousins had one more major personal challenge to overcome. "Ten years ago," he said, "I had a heart attack. The doctor told me my chances of living out the year were unacceptably low, unless I had an angiogram or surgery. I really enjoyed that because I knew he was wrong, so I wasn't bedeviled by expert advice. I relish that. That stress was converted into good feelings and good health."

Cousins recovered completely from his heart attack, without surgery. He wrote a book about this experience and called it *The Healing Heart*.

At the age of sixty-two, Cousins was asked to join the UCLA School of Medicine, though he didn't have a medical degree. As an adjunct professor, he spent his time writing and researching. The focus of the work? Optimism, health, change, and immunity.

The optimism we hold in our hearts *can* heal. But optimism alone will not lead to success. Blend it with hard work and determination. And it doesn't hurt if there's a part of you that, like Norman Cousins, refuses to believe the conventional wisdom and holds on to hope.

THE DOWN SIDE OF UP

Norman Cousins was a realistic optimist. He didn't deny the gravity of his problems. Instead, he acknowledged obstacles and set out to deal with them. He didn't say, "I don't really have this disease." He said instead, "I have some problems, and I know I can deal with them effectively if I work at it." This attitude helped him deal effectively with the dramatic changes in his life.

Some people, though, use denial as a *substitute* for true optimism. They deny the severity of a disease or problem, and thus avoid working at a successful outcome. The Bible says, "Faith without works is dead." The true optimist *works* toward a positive outcome.

Denial is a form of pessimism.

Psychologist Shlomo Breznitz, director of the Center for the Study of Psychological Stress at the University of Haifa in Israel, has done extensive research on denial and hope. In an interview in *American Health*, he explained the power inherent in these states of mind:

"The major difference between hope and denial, is that in denial you try not to pay attention—not to see, not to hear, not to think about the negatives.

"In hoping, you look at the situation, no matter how negative, to seek out the few remaining positive elements and build on them. It's the patient who tells himself, 'I may be in the coronary care unit, but lots of people recover with what I have. I'll be home next week.'

"The healthiest attitude is a hope based on a realistic evaluation of the situation."

Realism is key. Without it, optimism becomes false hope. In fact, Psychologist Raymond Niaura, at the Miriam Hospital in Providence, Rhode Island, discovered a link between emotional denial and health problems. In one study, men who denied their negative emotions and "put on a happy face" tended to have high cholesterol levels.

When asked to do difficult tasks, these "repressors" said they were doing fine, not feeling anxious. Yet their blood pressure and heart rate rose rapidly. "They tell you they are not experiencing stress when their bodies tell you they are," Niaura says. That's denial, and in this case it's a health hazard.

Having doubts doesn't mean you're pessimistic. Each of us wonders sometimes if we can make it through a difficult time, handle a problem, or deal with a dilemma.

HOW OPTIMISM HELPS US

Optimists have doubts, too, but optimism helps people achieve more, feel better, and live longer. Thus they handle change and stress more effectively. Here's how.

Optimism Fosters Higher Achievement

The arid Israeli landscape bakes in the harsh sunlight. Fatigue-clad soldiers trudge exhaustedly up a slight hill. Defeat is etched in every sun shadow of each face. These are the elite fighting men of perhaps the world's finest army. Yet they seem incapable of completing a march many civilians could handle.

These soldiers are part of a research project conducted by psychologist Shlomo Breznitz. Breznitz was studying Israeli soldiers to discover how hope affects productivity.

For the study, Breznitz had several groups of soldiers carrying heavy packs march rapidly for almost twenty-five miles. The researchers varied the information they gave each group.

"Some knew exactly how far they had to walk," Breznitz says, "and we gave them distance markers along the way. Some knew only that it would be long, and they had no way of estimating how far they'd gone. Some expected a thirty-kilometer march, and then at the last moment were told they had another ten to go. The last group expected a sixty-kilometer march, but were stopped at forty. So all these groups actually marched the same distance, but with different thoughts in their heads."

Breznitz found that the soldier's differing thoughts contributed to differing levels of performance. "The soldiers who had realistic information and who were kept fully informed of how far they had to go were in the best shape."

Among those who had no information at all, the subjective estimates of how long they had marched varied wildly. Some of the men thought the march had been short; others thought it was very, very long.

"What astonished us was that their cortisol levels were related to their *estimates* of distance traveled, not to *actual* distance traveled. [Cortisol is a hormone whose level in the body increases during stress.] This finding seems to be a metaphor for most of life's problems—stress comes from our interpretation of their difficulty, not the problems per se. Hope reduces their weight."

The groups of soldiers who were misled had real problems. "Again, stress was in the head, not the feet. Those who thought they were only going thirty kilometers had a hard time when they were told they had to go ten more—though they all finished the hike. But the group that started with the thought they had to go sixty kilometers did even worse. By the time they heard the good news—that they only had to go forty kilometers—they were so exhausted and hopeless it didn't matter much. Some of them actually dropped out after ten kilometers, a distance they marched almost every day before breakfast."

The fully informed group had an attitude of optimism that made them accomplish more. As Breznitz observed, "It's easier to bear your burden when you can see the light at the end of the tunnel."

University of Pennsylvania psychologist Martin Seligman's research also shows the value of optimism in fostering achievement. One of the tools used to assess optimism is Seligman's Attributional Style Questionnaire (ASQ). This reveals the subject's explanatory style and assigns a rating, with a high number indicating a positive style.

In one study, Seligman had a group of new insurance agents take the ASQ. After one year, the optimists were twice as likely as the pessimists to still be on the job.

Insurance company executives then agreed to a second study. Ordinarily, companies hire agents partially on the basis of an industry test. Seligman took a group of one hundred agents who had failed the traditional test but had a high score on the ASQ. Ordinarily, these prospective agents wouldn't have been hired, but for the sake of the experiment they got a chance.

When performance was evaluated some time later, the special group sold 20 percent more than the agents who had passed the industry test. And members of the special group sold 45 percent more insurance than regular agents who had failed the ASQ.

Seligman also studied swimmers at the University of California, Berkeley. Researchers asked each swimmer on the men's and the women's teams to take the ASQ. Then their coaches estimated how they thought each swimmer would do in a competitive situation. The athletes with high ASQ scores (the optimists) swam fewer poor events than those with lower scores. And the ASQ score predicted performance better than the coaches had.

Then the researchers played a trick worthy of Shlomo Breznitz. They had the athletes swim the best they could on their favorite event. After they finished, the swimmers were told that they had swum more slowly than they actually had. Later, after resting, they swam the same event again. The optimists did as well or better the second time. The pessimists did worse—consistently.

The results of these research studies indicate that those with a negative explanatory style are more likely to give up, because they blame failures upon themselves. A positive explanatory style helps us bounce back from failure, and optimism improves performance in just about anything. Expect the best, and you're likely to find it.

Jenny Craig, cofounder and chief operating officer of Jenny Craig International, is a true optimist. In fact, her husband and partner, Sid, claims that when you look under *optimist* in the dictionary, you see Jenny's picture.

Craig's optimism has been instrumental in her success. In 1983, Jenny and Sid founded Jenny Craig International, opening their first Weight Loss Centres in Australia. She told me about how her positive attitude helped the company take off.

"When we first went to Australia, nobody knew who Jenny Craig was. We were keeping our head above water, but we weren't making any money and couldn't afford to advertise enough to make the company grow. Yet even then, I always knew that we would make it. I used to tell Sid every day, 'It's going to work, it's going to work..'"

Jenny Craig backed her optimism with hard work, making certain the clients they *did* have were happy with the program. Word of mouth picked up the slack when they couldn't advertise as much as they wanted to. Soon the company became successful in the Australian market, opening fifty centers in a year and a half. Then, in 1985, Jenny and Sid brought Jenny Craig International to the United States. That wasn't easy either.

"We came back to the U.S.," Craig says, "and found out that during the two years we were in Australia quite a few weight-loss companies had sprung up. We started advertising, but people weren't beating a path to our door. We kept pouring money into it, and Sid would say, 'Where is the point that we fold our tent and say it's not working?'"

Once again, though, Jenny Craig believed they'd succeed. "I don't remember ever feeling, deep in my heart, that it wasn't going to work. I believed we'd make it.

"Eventually we realized that people were confused. All the weight-loss programs sounded alike. We had to have something to set us apart. So we developed our frozen food line, and made the meals available at each center."

Now differentiated from its competitors, Jenny Craig International took off in the United States. Within five years the company had more than 350 centers in major markets throughout the country. Jenny Craig's optimism helped her persevere until her company became successful.

Optimism Improves Health

Health and happiness go together. Partially it's because we feel better when healthy. But enjoying life actually helps build resistance to disease.

Conversely, a pessimistic attitude may lead to poor health. Need proof?

Imagine a plump, ripe lemon. Look at it—give it a squeeze. Then imagine taking a knife and cutting the lemon in half. Feel the weight of the blade cutting through the skin, and the droplets of juice splattering out. Think of squeezing the lemon juice into your mouth.

Did your mouth pucker? Did you begin to salivate? If so, your mind is influencing your body. David Bresler, Ph.D., former director of the UCLA Pain Control Unit, says, "If thinking of a juicy lemon makes you salivate, imagine what happens when you think of your life situation as hopeless. You are telling your immune system, 'Don't bother! Don't do the best you can to heal me!"

Many studies show that cancer victims who exhibit a "fighting spirit" have higher survival rates than those who adopt a helpless, hopeless attitude.

Psychologist Christopher Peterson studied 172 college students at Virginia Polytechnic Institute and State University in Blacksburg. The students were divided into two groups—optimists and pessimists. Both groups were assessed for overall health at the beginning of the study. One month later they were tested again. The pessimists had become sick more often. "And a year later," Peterson says, "they had made significantly more visits to the doctor."

Another study shows that expectations directly affect mind and body. Stanford University Medical Center put thirty hypertension patients through a blood pressure reduction program in 1982. First, they learned progressive muscle relaxation, a series of exercises that often lead to a temporary reduction in blood pressure. Then the patients separated into two groups.

The first group was told that they could expect immediate results from the relaxation exercises and that the effects would continue and increase with practice. Researchers informed the second group that positive benefits would be delayed and that they might initially notice a small blood pressure *rise*.

Both groups then had three twenty-minute sessions of progressive muscle relaxation. The results were dramatic. The first group, those with a positive expectant attitude, showed a 17-point mean reduction in systolic blood pressure. The second group showed a much smaller drop—about 2.4 points. Group two hadn't expected much, and that's just what they received.

Expectation often creates the reality we experience. And we're not the only ones who benefit, or suffer, from our attitudes.

Optimism Spreads to Others

Many diseases are contagious. So are most cases of optimism. Leaders who are upbeat and positive inspire similar emotions in their followers.

During World War II, Sir Winston Churchill rallied a nation with optimism. His belief in England's ultimate success was instrumental in bringing about victory.

Of course, your optimism needs to be realistic, or people won't follow what you say. But a positive attitude will always go farther than pessimism.

PESSIMISM AND EXPLANATORY STYLE

Martin Seligman's research shows that pessimists explain negative events to themselves in the following ways:

- **Permanent** rather than temporary. A pessimist who was laid off from a job might tell himself, "I can't ever keep a job." He believes that the problem will *continue*. An optimist, on the other hand, would say, "Too bad I lost the job. Ah well, I'll get another" (**temporary**—it's not a continuing problem).
- As **pervasive** rather than specific. "I can't do anything right," the pessimist tells himself. He sees himself doing everything wrong, rather than making a specific mistake. The optimist might say, "It's only one thing going wrong" (the problem is **specific** to this situation).
- As **personal** rather than external. "Losing the job was all my fault," the pessimist says. He blames the entire problem on himself (internal) rather than on external factors (or a combination of internal and external causes). The optimist might

say, "The company had a lot of problems anyway" (there were **external** factors contributing to the problem).

Of course, most people's styles aren't this clear-cut or drastic. But a little bit of pessimism can go a long way.

Interestingly, when thinking about a *positive* event, optimists and pessimists exchange explanatory styles. The optimist sees a positive event as *permanent, pervasive,* and *personal.* For instance, when the optimist's boss compliments her on a presentation she made, the optimist might say to herself, "I'm really doing a good job at work."

After a similar compliment, the pessimist might say, "My boss really liked this presentation, but it's just because he was in a good mood." The pessimist explained the positive event in *temporary, specific,* and *external* terms.

FAMILY TIES CAN BREED PESSIMISM

Most people never consciously choose their explanatory style. Instead, they learn it as they're growing up. When a parent speaks frequently to a child in a negative way, the youngster learns pessimism. The phrases that damage are ones like:

"You stupid kid" (permanent, personal).
"Can't you do anything right?" (permanent, pervasive, personal).
"You really make it tough on us" (permanent, personal).

Or, in talking to someone else about a child (with the child present):

"Jennifer just doesn't get along with other children"

Often parents don't mean it when they use phrases like these with their children. The words rise from anger or frustration. Yet the children believe that what their parents say is true. The damage is done, even if it was unintended.

Silence can breed pessimism, too. If children hear little praise as they grow up, it's unlikely they will feel optimistic. Children learn that they have power and value by hearing about their strengths.

Without praise, it's difficult for children to become optimistic. They need to have a positive model—someone showing and telling them that they *can* succeed and recognizing their accomplishments. It's essential for parents to acknowledge even the small victories. True achievement requires building on past successes, however inconsequential.

Children blossom when parents talk to them in optimistic ways, saying for instance:

"You did a great job on that paper for school. You're really smart."

Or, when the child does something wrong:

"You made a mistake. We all make mistakes sometimes. What can you do differently next time?" (temporary, specific).

But even if you were raised with high negativity or low praise, you *can* change. It takes hard work, but millions have succeeded in rising above the past.

HOW TO BECOME MORE OPTIMISTIC

This section demonstrates how to emphasize or reemphasize the bright side. You don't need to use all these strategies. Just pick a few that you feel will help you handle change by becoming more optimistic. And they will!

--- **S T R A T E G Y   1** ---

Watch Your Mouth

Self-talk is what we say to ourselves about situations. Negative self-talk breeds pessimism. But, Martin Seligman says, "If you learned it, you can unlearn it."

First, remember the three parameters of explanatory style: permanent/temporary; pervasive/specific; and internal/external.

- Begin by monitoring your self-talk for a few days. Whenever you talk negatively to yourself, make a note of it, either mentally or in writing. Label the self-talk as permanent, pervasive, personal, or a combination of these.
- At the end of each day, review your notes. How many times

did you put yourself down or view things in a negative light? Many people find this process frustrating because it brings problems to light. Yet awareness is essential for progress.

- After you've monitored your self-talk for a few days, experiment with making changes. If you say, "How could I have done that? I'm really dumb," (permanent and pervasive), change the thought to, "I made a mistake. Ah well, I'll do better next time" (temporary and specific).
- Perhaps you have an argument with someone and say to yourself, "It was all my fault" (internal). Try substituting "We both had a part in this, even though I made a mistake" (more externally oriented).
- Finally, if you say things like "I always mess up the important assignments" (permanent), instead try, "I had trouble on this project, but I did well on _____, _____, and _____" (temporary).

Psychologists call this process a *cognitive* approach because you're changing your cognitions, the way you think. We'll cover this technique in greater depth in Step 11.

The process of changing self-talk can be easier if you work *with* someone. Depressed clients in counseling show a clear rise in optimism as they continue in therapy. Cognitive therapy helps the client learn how depressed thinking differs from optimistic thinking.

Amdahl CEO Jack Lewis strives to keep his thinking positive through self-talk. "I'll say to myself, 'Come on, this problem is solvable. All you have to do is break this down into parts and understand what is going on and it will be okay."

And before electing not to run for a third term, Sacramento Mayor Ann Rudin told me, "Sometimes I have to give myself a little encouragement by saying, 'You can do it.' If I have some hesitation about doing something, this little voice gives me a nudge."

STRATEGY 2

Concentrate on the Good

Staying positive is sometimes a matter of fixing your mind on the good. Top stress researcher Hans Selye believed in keeping a positive focus, particularly when dealing with stress and change.

"Try to keep your mind constantly on the pleasant aspects of life and on actions which can improve your situation," he said. "This is perhaps the most efficient way of minimizing stress. . . . As a wise German proverb says, 'Imitate the sundial's way; count only the pleasant days.'"

Several years ago, I realized that I accentuated the negative when in a bad mood. I'd search for what was wrong and dwell on it. Many people do the same.

The antidote has been to *search for the positive* instead, especially when I'm feeling bad. Sometimes that's a hard task. But as I push myself to continue, I always find *something* to be grateful for. And often that discovery leads to a domino effect of further positive breakthroughs. It certainly becomes more difficult to maintain an entirely gloomy view of the situation.

You always choose where to put your attention. Do you put yours on the positive or negative events around you? If you often focus on the negative, try these strategies:

- Throughout the day, look for one positive aspect of each situation in which you find yourself.
- When you find yourself thinking about all the negative things which might happen, *stop*. Ask yourself what *positive* things might occur.
- When you're dealing with someone you don't like, look for one positive aspect in that person's character or appearance.

Lastly, before you go to sleep at night, think about what it was that you enjoyed most during the day. When I began doing this regularly, it strengthened my relationship with my sons, because I realized how often time spent with them was full of joy. Remembering those good moments helps me get through the times when they're full of mischief.

STRATEGY 3

Find People with the Same Problem

I once counseled an intelligent young woman, Laurie, who worked as a typist in a large corporation. When she first came to see me, Laurie was very pessimistic. She dreamed of becoming a manager but felt she'd never succeed.

Laurie had another problem, too—she was an alcoholic. No one knew about it. She was a binge drinker and could stop drinking for weeks at a time. Even when she drank she was often able to control it. But sometimes she'd set out to have one or two drinks and wind up having many more. When that happened, she sometimes called in sick at work or went to work with a hangover.

Laurie blamed her drinking on her job and the lack of a relationship in her life. When I first suggested she might have a drinking problem, she denied it furiously. But after doing some reading on the topic, she agreed to try Alcoholics Anonymous. At first Laurie didn't like the meetings. She said the people there had more problems than she did. But she agreed to try a few more meetings.

Laurie continued to attend A.A., and her life improved. She stopped drinking and became more optimistic about the future and her life. Support groups like A.A. help their members to beat pessimism. And, as we discussed in Step 4, support groups of all kinds are available, often free of charge, for almost any problem, in almost every town.

When I heard from Laurie recently, she had been sober for over two years. She told me she was very happy. She had finally landed the management job she's dreamed of. Her future, both personal and professional, looked bright.

STRATEGY 4

Remember—Negatives Can Become Positives

===

Several years ago, Jenny Craig's husband, Sid, tried to buy the San Diego Padres baseball team from then owner Joan Kroc. Jenny Craig told me what happened.

"I knew it was important to him, and because he wanted it I wanted it for him. We were down to the final negotiations. Suddenly Joan decided she was going to go in another direction; no explanation was given. We weren't able to buy the team. And for a couple of days Sid was really down."

But Jenny remained optimistic. "I kept telling Sid, 'If it happened this way, it was meant to be. It happened for the best. Maybe something better is going to come along later.'"

Something good *did* come from the setback. Craig described it: "When major league baseball was going through the strike and the salary negotiations, Sid said, 'God, I'm glad I don't have that team.' You couldn't anticipate that that was going to happen. But it really *did* all come out for the best."

Actor Michael Tucker learned a similar lesson. Years before
"L.A. Law," Tucker was acting in a production of *A Midsummer
Night's Dream* at the Arena Stage Theatre in Washington, D.C.
His role required him to sing several songs.

"The composer of the music heard me sing," Tucker told me.
"He said, 'If that guy's singing the songs, I'm pulling my score.'
So the director fired me. I was furious about it. I had to get a job
as a waiter to survive."

A few years later, Tucker was in New York and he got a call
from his agent. "He'd gotten me an audition for a play," Tucker
says, "directed by the same man who had fired me earlier. I said,
'No, I don't want to see him.'

"And he said, 'He said you'd say that, but he wants to see you.'

"So I went in . . . and he hired me. We had a fantastic time. We
became good friends. He also hired me about two years later for
a production called 'Concealed Enemies,' about the Alger Hiss
case. That appeared on PBS, was an enormous success, and really
led to 'L.A. Law.'"

Though Michael Tucker didn't realize it at the time of the setback, his firing—and his sportsmanlike reaction to it—led eventually to a huge boost to his career. The optimists are right. Often,
negative events really *can* lead to something positive. To remind
yourself of this fact, try the following:

- Think about how some of your past setbacks and failures led
  to something positive, perhaps something you hadn't even
  anticipated. What did you learn from the problems you dealt
  with?

STRATEGY 5

Tell Yourself Stories with Happy Endings

Psychologist Shlomo Breznitz says, "Hope takes work: One has
to dwell on the situation, think it over, weave possible scenarios,
and tell oneself stories with happy endings."

We have to focus on a troublesome situation and encourage
ourselves to create happy endings to it. Stories are powerful. They
go directly to the unconscious mind and can change our inner-
most thoughts and feelings.

Jack was a successful salesman who attended one of my seminars. He and his wife had recently divorced, and he felt lonely,

sad, and anxious about the future. I helped Jack create a positive story. He imagined himself one year in the future feeling happy and content. He saw himself selling more effectively and regularly dating an interesting new woman.

I encouraged Jack to think of this story frequently. Ten months later he called to tell me it had come true.

You can also use positive stories when dealing with others, children or adults. Tell them stories about how other people faced challenges and changes similar to those they're facing. Tell them how the people in the stories met their difficulties and triumphed. Make your story enthusiastic but *not preachy*.

STRATEGY 6

Prove It to Yourself—Optimism *Can* Bring Positive Results

Norman Cousins became more optimistic over the years. Part of this growth came from experiencing the positive results of active hope. Each time he succeeded, his confidence and otpimism grew.

To become more optimistic, first prove to yourself that you can succeed. Set a goal. A small, easily attained outcome is best. You might:

- Attend a new professional group meeting.
- Take on an extra project at your job.
- Learn a new sport.
- Try a hobby you find interesting.

Make certain you truly want to achieve the goal and that it's something you can achieve with moderate effort.

Then go all out to succeed. Prove to yourself that you can do it. One positive experience will lead to many more. Change will become much easier to manage.

SUMMARY: USE REALISTIC OPTIMISM

A positive attitude makes change less stressful. However, as Norman Cousins said, "You should not underestimate the problem. To successfully beat a problem you must look at it from its darkest side. *But don't underestimate your ability to deal with it.*"

To help boost your own ability to deal with change, remember the six strategies for increasing realistic optimism:

1. *Watch your mouth*—talk to yourself optimistically.
2. *Concentrate on the good*—to discover more of it.
3. *Find people with the same problem*—help each other.
4. *Remember*—negatives can become positive.
5. *Tell yourself cheerful stories with happy endings.*
6. *Prove it to yourself*—optimism can *bring positive results.*

"If you are pessimistic, your head is down, you can't see your prospects," Norman Cousins said. "Optimism means that you send your periscope up as high as you can to scan the horizon.

"Unless you believe there is something out there you are not going to be looking for it. . . . I think that we have far greater powers than we realize."

NOTES

The experiment with learned helplessness in dogs was described in "Effects of Inescapable Shock upon Subsequent Escape and Avoidance Responding," by J. Bruce Overmier and Martin Seligman, in the *Journal of Comparative and Physiological Psychology*, Vol. 63, No. 1, 1967.

Information on the value of a positive explanatory style was covered in "Stop Blaming Yourself," by Robert J. Trotter, in *Psychology Today*, February 1987.

Research on happiness and aging was summarized in "Want to Be Happier? Just Keep Aging, Poll Suggests," by Anne Roark, in the *Los Angeles Times* (reprinted in the *Sacramento Bee*), April 28, 1989.

Taylor and Lazarus's views on positive illusions were summarized in "Living on Cloud Nine," by Daniel Goleman, in the *New York Times* (reprinted in *Sacramento Bee*), December 26, 1987.

Research on denial in heart patients is from "The Role of Denial in Recovery from Coronary Heart Disease," by Jacob Levine, *et al.*, in *Psychosomatic Medicine*, Vol 49.

Breznitz's quotes are from "Denial and Hope," by Daniel Goleman, in *American Health*, December 1984.

Research on repressors was covered in "Hidden Emotions, High Cholesterol," by Susan Chollar, in *Psychology Today*, September 1989.

Breznitz's quotes are from "Denial and Hope," by Daniel Goleman, in *American Health*, December 1984.

Information about the ASQ is from "Foresight Boosts Metropolitan's Sales," by Daniel Oran, in a Special Report (available from Foresight, Inc., Falls Church, VA).

Brezler quote is from "The Astonishing Healing Power of Hope," by Richard Trubo, in *Glamour* magazine, August 1985.

Peterson's research on college students was summarized in "Do Optimists Live Longer?," by Nan Silver, in *American Health*, November 1986.

Blood pressure study reviewed in "Expectation and the Blood Pressure Lowering Effects of Relaxation," by W. S. Agras, *et al.*, in *Psychosomatic Medicine*, Vol. 44.

The study of children who lose parents was covered in "Stop Blaming Yourself," by Robert J. Trotter, in *Psychology Today*, February 1987.

Seligman's quote is from Trotter's article, cited above.

The study of depressed students was reviewed in "Accentuate the Positive," by Valerie Adler, in *American Health*, May 1989.

The Breznitz quote about stories is from "Denial and Hope," by Daniel Goleman, in *American Health*, December 1984.

10 STEP SEVEN

Using Humor to Cope with Change

Life is too serious to be taken seriously.
—OSCAR WILDE

Doctors said his chances of survival were minimal. Suffering from collagen disease, Norman Cousins was in the hospital. One morning, while the renowned editor and writer ate breakfast, a nurse arrived with a specimen bottle.

"While she wasn't looking," Cousins says, "I took my apple juice, poured it in the bottle, and handed it to her. She looked at it and said, 'We're a little cloudy today, aren't we?'"

Cousins took a gulp from the bottle and said, "By George, you're right. Let's run it through again."

Very funny. Life often is. And finding or making the humor lends instant perspective and optimism to any situation, even when rapid change is taking place. Some people are good at taking life and themselves lightly. When uncomfortable changes occur, they find something funny and laugh themselves through the tension.

Others, though, think life is a pretty serious business. After all, think of all the terrible things that happen. But that's just the point. If we didn't laugh, we'd moan, cry, and wail. We have a choice. As famed Harvard psychologist and author William James said, "We don't laugh because we're happy—we're happy because we laugh."

Most of the peak performers I interviewed and surveyed laugh a lot, often at themselves. When asked to rate themselves on the question "My sense of humor is a key part of my success," 78 percent agreed. And humor makes them more successful in dealing with change, too, by reducing tension and creating an improved attitude.

LAUGHTER REDUCES TENSION AND MAKES CHANGE LESS STRESSFUL

Several years ago I gave a series of seminars for the city of Oakland, California, and taught the meter readers, among others, to handle change and stress more effectively. These courageous meter monitors ventured forth every day on the streets of Oakland, writing traffic tickets and confronting violators. Their job wasn't easy. They told me that people would sometimes threaten them, point guns, and even try to run them over.

Yet the meter readers handled the stress remarkably well. How? They laughed about it. They had "in" jokes about their jobs, and they used them to create perspective. They had learned to make a tough task fun, thereby rising above the stress and doing their jobs more effectively.

Research proves the value of humor. A study at Texas Tech University found that students were better able to tolerate pain after viewing a comedy tape. Why? During laughter, the body releases endorphins—natural painkillers. And laughter slows the release of some stress hormones, too.

Laughter also reduces tension by relaxing muscles. After laughing, our blood pressure drops below normal for a brief time. Psychologist Kathleen Dillon of Western New England College found that students who watched a video of *Richard Pryor Live* had higher levels of helpful antibodies than did a control group. Their immune systems functioned better.

Art Linkletter told me, "Humor is the best way I can think of to release tension. If you can laugh at something, you don't have to scream.

"Probably the greatest example of that are the Jews. They've been discriminated against, been chased from one end of the world to the other, and they have developed some of the most delicious and delightful folk humor in the history of the world. And today, if you look at the leading humorists and comic writers, you're apt to find that a big percentage of them are Jewish. They have learned to laugh at life instead of being battered by it."

LAUGHTER HELPS PEOPLE GET ALONG TOGETHER

Humor also helps us deal more effectively with other people. And when we get along with others, change is easier to handle.

The Illinois consulting firm of Hodge-Cronin & Associates recently interviewed 737 CEOs. Ninety-eight percent said that, assuming all other criteria are equal, they prefer to hire a job applicant with a sense of humor over a candidate with none.

Entertainer and author Steve Allen told me how humor helps outside corporate America. Allen said that many older comedians used humor to get along with others while growing up in tough neighborhoods.

"When you are nine years old and get beaten up a lot or at least threatened, if the other kids know that you are the funny one there is some protection in that. They like you to hang around and make them laugh."

And humor helps lovers keep loving. Broadcaster Walter Cronkite married his wife, Betsy, in 1940, and they're still together. What keeps them close? "I think it's a sense of humor, Betsy's more than mine," Cronkite says.

His daughter, Kathy, agrees. "They both have a well-developed sense of playfulness," she says. "This is a side of Dad most people never see."

And wife, Betsy, observes, "I think the glue that holds Walter and me together is that we both still laugh a lot at each other's jokes."

Humor *does* help smooth and soothe our relationships. And who should know that better than a president?

PRESIDENTIAL HUMOR

Think about the best-loved U.S. presidents. Then remember which recent chief execs had a good sense of humor. Is there a correlation?

Presidents, like the rest of us, find that humor helps them handle change and get along with others. Whatever your political persuasion, it's easier to put up with a funny politician than a humorless one.

If Ronald Reagan hadn't been able to use humor skillfully, would he have survived the Iran-Contra scandal? If Richard Nixon had been funnier, would his odds have been better during Watergate?

Even before taking office, Ronald Reagan used humor to handle pressure and change. Then, in March of 1981, a would-be assassin fired several shots at the president and his party as they were leaving a Washington hotel. Reagan was hit, and taken to the hospital for emergency chest surgery.

As hospital aides wheeled him into the operating room, Reagan looked around at the surgeons, smiled, and said, "Please assure me that you are all Republicans."

Several days later, reporters asked Reagan about the assassination attempt. "I should have ducked," he said simply.

Is it any wonder that Ronald Reagan made a speedy recovery from his wounds? His humor helped him heal fast, handle the dramatic changes he was experiencing, and reassure the citizens of a worried nation.

Several years later, in the 1984 presidential campaign, Reagan's first debate with Walter Mondale left him looking ineffectual. He seemed disoriented and gave sloppy answers to questions. People wondered if his age was becoming a problem.

Then, in the second Reagan–Mondale debate, the president turned the negatives around. One moderator asked Reagan whether his age might influence his ability to do the job. Reagan's eyes lit up as he listened to the query. Then he said, "I am not going to make age an issue in this campaign. I am not going to exploit for political purposes my opponent's youth and inexperience."

The age issue disappeared, at least for that campaign.

Later, during a speech, Reagan talked about his term in office. "Since I came to the White House I got two hearing aids, a colon operation, skin cancer, a prostate operation and I was shot." He paused. "The damn thing is, I've never felt better in my life." The audience howled with laughter. Reagan had them in the palm of his hand.

Jack Kennedy also used humor wisely and well. In 1961, Kennedy appointed his brother, Bobby, attorney general. Many accused him of nepotism. Jack Kennedy handled it with humor. "I can't see that it's wrong to give him a little legal experience before he goes out to practice law," he said.

Years earlier, President Abraham Lincoln also demonstrated a knack for making light of himself. During one campaign, Stephen Douglas accused Lincoln of being two-faced. Lincoln said, "If I had two faces, I certainly wouldn't wear this one."

HOW TO USE HUMOR

The six strategies for using humor to handle change effectively follow.

STRATEGY 1

Use Humor Appropriately

Before discussing *how* to use humor, we must cover when *not* to use it. Humor isn't always appropriate.

It's important to avoid humor that hurts other people. That can include ethnic, racial, or sexist humor. And there are some situations on the job where humor may not be appropriate.

Finally, many people are offended by "dirty" jokes or profanity. If you use this sort of humor, be very careful that those you share it with appreciate that approach.

STRATEGY 2

Find Amusing Things in Everyday Life

Most of us are born with humor. You don't look at a laughing six-month-old baby and say, "Gee, that kid has a great sense of humor." As we grow to adulthood, though, we're taught that we must be serious, all or part of the time. Baloney.

Luckily, we human beings are a funny bunch. For proof, just look around and listen.

Humor is everywhere, but we do need to look for it. If we're grimly focused on something else, the delightful lightness around us will go unnoticed.

To help yourself find and use everyday humor, try the following:

- Think about and write down funny, silly, and ridiculous situations you've dealt with in your life.
- Reflect on funny things you've read or heard. These can include misprints, humorous articles, television shows, and movies. You may also recall humorous situations or amusing people from your work world.
- Think about your funniest friends and relatives. What have they said (or done) that made you laugh? The witty people in our lives are a rich resource.
- Start a humor notebook and/or file. Whenever you hear or read a funny story, add it to your collection. Watch for funny

cartoons, too. When you're feeling down or stressed, take a look at these items and enjoy their humor.

STRATEGY 3

Practice Makes Funny

During the interviews for this book, many of the peak performers used humor to make their points. But most didn't tell jokes. They just took an easy approach to sometimes serious topics. When they did, the interviews took on a light quality of their own.

Producer, speaker, and comedian Gene Perret believes that to use humor more effectively, we must practice.

"The first time you learn a new way to do a backhand in tennis, you gradually slip back into your old way of doing it. But as you practice it more, the new way becomes second nature. That's what's happened to me. I've told many people about the benefits of humor. Thus I have to practice it myself, and the more I practice, the easier it gets."

Fortunately, everyone can use humor. I asked Steve Allen what he'd recommend for those who'd like to use humor more often to manage pressure-packed change.

"In my book, *How to Be Funny*, I say that the purpose of the book is not to guarantee that everyone who reads it will close the covers and afterward be as funny as Eddie Murphy. That would hardly be likely unless they were already pretty darn funny. . . .

"But I have never met anyone who is totally humorless. We've all met people who were grouchy or depressed or not too lively. But if you hung around them for three days with a tape recorder, you'd notice that from time to time even those down people do smile a little bit, or chuckle sarcastically, or tell a joke at the office."

Allen's son, Steve Allen, Jr., is a physician who specializes in using humor to heal.

"Dr. Steve suggests that we should try to recapture the child within," the senior Allen continued. "We don't totally change from what we were at three or four. But we put most of it aside. Dr. Steve says that's a very great mistake. There is no reason to act like an automaton, just because you are grown up.

"Indeed, people we admire almost always have a component of humor. If they don't, we may admire them for their expertise on the violin. But we'd like them even more if they smiled a little bit, even while bowing."

To practice humor yourself:

- Tell jokes or funny stories to other people, always remembering to use humor appropriately. Try selecting a "funny story of the week." Then tell it to several people. Watch their reaction, to see if you need to change or discard the story. But remember, most stories become funnier as you practice them more.
- Laugh at yourself. Most of the men and women I interviewed make frequent fun of themselves. At first you may not feel like doing the same. But just let out a chuckle anyway, even if it sounds forced at first. Soon laughter will come more easily.
- Discard your adult roles every now and then. When's the last time you allowed yourself to act like a kid? If you've forgotten how, watch children play, or better yet, join in with them. Kids use humor and play naturally. If you observe these little experts, you'll be laughing at their level in no time.

STRATEGY 4

Meet Your Problems with Humor

Humor is a great way to turn turmoil into victory and negative changes positive. Steve Allen has done this for years.

"During the years I did talk show duty, practically ninety-eight percent of what I did on the air was ad-lib," Allen told me. "Most of the shows were done live. There was something inherently stressful about having millions of people watching you and carrying them through a sixty- or ninety-minute show with relatively little planned."

Allen discovered early in his career that when something went wrong, he could say or do something funny and turn the negative into a plus.

"It could be something so trivial as a pencil falling off my desk. I could say something routine about it or say, 'Well, if that's how it's going to be, I'll throw everything off the desk,' and the audience can easily be made to laugh from that.

"If a waiter drops a tray in a nightclub, or a woman gets up from her table and heads to the lady's room right in the middle of your monologue, those could be negatives."

But, Allen says, you can make a joke out of interruptions.

"Often this works so well that you should pay that lady to travel around the country with you and stand up every night wherever you work," Allen continues. "You can sometimes get bigger laughs with that than you might with the next three jokes you were going to do."

Allen tells about the time he turned embarrassment to laughter on his radio show. An advertising whiz, Jim Moran, was on, promoting Persian rugs. He came on stage, dressed in Arabian garb, leading a huge camel. As Moran and Allen talked, the camel began voiding on the linoleum floor. Because camels can store so much water, they also have enormous bladders, which take a long time to empty.

The audience began laughing hysterically. Allen and Moran stopped talking. The camel continued doing its duty for almost five minutes, and the longer he went, the louder the audience laughed. Stagehands were called to mop up the mess, which was beginning to run off the stage.

Finally, the camel's bladder was empty and stagehands finished cleaning everything up. But the linoleum, formerly dark brown, had become many shades lighter. It was now pale yellow.

For a moment, Allen, Moran, and the audience stared at the bleached floor. Then Allen looked out at the crowd, and in his best TV commercial voice said, "Say, homemakers, having trouble keeping kitchen floors spotlessly clean?" The audience roared. The show ended with everyone happy and relaxed.

In any negative situation, we have a distinct choice. Get serious or lighten up. Frequently, even the worst situation can benefit from some humor. Laughter and lightness help us perform better and handle change more effectively.

- If you know you're going to be dealing with a negative situation, plan a funny line or statement in advance. And, if it's not appropriate to say it out loud, you can use it to lighten your *own* perspective.

STRATEGY 5

Mix Business with Pleasure

Having fun at work boosts productivity and buffers uncomfortable change. Yet, in many organizations, fun is the last thing you're supposed to have.

Psychologist Alice Isen, of the University of Maryland, has found that people organize information better and are more creative when they're in a good mood. Isen compared subjects who had either watched a video of "TV bloopers," seen a math video, or done boring exercise. Those who'd seen the funny video exhibited better memory and were more creative in accomplishing a task.

"Mild elation seems to lead to the kind of thinking that enables people to solve problems requiring ingenuity or innovation," Isen says. In another study, Isen found that people who looked at humorous cartoons were less contentious and more likely to find solutions in negotiations.

David Abramis, of California State University at Long Beach, surveyed 341 adults, finding that those who believe it's okay to have fun at work actually enjoy themselves more there.

And a recent Burke Marketing Research survey of personnel directors found that 84 percent believe that employees who have a sense of humor do a better job than those who don't.

Gertrude Crain has presided over extraordinary growth in Crain Communications, Inc., the large trade magazine publisher. Though she's proud of what her company has accomplished, she also believes in enjoying the journey. "My husband [Crain founder, G. D. Crain, Jr.] always believed the business should be fun," she says. "My sons, Rance and Keith, and I do our best to make it that way."

There are many ways to lighten your work environment. Corporate humor consultant Matt Weinstein tells of one company that asks employees to bring in their baby pictures. Employees and managers post them on the bulletin board.

"What that company was saying was, yes, we have a rigid hierarchy here and, yes, we have a chain of command," Weinstein said. "But the bottom line is, everybody here started as a baby. That company will be able to go well beyond the standard definition of teamwork and camaraderie."

Another CEO Weinstein works with keeps a framed picture of himself in his office, with the caption "Our founder." The photo is taken from the exec's junior high school yearbook.

David Abramis, who conducted some of the research mentioned above, suggests several other ideas that can lighten the world of work:

- *Suggest or create events:* contests, parties, sports activities, theme days.
- *Talk it up:* Tell people that it's okay to have fun at work, when it's appropriate.
- *Encourage supervisors to create fun.*

- *Set an organizational or departmental goal: increasing productivity by having more fun.*
- *Ask people what they think is fun,* then create more of those kinds of activities
- *Hire people who like to have fun;* they're likely to be more productive
- As psychologist and humorist Terry Paulson says, *"Take your job seriously, and yourself lightly."*

STRATEGY 6

Meet with Humor

January 1977—the Orange Bowl. Lou Holtz's University of Arkansas team is slated to play against Oklahoma. They're due on the field at 8:22 P.M. Holtz gives a rousing pregame speech to fire up his players.

At 8:22, the Orange Bowl president and an NBC exec walk into the locker room. They tell Holtz that the Rose Bowl telecast ran late, and everything has to be moved back fifteen minutes.

The team is pumped up, ready to go. Now they have to sit and wait. Holtz and the other coaches meet to decide what to do. They're concerned that the players will lose their emotional charge. Suddenly Holtz snaps his fingers. "I've got it," he says, walking out of the coaches' room toward the players. "I'll tell you what we're going to do. I travel around and speak a lot, and I'm always looking for new material. You guys tell me jokes and I'll use them in my speeches.'"

At first the players seem skeptical. Then one takes a chance and tells a joke. Smiles break out on the serious young faces. Then Holtz delivers another gag, and soon everyone is doing it. When the NBC exec comes back, the whole team is laughing. They carry their high spirits into the game, and recover a fumble on the third play. By the end of the first quarter Arkansas is leading, 14–0.

Lou Holtz kept his team loose through laughter. They handled the pressure, kept their emotional peak, and dominated the game. The business executives I interviewed get similar results when they use humor in meetings. Jack Lewis, CEO and president of the Amdahl Corporation, told me, "One of the things I use to alleviate stress in a group is humor. It lets people relax and think more effectively."

DON'T TAKE YOURSELF TOO SERIOUSLY

Using humor requires taking yourself lightly. When conducting church services, Nobel Prize winner Archbishop Desmond Tutu often laughs and jokes, encouraging the congregation to laugh and rejoice along with him. Sometimes he even dances down the church aisle.

"People are not absolutely sure that an archbishop ought to dance," Tutu says with a chuckle. "They see you dance, and the next moment you're dignified again . . . the more sedate, more proper kind of archbishop. They see you moving relatively easily from one mode to another, and that fills our people with a tremendous sense of being in charge, in control."

As professional speaker and former NFL referee Jim Tunney told me, "Someone said a long time ago, 'The Lord should have had an 11th Commandment: Thou shalt not take thyself too seriously.'"

Humor isn't a cure-all, but it *is* a help-all. Next time you're dealing with a tough transition, use humor to make it easier by remembering to:

1. *Use humor appropriately,* so you don't hurt anyone's feelings or make someone angry.
2. *Find funny things in daily life,* from newspaper misprints to humorous people.
3. *Practice* using funny stories, jokes, and a humorous outlook on life in general. You don't have to be a great joke teller to use humor. Notice what makes you and other people laugh.
4. *Meet problems with humor* by looking for laughter when life or circumstances look bleak.
5. *Mix business with pleasure.* Don't forget humor and fun when you go to work. If you're an executive or manager, help your employees enjoy what they do more. They'll repay you with higher productivity and increased loyalty. And, if you're one of the hired hands, see what you can do (within reason) to boost the fun quotient on your job. After all, you're probably not the only one who thinks things are a bit boring around the plant.
6. *Meet with humor* by keeping meetings on track with appropriate laughter.

We can take life very, very seriously. But it's boring that way, and change seems much more threatening.

KEEP YOUR SENSE OF HUMOR

In 1981, when John Hinckley, Jr., shot President Reagan, one bullet also hit presidential press secretary James Brady. At first, TV news teams reported that Brady had died. But a medical team worked feverishly to keep him alive. The bullet had penetrated Brady's brain and exploded there, leaving his left side mostly paralyzed. His brain functioning was seriously diminished, but Brady survived.

Over the years, James Brady worked hard to recover. Today, his brain functioning has grown much sharper and clearer. Though he's usually in a wheelchair, Brady often works a full day, and he writes a regular column for *Parade* magazine.

Dr. Arthur Kobrine is the neurosurgeon who operated on Brady and has since helped him to recover. Kobrine says that Brady "is in a class by himself. I just admire the hell out of Jim Brady. He is . . . always able to laugh at himself, to make light of his situation, to poke fun at others in a loving way, but never—I repeat, never—willing to quit."

Today Brady speaks with a clear articulation that shows his remarkable recovery. He's learned to handle the immense changes he's gone through. "You've got to persevere," Brady says. "Persevere, and keep your sense of humor. They can't shoot that away."

NOTES

The experiments on laughter and pain were summarized in "Lighten Up," by Nick Gallo, in *Better Homes and Gardens*, August 1989.

Information about stress and the immune system appeared in "Laughter Is the Best Defense," by Susan Lang, in *American Health*, December 1988.

Quotes on humor from Cronkite and his daughter are from "Happily Ever After," by Stephanie Mansfield, in *Woman's Day*, February 16, 1986.

Betsy Cronkite, quoted in "Walter Cronkite Clears the Air," by Dalma Heyn, in *50 Plus*, March 1985.

The study on mood and creativity was reported in "Laughing Matters—At Work," by Susan Lang, in *American Health*, September 1988.

The tips for fun on the job are from "Finding the Fun at Work," by David Abramis, in *Psychology Today*, March 1989.

The Burke Marketing Research survey was reported in *Making Humor Work*, by Terry Paulson, Ph.D., Crisp Publication, Inc., in 1989.

11

STEP EIGHT

Learning from Mistakes

Failure is the opportunity to begin again more intelligently.

—HENRY FORD

People who win big, fail big.

- Babe Ruth struck out 1,330 times.
- A newspaper editor once fired Walt Disney, saying he "had no good ideas."
- Abraham Lincoln, a captain in the Army at the beginning of the Blackhawk War, had been busted to the rank of private by the end.

Mistakes are essential. They provide important information to help us deal with changes in our lives. *Within each error we can find the data needed to become more successful in the future.*

But today much of America, particularly the business community, is cautious and conservative. No one wants to make a mistake. Most take the established route, the path worn bare by millions as they carefully plod through life.

Yet the successful people I talked to take risks. They aren't fazed by mistakes. Mail order expert Lillian Vernon, chairman and CEO of the Lillian Vernon Corporation, told me, "Which of us is so perfect that we don't make mistakes? I don't believe that the end of the world has come if I make a mistake.

"I make a decision based on the best information I have at my disposal," Vernon continued. "Sometimes it just isn't enough information. If I make the wrong decision, I learn from my mistakes and solve the problem another way. I never castigate myself over a mistake. Running a business requires making thousands of decisions, and not all of them are going to be correct."

How do mistakes differ from the kind of setbacks we talked about in Chapter 2? Setbacks are due to events largely beyond our control. Mistakes stem from our own errors.

We can prevent some mistakes but not all. Luckily, coping effectively with our errors can help us handle change more effectively.

FAILURES LEAD TO SUCCESS

As a toddler, you failed many times. You tried to walk and fell down, attempted new words and mangled them, tried to build a tower of blocks and knocked it over. Yet by learning from your mistakes, you eventually succeeded.

Warren Bennis, a professor of business administration at the University of Southern California, was formerly president of the University of Cincinnati. In his book *Leaders: The Strategies for Taking Charge*, Bennis interviewed ninety outstanding leaders from business and the public sector. He reported that the top leaders don't dwell on, or even *use*, the word *failure*.

Failing Two-thirds of the Time Is Okay

To succeed, we must risk sometimes striking out. Harvey Mackay runs one of America's most successful envelope manufacturing companies. In the mid-1980s Mackay decided to write a book. Though it was his first, he wanted it to be a best-seller. People who didn't know him said he would fail. Yet his book, *Swim with the Sharks Without Being Eaten Alive*, became one of the most successful business books of all time. He followed it with another best-seller, *Beware the Naked Man Who Offers You His Shirt*.

I asked Mackay how he handles mistakes. "If you want to double your success ratio, you have to double your failure rate." he said. "If you're an entrepreneur and you want to be a success, you'd better not worry about failure.

"Mistakes happen all the time. Every time you make a mistake, and learn from it, it builds strength and character. Strategizing your way around adversity is what makes winners."

Learning to weather mistakes *is* an essential skill for success. And today there *are* tools to help all of us learn from our mistakes and keep going. We'll cover them further in this chapter. But first, let's discuss how perfectionism keeps many people from ever attaining what they want.

PERFECTIONISM AND LACK OF PERFECTION

When it comes to mistakes, there are three kinds of people:

1. Perfectionists
2. Balanced achievers
3. Those who don't care

Most of those whom I interviewed fall into the second category—balanced achievers. They do their best and then let go, knowing that they can do no more. They believe, devoutly, in quality and hard work, but know there are limits to what one person can do.

Unfortunately, finding that kind of balance is difficult. Most of us occupy one of the other two categories. The perfectionist, for instance, thinks that if he makes *any* mistakes on a project he and it are failures. He strives toward one goal after another and suffers habitual disppointment because perfection is impossible.

As a teenager, I was one of the finest young flutists in the United States. But I didn't know it. In fact, when I played in a concert or contest, I often told myself I'd done a poor job. At fifteen, I auditioned to play a solo with the Milwaukee Symphony. Afterward I was convinced I'd played badly—after all, it hadn't been perfect.

Imagine my surprise when the next night my mom called me to the telephone. On the line was a newspaper reporter. "How does it feel to have won the Young Artist's Competition?" he asked. I was so stunned I could barely reply.

In the years that followed, my perfectionism persisted, in spite of continued success. I even performed in Carnegie Hall, but the perfectionist inside me wasn't satisfied. Eventually I stopped playing music.

In the years since then, I've gained perspective on the issue. For instance, it's difficult to write a book and stay perfectionist. There's always something you can add, fix, or polish—but editors and deadlines inject a dose of reality. Today I can usually say "no" to the perfectionist within. What a relief!

Perfectionists fall prey to a host of difficulties. Psychiatrist David Burns, author of *Feeling Good: The New Mood Therapy*, researched this issue at the University of Pennsylvania. Burns reports that perfectionists are likely to respond to mistakes by becoming depressed or anxious.

Yet many insist that dedication to perfection increases productivity. Burns wondered about this. So, in 1980, he tested a group of successful insurance agents, whose salaries ranged from $29,000 to $250,000 per year. He gave them a test that measures levels of perfectionism. About half the agents showed perfectionistic thinking styles. Burns found that the perfectionists earned an average of $15,000 less per year than did the nonperfectionists.

In another study, Michael Mahoney of Penn State University compared male gymnasts who qualified for the Olympics with those who did not. The successful group differed from the others by: (1) being less perfectionistic and (2) downplaying the importance of past failures in performance. The *less* successful gymnasts often experienced severe self-doubt and imagined things going wrong.

Author and television personality Julia Child told me that perfectionists are a pain to work with, especially in the kitchen. "They're impossible to work with," she said. "They usually cannot delegate anything and you can't hurry them up because they want everything to be perfect. That's not realistic. You have to do things as well as you can, but you are not going to be able to dot every 'i'."

In addition to inhibiting performance, perfectionism can also affect health by boosting stress levels. And perfectionists often have difficulty in relationships because:

- They assume that others will reject them for being imperfect.
- They often expect perfection from others.

The Roots of Perfectionism

Like pessimism, we learn perfectionism at home. If parents set impossible standards for their children, the youngsters either give up or continue to strive against all odds. If the parents continually reward the child's achievement and punish mistakes, the child gets a clear message: The only acceptable behavior is doing it right—*always*.

BEATING PERFECTIONISM WHILE DOING IT RIGHT

It's possible to become less perfectionist while still doing a good job. Here's how:

Adopt a Realistic Attitude

Steve Allen, whom I mentioned earlier, is one of the most productive people alive. Besides creating books, songs, and record albums, he has starred in motion pictures and on Broadway, and starred on the "Tonight Show" and other hit television shows.

Allen, a balanced achiever, told me that he thinks we *do* have some limits.

"We all have a genetically established ceiling on our abilities. People notice that I do fourteen different kind of things. They ask, 'Has it ever occurred to you that if you just concentrated on one thing you might be the world's greatest?'

"I say, 'Well, thank you for the implied compliment but I would never have been the world's greatest because I am not capable of it.' I'm a damn good composer, but I wouldn't have been as good as Cole Porter if I stopped everything else. I'm a creditable writer, but I never would have been as good as some of the real masters. If I stopped everything else, all that would have happened is that my short stories would have gotten about 4 percent better. And why, for such a slight improvement, give up so much?"

I remarked that Allen had avoided perfectionism, that he didn't seem to believe that every project had to be the best ever.

"Right," he replied. "I'm very relaxed about that. Because my perception of my abilities is—I'll make up a dumb-sounding phrase—'realistically modest.' I'm not any more modest or any more conceited than the average guy about anything."

Allen's attitude of balanced achievement is one of the keys to his success.

To beat your own perfectionism, realize that you may not be the best in the world. Follow Steve Allen's advice: Just do *your* best, *not someone else's.*

When I first became a professional speaker, I wanted to be as good as Ken Blanchard and Zig Ziglar. I tortured myself trying to get to their level, until I finally gained perspective. I'll *never* speak like Ken or Zig—they've got their own unique styles. But I have my own strengths and important things to say. Today I work at reaching my *own* potential and find I'm closer to it every day. Much of that progress is due to loosening up, because I've stopped being so perfectionistic.

Deal with Errors in Thinking

David Burns, M.D., to whom I referred previously, has pinpointed three errors of thinking in perfectionists.

1. *Overgeneralization.* A perfectionist supervisor makes a mistake with an employee and tells himself, "I'll never get this right," setting up negative thinking.
2. *All-or-nothing thinking.* An administrative assistant makes a mistake in a report and says to herself, "I'm really a failure," setting up defeatist thinking.
3. *Should statements.* An executive makes a mistake on a yearly profit projection and doesn't analyze how she went wrong or what to change in her methodology. Instead, she tells herself, "I *should* have done that better," instead of analyzing the error in her thinking and learning from it.

Many researchers, including psychologist Michael Mahoney at Penn State University, have found that positive reinforcement is more effective than punishment at changing behavior. But the perfectionist tries to change his or her behavior through negative self-talk (punishment). That approach doesn't work. It leads only to more perfectionism.

One way to change perfectionism in ourselves is to confront the negative statements. We'll cover that process in more detail in Step 12. To begin though, change your self-talk.

- When you notice yourself practicing overgeneralization, all-or-nothing thinking, or *should* statements—STOP. Do you really want to talk that way to yourself? If not, *change* the statements. *Talk back* to the internal critic.
- Practice saying things like, "I made a mistake. Well, I'll do better next time." Or perhaps, "I'm still successful in many areas, even if I did make a mistake."

Write It Up

- You might also make a list of the advantages and disadvantages of perfectionism. On one side of a piece of paper, write a + sign, on the other a −. Then write the benefits and drawbacks of your search for perfection. When I ask people to do this, they inevitably find that the *costs* of striving for perfection clearly outweigh the benefits.
- Another strategy is to write a daily note to yourself. Point out the things you've done right. Praise yourself for what you've

done well, even when you've made mistakes. Talk to yourself the way an unconditionally loving parent would.

Make Yourself Criticism-Proof

Everyone gets criticized. Learning to handle it can help us cope more effectively with mistakes.

Throughout the Civil War, Abraham Lincoln was at the center of a fire-storm of criticism. Copies of his thoughts on this topic have hung above the desks of Winston Churchill, General Douglas MacArthur, and many others. Lincoln said:

"If I were to try to read, much less to answer, all the attacks made on me, this shop might as well be closed for any other business. I do the very best I know how—the very best I can; and I mean to keep on doing so until the end. If the end brings me out all right, then what is said against me won't matter. If the end brings me out wrong, then ten angels swearing I was right would make no difference."

Lincoln learned to do what he believed was right. Psychiatrist David Burns recommends another technique. Because perfectionists fear rejection, they often continue to strive for the impossible, even after they understand this behavior doesn't work. Thus Burns suggests learning "verbal judo."

In the martial art of judo, the opponent's own energy is redirected against him. In verbal judo, you redirect a critic's *verbal* energy. This is accomplished through *inquiry* and *disarming*.

- To use *inquiry*, respond to a negative statement with a question. If someone says, "You're an idiot," ask him, "What did I do that you thought was idiotic?" By responding with a question, rather than defending yourself, you dramatically change the energy of the exchange, put your critic off guard, and may learn something.
- To *disarm* a critic, find a part of his statement that is true, even if the rest is unwarranted. For instance, you might respond to a criticism of a report by saying, "Yes, I agree with your point about the last page." Then just stop. Don't say anything else. Let the critic decide what to do next. You haven't admitted that the report is bad, only that there's something wrong on the last page.

Burns recommends practicing rounds of criticism with a therapist. By prearrangement, the counselor plays the critic and zaps the client with abuse and insults. The client then responds, using verbal judo. If the client becomes upset, they switch roles and the therapist demonstrates an effective response.

You might try this with someone other than a therapist—a friend, for instance. You can help each other beat perfectionism by becoming "rejection proof." After you've dealt with rejection in a safe setting, it becomes easier to do out in the real world. Be careful, though, that you pick a partner who hasn't got a vested interest in really getting to you.

The most important tool for beating perfectionism is *knowing you can't do it all*. Motivational speakers are fond of saying, "You can do anything." Untrue. *Many people can do more than they think they can*. But perfectionists think they "should" be able to do *anything*.

If you're a perfectionist, know that there are limits to everyone's abilities, even yours. That realization will help you to be happier and more successful.

THE FIVE A'S OF TRANSFORMING MISTAKES

In talking with successful balanced achievers, I discovered a five-point plan for coping with mistakes. Most of the top achievers I interviewed use variations of these steps.

Follow the five A's to transform mistakes into raw material for future success.

––––––––––– **STRATEGY 1** –––––––––––

Admit It

The first step in the five A's is to admit you made a mistake. Identify what the error was. And learn from it!

Several years ago, "L.A. Law" star Michael Tucker planned a sumptuous dinner for friends, including restaurateur and master chef David Liederman. Tucker loves to cook, and he wanted to impress his guests with the meal.

By the time all the guests had arrived the sun had gone down. Tucker went outside and began grilling the main course—about $200 worth of fresh seafood. "By the time I got started, it was getting hard to see," he says.

When he finished grilling, Tucker made his big mistake. He knocked the plate containing the freshly cooked seafood onto the ground. No one had seen what happened, so Tucker got down on his hands and knees and began searching for the fish in the darkness.

"I picked up what I could," he says, "and rinsed it off with the garden hose." But soon Tucker realized he would have to admit his mistake. Sheepishly he went back into the house and told his guests they'd have to go out to eat.

As Michael Tucker knows, the first step to cleaning up a mistake is to admit what you did. That's tough, because we usually become defensive after making an error.

<hr>

STRATEGY 2

Analyze What Happened

<hr>

After admitting and identifying your mistake, analyze what went wrong and why. Unfortunately, some people just ignore the error. Other people can't *ever* seem to forget an error. They admit the mistake and then mentally berate themselves for making it. Their inner critic runs wild.

Analyzing the error will help you learn from it and prevent similar mistakes from occurring. Ninety-three percent of the peak performers who responded to our survey said they learn from mistakes.

Inventor Thomas Edison tried five thousand different light bulb filaments before he discovered the right one. When a reporter asked Edison about those thousands of failures, the inventor said, "I didn't have any failures. I learned five thousand things that didn't work. Each one of those discoveries gave me valuable information that eventually led to the success."

Jack Lewis, chairman and CEO of the Amdahl Corporation, the giant mainframe computer manufacturer, told me how he analyzes and learns from errors. "I say to myself, 'Why did I do that? What did I miss early on?' I analyze it, figure out what caused me to make that mistake, and what I should learn so I don't fall into the same thing again."

Julia Child, the famed culinary expert, told me about a mistake she made once during a cooking demonstration before a large audience in San Francisco.

"I was doing a caramel cage, where you dribble the caramel on an upside down bowl that is buttered. And when I took the caramel cage off it just broke."

Child was embarrassed by her mistake, but she analyzed what went wrong. "It was a mistake to try something so fragile and difficult in front of a group. But I did learn from it. You have to let the caramel cool down and then reheat it, so it's not so hot and doesn't burn off the butter. I tried it again, and it worked."

As Julia Child did, when *you* make a mistake, analyze *exactly* what happened. Review the details of the error in your mind. Ask yourself:

- What *specifically* was the mistake?
- What was my part in it?
- Why did I make the mistake?
- What effect will the mistake have?

In addition, pinpoint the severity of the mistake:

- Serious
- Moderate
- Trivial

Note for perfectionists: Perfectionists overstate the importance of their mistakes. If you're a perfectionist, honestly ask yourself how important the error is. Is it going to matter in ten years, five years, or even a few months?

Perfectionists also need to watch out for "shoulds" as they analyze. Ask yourself whether the error is something *you* think is wrong, or whether you're using someone else's criteria for judging yourself.

If, however, you fall into the "who cares" group, realize that you'll need to look carefully to see past any possible denial of the truth. Perhaps you have a bigger part in the error than you think. Try imagining what would happen if you continue to make similar mistakes. Would it hurt you or anyone else?

Whichever your approach, *decide what you can learn from the mistake.* Once you've done this, you're ready for the next step: building an effective plan to deal with the problem.

--- STRATEGY 3 ---

Assemble a Plan

This is another point at which many people stop the process of dealing with mistakes. After admitting the error and analyzing it, they give up. Instead, practice damage control. Does anything need to be done to correct the error?

Harry Hoffman, former president and CEO of Waldenbooks, told me how he once handled a downturn in sales.

"One year book sales fell flat for the forty-five days before Christmas, which is the most important time of the year for booksellers. We had a number of good months before that, and then the bottom fell out. We did okay and made money, but it wasn't as good as we had planned.

"After that we developed a new program that would make sure that didn't happen again. Dealing with adversity helped us become a better, stronger organization."

Doctor Norman Vincent Peale suggests using mistakes to strengthen the overall plan.

"Many of the world's finest Oriental rugs come from little villages in the Middle East. Each rug is hand-produced by a crew of men and boys under the direction of a master weaver. Since ordinarily they work from the underside of the rug-to-be, it frequently happens that a weaver absent-mindedly makes a mistake and introduces a color that is not according to the pattern. When this occurs, the master weaver, instead of pulling the work out to correct the color sequence, will find some way to incorporate the mistake harmoniously into the overall pattern.

"It is a useful object lesson, for we all can learn to take unexpected difficulties and mistakes and weave them advantageously into the greater pattern of our lives. There is an inherent good in most difficulties."

To assemble a plan, refer to your earlier analysis. Then ask yourself:

- How can I clean up the mistake and see that it doesn't happen again?
- How can I deal effectively with the other people involved?

Answering the last question leads to an important action step: the Fourth A—Apologize.

─────────── **STRATEGY 4** ───────────

Apologize

Saying "I'm sorry" is an effective way to clean up an error. Ninety-five percent of our survey respondents said they apologize after making an error. They believe it is key to dealing with errors.

U.S. Senator Barbara Boxer of California says, "When I make a mistake with someone, I sit right down and write that individual a note, or give them a call. I say, 'Forgive me. I made a mistake.' And usually they forgive you. If they don't, you know that you tried your best. You can't please everybody."

Many support groups stress the importance of making amends. When people have had big problems in their lives, through compulsiveness in gambling, eating, sexuality, drinking, or drug use, they often carry enormous guilt.

I've worked with many clients who are members of the support groups that address these issues. They report feeling great relief after making amends for their past behavior. The relief comes even when the person to whom they apologize doesn't take it well.

Usually though, saying "I'm sorry" is also an effective way to win back someone's cooperation. Zig Ziglar, the successful motivational speaker and writer, told me how an apology helped keep one of his important clients happy.

"We have a publication called *Top Performance*. A man who worked for a major client of ours in Houston wanted ten copies sent, under some unique guidelines.

"And we blew it every way from Sunday," Ziglar said. "There was a problem with our computer, so everything he told us don't do we did, and everything he said do, we didn't." Ziglar said.

The man was furious. He wrote to the Better Business Bureau— the first time Ziglar had ever had a complaint lodged there.

"The Better Business Bureau sent me a copy of the letter he wrote. So I dictated a letter. I said, 'You are totally right. If I had been in your shoes, I would have been even more furious. I can't believe that we managed to totally foul up. Tell me exactly what you want me to do. I will do whatever is necessary to make you happy on this deal.'

"I got the nicest letter back from him, and he sent a copy to the Better Business Bureau. He said, 'Zig, it's not that big a deal, if you will just do so and so,' a very reasonable request.

"I think most people are fairly compassionate, and if somebody will say, 'I made a mistake, forgive me,' I think most people will."

Let people know that *you* know you blew it. Come right out and say it. Say "I'm sorry," and *then* ask what you can do to make things right. When they tell you what they want (and often it will be nothing at all, or something small), *listen* to what they say. Do it, if you think the request is reasonable. If you don't agree, tell them, and suggest something else.

Make your amends, reap the rewards, and then move to Strategy #5: adjusting your strategy for the future.

Adjust Your Strategy

This is where you can (a) release any remorse you have about your error and (b) reprogram yourself to avoid making similar mistakes in the future.

Release for Relief: Let Go of Past Mistakes

Many of us find it difficult to forgive ourselves for making an error. And even some of those who completed my survey reported difficulty letting go. Seventy-two percent said they agreed or strongly agreed with the statement "I'm able to deal with my mistakes and move on, without remorse." The rest disagreed or were undecided.

Psychologist Richard Wenzlaff, of the University of Texas in San Antonio, researches how people handle mistakes. Wenzlaff says, "A student who gets a C when he expects a B or A, and then inflates the significance of that information, can initiate a self-defeating chain of thought: 'I'm going to do poorly in this class, I'm just not a good student, I'll flunk out of college—and, finally, I'm a failure in life.'"

This attitude is similar to that seen in perfectionists and is equally destructive. Famed attorney F. Lee Bailey told me about the importance of letting go of mistakes.

"When I was young I always wished that I could back the clock up and try it over again when I had done something wrong. Today I direct that energy positively toward the future instead of agonizing over the terrible faux-pas that I committed."

Professional speaker and former NFL referee Jim Tunney changes his focus to release mistakes. "I don't think failure, I think success. If I do have some sort of a glitch or a mistake, I forget about it—block it out and focus on where I am going.

"In a football game, I sometimes made a call that coaches and players and fans were unhappy about. If I kept replaying that in my mind and kept thinking about it, I might make an error on the next play. I had to block that out. That play was history and I just had to forget it.

"So I'd talk to myself about the next play. 'What am I focusing on? Here's the snap from center. Here's the quarterback taking the ball. What am I looking for in the quarterback? Look for the blocking of the guard.' I'd focus on the things I was looking forward to, rather than thinking about what happened the last play."

Tunney used, and still uses, self-talk and concentration to release mistakes. He focuses on the present, so he won't make another error. To do this yourself, try his system.

- *First*, use positive self-talk. Say things to yourself like, "Yes, I made a mistake. Everyone makes mistakes. I'll just go on, and try to do better next time."
- *Second*, immerse yourself in what you're doing *now*. That will help to keep you from making another error.

Reprogram Yourself for Future Success

Make certain the mistake won't happen again, by changing your future reactions. But be careful here, lest you decide to stop taking certain kinds of risks.

How do we use the message mistakes provide without pulling back from other risks? William Miller, a management consultant with the prestigious Stanford Research Institute, tells a story about a marketing manager who put together a system for handling mistakes. Miller quotes the manager:

"About two years ago I had the worst day of my life. Everything went wrong ... Projects didn't work; people didn't respond the way I wanted. I went off to a coffee shop—and I wrote on the top of a piece of paper 'Lessons Learned and Relearned.'"

Hours later the manager completed his task. On seven pages of paper he'd listed "27 Lessons Learned."

"At the end of that session," he says, "I felt totally contented, joyful, and successful and realized that I had just had one of the best days of my life.

"As a result, I started writing a 'Lessons Learned' journal every day. Now, at the moment something starts to go wrong, I say, 'Ah, it's going to be great this evening when I write the lessons learned and can note this one—and actually feel good right at the moment and not have it weigh on me.'"

Leslie Cameron-Bandler is one of the cofounders of Neuro-Linguistic Programming, or NLP. NLP is a system of improving communication and brain functioning. Cameron-Bandler has devised a method she calls "Converting Mistakes into Learnings."

Part of the system focuses on reprogramming for a more effective future. Cameron-Bandler recommends using three steps after you've completed the first four A's we've covered.

1. *Decide what you'd like to do differently next time.* This can stem from your earlier **analysis.**

Jackie, a secretary in a midsized service company, approached me during a break in one of my seminars. She complained of the problems caused by her bad temper. Though she liked people, she often blew up when they didn't do what she wanted. This had become a problem at her job.

I helped Jackie use the reprogramming system. As a first adjustment, Jackie decided, "When I feel angry in the future, I'll take a few minutes time out before I respond." She elected to go back to her desk, or to the restroom for at least two minutes before she dealt further with the individual who was bothering her.

2. *Commit to using the new instead of the old behavior.* Imagine yourself making the mistake again. Then imagine using the new strategy.

Jackie practiced seeing herself getting angry and yelling at her coworker. She allowed herself to reexperience the feelings. Then she imagined herself following the new strategy—taking time out before responding to her coworker.

3. *Imagine yourself using the new behavior in a future situation.* Make this far enough in the future so that you've had a chance to use the new behavior several times and feel comfortable with it.

Jackie imagined herself several months in the future, having dealt successfully with her anger. She imagined a coworker being unreasonable. Jackie visualized herself taking time away from the situation to reduce her anger to a manageable level.

After practicing this strategy, Jackie was still skeptical. But she called me several weeks later to say she was handling her anger much more effectively. Several of her coworkers had commented on the change.

SUMMARY: USE THE FIVE A'S TO TRANSFORM YOUR MISTAKES INTO SUCCESS

We're born to win—and then fail—and win again. We all make mistakes. And straining to avoid errors through perfectionism can make us tense, depressed, and less productive.

I've used the Five A's with many people in my seminars and my counseling practice. Most report that they're better able to avoid mistakes when they practice them. To use the system:

1. **Admit** you made an error.
2. **Analyze** what went wrong and what you did.

3. **Assemble** a plan to clean up the mess (if there is one).
4. **Apologize** if it's appropriate.
5. **Adjust** yourself.
   a. Release for relief.
   b. Reprogram yourself:
      • Decide what to do next time.
      • Imagine yourself doing it differently in the original situation.
      • Imagine yourself acting the way you'd like to in the future.

NOTES

Leaders: The Strategies for Taking Charge, by Warren Bennis and Burt Nanus, Harper & Row, 1985.

The Tom Peters quote is from "Glorious Failures Spawn Later Success," by Tom Peters, in the *Sacramento Bee*, April 19, 1989.

Burns's research on perfectionism is from "The Perfectionist's Script for Self-Defeat," by David Burns, in *Psychology Today*, November 1980.

The research on racquetball players is summarized in the Burns article cited above.

Some of Ellis's ideas are covered in *A Guide to Rational Living*, by Albert Ellis and R. A. Harper, Wilshire Books, 1970.

Burns's approaches are covered in depth in his book *Feeling Good: The New Mood Therapy*, Signet, 1980.

Wenzlaff's quote is in "Taking Setbacks in Stride," by Daniel Goleman, in the *New York Times*, July 23, 1988.

Leslie Cameron-Bandler's formula is from "Converting Mistakes into Learnings" (pamphlet), P.O. Box 1173, San Rafael, CA 94915: FuturePace, Inc., 1985.

12 STEP NINE

Maintaining Perspective

In the midst of winter, I finally learned that there was in me an invincible summer.

—ALBERT CAMUS

In February 1971, Astronaut Edgar Mitchell became the sixth man in history to walk on the moon. Those small steps led to a leap in perspective for him. During his trip to the moon, Mitchell experienced a profound shift in his view of life itself.

"Seeing the Earth in space was a powerful experience," he said. "Your reality shifts from Earth-center to cosmic-center. You no longer see things in terms of Earth-center reality. And your time frame shifts to a universal time frame."

Edgar Mitchell believes that seeing the Earth from space taught him to handle change more effectively by providing a different perspective on the everyday problems we all experience. And after his space flight, Mitchell is also better able to cope with major problems and crises.

Most of the men and women I interviewed agree with Mitchell about the benefits perspective lends to their lives and work. In fact, this chapter grew directly out of the interviews. Though I'd intended to write a section on taking time for relaxation, so many peak performers mentioned perspective that I knew we were on to something.

In this chapter we'll cover:

- Finding perspective where little or none existed before
- Building perspective to boost your ability to manage change
- Using humor, vacations, and relaxation to renew and fortify healthy perspective.

MAINTAINING PERSPECTIVE

It's a typical day. Too much to do and too little time to do it. Everyone wants a piece of you—boss, coworkers, family, and friends. And there's not enough to go around.

You feel overwhelmed, your heart starts pounding, and you snap at someone. How can you get back on track?

Writer and speaker Ken Blanchard suggests finding perspective through gaining a wider view. He talks about taking a mental helicopter ride to the ceiling. "Imagine floating up there looking down on what's happening from a distance," he says.

That's what perspective is all about. It enables us to see the bigger picture. The people I interviewed have many ways of doing this—some through spirituality or rejection, others with a more secular approach. But all agreed that a sense of perspective helps them keep going when pressure-packed change takes place.

We'll start by surveying some of the spiritual perspective builders.

SPIRITUAL PERSPECTIVE

For millions of years, people have gained perspective through religion and spirituality, especially in times of transition. Many I interviewed do the same. But not all. Our survey asked participants to rate the statement, "I have strong spiritual beliefs." Fifty-eight percent agreed or strongly agreed; 32 percent disagreed or disagreed strongly; and 11 percent were undecided.

About her spiritual beliefs, author and television personality Julia Child says, "I like the credo that says to love thy God with all thy heart, all thy soul, all thy mind; and to love thy neighbor as thy self."

When evaluating the statement "I pray frequently," 43 percent of the peak performers agreed or strongly agreed, 10 percent were undecided, and 48 percent disagreed or disagreed strongly. According to a recent survey published in *Psychology Today*, about 32 percent of the general population say they pray frequently.

Research shows that taking an active, spiritual approach can help us deal with change. Psychologists Daniel McIntosh, of the

University of Michigan, and Bernard Spilka, of the University of Denver, studied three groups: active Christians (those who look upon God as a partner with whom they can work); passive Christians (who are less involved with their faith and believe that God preordains events); and questors (those who aren't quite sure *what* the truth is).

Researchers found that active Christians tend to be healthier than those in the other two groups. They also prayed more, which other researchers say reduces tension. In addition, prayer gives a sense of control, essential to handling change effectively.

The perspective provided by active spirituality can increase health and boost our ability to handle change. Other research demonstrates similar results for those who actively pursue religious beliefs.

How Some See Spirituality

The religious beliefs of those I interviewed vary considerably. But, whatever the belief, the peak performers insisted that spirituality provided perspective and direction in their lives.

Gertrude Crain, of Crain Communications, Inc. has a concept of God that is very helpful to her. A life-long Catholic, she told me her spiritual beliefs help keep her from worrying.

"Religion is very reassuring," she said. "I can appeal to God and ask for help. I don't have to make all the decisions myself."

Several of the peak performers described their spiritual beliefs as a way to get in touch with a quiet core within themselves—a part that is still and at peace no matter what's happening.

In my own life, losing that quiet center makes change seem much more stressful. I forget what's truly important and let silly things bother me. But when I have the perspective that comes from inner peace, life is good, even when negative changes occur.

This chapter reveals several ways to find your own quiet center. One, of course, is spirituality: prayer, meditation, and worship. Perhaps you're already using one or more of these. If not, are there spiritual beliefs you've drifted away from? This might be the time to try them again. Many people find that going to a church, temple, or other organized group helps them. Following a spiritual belief system is often easier when we can receive guidance from someone who has been down that path before. But if the spiritual beliefs you've known before don't appeal to you now, try something new instead. Your beliefs don't necessarily need to dovetail with an established religion. Your own unique approach might work best for you.

Whichever approach you take, some common elements seem to work.

- A number of those I interviewed mentioned taking time in the morning to pray or meditate. They said this helps them to maintain a sense of peace throughout the day, no matter what changes they encounter.
- Some peak performers pray before going to sleep at night.
- Reading spiritual writings can help us regain inspiration, particularly when life is tough. Reading an inspirational book or article just before bed helps the ideas stay in our unconscious mind throughout the night.
- People in a 12-Step Recovery program, such as A.A. or N.A., may find that the handbook *Day by Day* (Hazelden, 1974) provides inspiration and perspective. For Al-Anon members, or anyone dealing with the compulsive behavior of a loved one, try *One Day at a Time in Al-Anon* (published in 1981 and available through Al-Anon Family Group Headquarters, Inc., P.O. Box 182, Madison Square Station, New York, NY 10159).
- Whatever your spiritual beliefs, practicing them with a group can also strengthen your ability to master change. The power of the group can help you through times of turmoil and stress.

Of course, spirituality is by no means the only way to gain a better outlook during times of change. There are other paths to plentiful perspective.

OTHER PERSPECTIVE BUILDERS

During World War I, Sir Winston Churchill traveled to France to observe the fighting firsthand. At one point he was in a front-line sandbagged shelter. There he received a message from a long-time friend, now a general, asking if they could meet. So Churchill walked three miles to the crossroads where a car was to pick him up and deliver him to the general. Churchill waited at the crossroads for nearly an hour. The general never arrived. Finally Churchill discovered that the car had been sent to the wrong place. It was now too late for the meeting.

Rain had begun to fall, and Churchill had to walk back to the trenches in the dark. He cursed the careless general as he trudged. But when he got back to the shelter, his curses stopped abruptly. The shelter was gone. Five minutes after Churchill had left, a shell destroyed it, killing the man inside.

As Churchill wrote: "Suddenly I felt my irritation against General X pass completely from my mind. All sense of grievance departed in a flash. As I walked to my new abode, I reflected how thoughtful it had been of him to wish to see me again, and to show courtesy to a subordinate when he had so much responsibility on his shoulders."

Producer, comedian, and writer Gene Perret told me about a fellow writer who also found instant perspective.

"A friend of mine, who's a Hollywood writer, was out here trying to get a job. He did a few shows, and made a few bucks, nothing big. Then, all of a sudden he got red hot—he became a big producer.

"One day he arrived at work and someone was parked in his parking space. Now, there were twenty-two other parking spaces, but he wanted *his* parking space. And at first he was furious. Then he stopped to think and got some perspective. 'It dawned on me,' he said, 'that three months ago I didn't even have a car.'"

Various approaches to gaining perspective have the same basic elements:

- Getting an overview of the situation
- Realizing that you're not alone—that others suffer, too
- Understanding there's more to life than our own limited view

Gene Perret summed it up: "I saw a cartoon once. There was a picture of the galaxy, with about a million stars. And there was a little arrow pointing to one small part that said, 'You are here.' It puts you in perspective."

PERSPECTIVE AND HUMOR

One perspective builder we've already discussed is humor. Before retiring as an NFL referee, professional speaker Jim Tunney dealt with big-time pressure and plenty of change on the football field. Often he kept his perspective through creating laughter.

"I remember one game," Tunney told me, "where the coach of the opposing team was upset with a call that one of our officials made, and was yelling at me. I didn't make the call, but he was angry at me. The veins were sticking out of his neck. So during the time out, I went over to the side lines and tried to see what I could do to help.

"The coach said, 'That was a foul, and the official should have called it.'

"And I said, 'No, the official looked at it and he decided it was not a foul.'

The coach turned to me and said, 'You've been screwing me for eighteen years.'

"And I said, 'It's nineteen now.'

"He laughed and I laughed, and it really took the edge off of things. It put everything in perspective."

TAKE TIME OUT FOR PERSPECTIVE

We've got a perspective problem. But it's not the problem many forecast. In the 1950s and '60s, experts predicted an explosion of leisure time. They said that soon we'd have so much time off we wouldn't know what to do with it.

Of course those predictions haven't come true. In fact, the National Research Center of the Arts, an affiliate of Louis Harris and Associates Inc., recently completed a survey that found that:

- In 1973, people spent an average of 40.6 hours per week at work. By 1989 the figure had risen to 46.8.
- In 1973, weekly leisure time was 26.2 hours. By 1989 it had dropped to 16.6 hours. Women had even less: 14 hours.

The survey also reported that the average small business owner works 57.3 hours per week, followed by professionals, who labor 52.2 hours weekly.

"Time may well have become the most precious commodity in the land," the report concluded.

Remember when "labor-saving" devices were supposed to give us more leisure time? Automatic washers and dryers, electric garage door openers, microwaves, and trash compactors promised to free the average householder from the drudgery of repetitive work. Instead, we seem to work harder and harder, toiling to buy and use all the new labor-saving devices.

Something is wrong. People weren't designed for nonstop work. Today, stress-related illness is rising at an alarming rate. And as the pace of change accelerates, stress often grows, too.

But perhaps things are changing. A recent survey by the Hilton Hotels Corporation found that 67 percent of 1,010 adults queried would be willing to give up one to two days income for a day or two of free time each week. As Harvard professor of economics Dr. Juliet Schor comments, "A shift in materialist values is taking place even as economic pressure on people to work longer hours is increasing."

Like most of us, the peak performers I interviewed feel the time crunch. Many told me they wished they had more time to do the things they want and need to accomplish. And that's not surprising. They work an average of 52.95 hours per week. But many have also found ways to create "down time," even when they have more than enough other things to do.

In this section, several peak performers describe what they do— and what *you* can do to enhance your ability to manage change— by taking (and creating) time out.

VACATION: THE LONG AND SHORT OF IT

Most experts on productivity recommend periodic holidays. Robert Ornstein, Ph.D., and David Sobel, M.D., in their book *Healthy Pleasures*, write that "most people report relief from mental and physical stress [as a result of a vacation]. In one study, findings showed that getting away reduced fatigue, digestive problems, insomnia and loss of interest in sex by half. Headache pain plunged to 3 percent [of those studied], compared to 21 percent before the vacation."

According to our own survey, 73 percent of the peak performers take at least two weeks of vacation per year, and 8 percent sometimes do. They find that the time off helps them cope more effectively with change and stress.

Ken Blanchard makes vacations a centerpiece of his summers. "The biggest release for my wife and me is to go to our cottage in upstate New York for six or seven weeks in the summer. Ever since we started the company (Blanchard Training and Development), we stop the world and get off for a few weeks.

"When I'm back at work and I feel overwhelmed, I just imagine floating on the lake. It really helps."

Others who take regular holidays swear by them. And vacations don't necessarily have to take you anyplace. With two small children, my wife and I sometimes have home holidays. We take a week off, schedule a baby-sitter for part of each day, and spend the time relaxing and taking day trips.

Time for Adventure

Some peak performers like to keep moving on vacation. In fact, adventurous vacations are increasingly popular for many people.

Once an avid auto racer, broadcaster Walter Cronkite now prefers spending his vacations sailing. But he still believes in the value of the race track for a change of pace. "Automobile racing is the best relaxation anybody could find. It's the exact opposite of what people think it would be. There is stress in automobile racing, but it's of such a different variety that it's a relief.

"When you're behind the wheel of an automobile going 140 miles per hour on a racetrack, you don't have time to think of anything else. You know exactly what you're doing. A wandering mind at that point could be fatal. You need to concentrate and put absolutely everything else out of your mind. And in that sense it's extremely restful."

Whether your vacation is risky or relaxing, taking time out provides a change from our normal routine. And that rebuilds strength and energy, helping us handle negative changes better when we're back on the job.

What If You Can't Stop?

But what if you can't stand to stop working?

- If you have difficulty leaving your work at work, compromise. Try scheduling three hours of work for your first vacation day, two for the next, one for the third. Then play with a day without any work, just as an experiment. Notice how you feel.
- If, after the experiment, you find that you still like to work on vacation, don't beat yourself up. A change of scene will help, even if you *do* take work with you.

Weekend Wonders

Weekends can be minivacations if you schedule them to do things you enjoy with friends or family you enjoy.

Nap It Up

Another kind of vacation takes even less time—the nap. "Nature definitely intended that adults nap in the middle of the day," says William Dement, director of Stanford University's Sleep Disorders Clinic and Research Center.

And in one report, researchers stated that an afternoon nap can significantly improve mood and boost mental alertness, particularly in those who otherwise get too little sleep. This is especially important because of the well-documented midafternoon performance drop people suffer. *Even those who get a normal amount of sleep have quicker reaction times and make fewer mistakes when they've had a brief nap.*

But naps are for babies, right? Wrong. According to David Dinges, University of Pennsylvania sleep researcher, after napping, "People feel better and do significantly better on mental performance tests." Those tested by Dinges show postnap benefits, including improved concentration and increased ability to make complicated decisions.

And James Krueger, M.D., of Harvard Medical School, discovered that sleep may help boost the functioning of the immune system.

But how can you nap at work? Lunch is one time to rest. When giving all-day seminars, I'm on my feet for eight or nine hours, using a lot of energy. When I first started leading these sessions, I felt tired by midafternoon. Now, though, I take part of the lunch break to nap or relax, either in my car or an empty office. Afterward, my energy level and effectiveness rise. I feel strong throughout the afternoon.

- Sleep isn't the only way to boost your energy level. Resting with your eyes closed, even for just a few minutes, can help. Some companies have special "quiet" rooms that are ideal for this. If yours doesn't, try a nap or relaxation in your car at lunch.
- With a private office, it's easier to get time alone. But if you don't have your own space at work, try the restroom as a place where you can find a few moments to close your eyes.

If you feel guilty resting, remember that it may make you more productive. Steve Allen wrote his biggest musical hit, "This Could Be the Start of Something Big," after dreaming about it.

THINK, RELAX, MEDITATE

Naps aren't the only way to relax during the day. Brief, conscious time-outs also help peak performers stay energized and productive.

Find Time to Be Alone

Our survey also asked the peak performers if they take time to be alone every day. Sixty percent said they did. CEO Jack Lewis remarked, "I think a lot and mull over problems when I drive. The reason I won't put a radio or telephone in my car is that I use driving as my quiet time to think."

At one of my recent seminars, a participant told the group about the time she asked her 106-year-old grandmother for the secret to her long life. The senior citizen's reply came quickly.

"Everyone needs to have at least twenty minutes each day to oneself," she said. "I always made sure that I did, and that's helped keep me feeling strong and healthy."

To get time for yourself:

- If you drive to your job, on the way to or from work, find a quiet place where you feel comfortable, and park. Then take ten or twenty minutes to relax. Listen to a music tape, think, or just close your eyes and tune out.
- If you take public transportation to work, try closing your eyes and relaxing while en route. You might even carry a portable cassette player and wear headphones to provide soothing background music.

If you're at home most of the day with kids, time out is especially important. Arrange for a spouse, babysitter, or friend to spell you for even a few minutes. Many parents, especially single ones, tell me they feel guilty taking time for themselves. So I ask them what happens when they're "on" all the time. Most say they get short tempered and grumpy. Is a frequently angry parent good for kids? Give them, and yourself, a break. You'll *all* feel better.

And if you're a working woman whose husband won't help with the housework and kids, try sitting down for a talk. Let your husband know (hopefully without yelling) that you'd like to have a few minutes to yourself each day. Ask if he'll take over while you relax. If he won't, it might be worth having a few sessions with a marriage counselor to work toward an agreement on this important issue.

Deep Relaxation and Meditation

Few people do it. But those who do take regular time for deep relaxation report that it helps them handle change more effectively. Meditation and deep relaxation have much in common. To do either, you take ten minutes or more to relax and focus the mind. And research shows that most of the many methods work equally well.

Deep relaxation is the opposite of the fight-or-flight response. During relaxation, heart rate goes down, blood pressure decreases, muscles relax, and the brain wave state changes. Meditation is literally a brief vacation.

More than five hundred articles and studies have chronicled the beneficial changes that take place during meditation. **People**

who practice deep relaxation regularly also gain these benefits.
Among them:

- Meditation is more refreshing and energy-restoring than deep sleep. Meditators report that they need less sleep after they begin meditating.
- Meditators are more psychologically stable than others.
- Meditators react less radically to stressful changes.
- Meditators have an internal locus of control (feel more in control of their surroundings).
- Meditators rate themselves as more contented.
- Meditators concentrate better.
- Regular meditation can reduce high blood pressure (researchers at New England Deaconess Hospital helped 80 percent of their hypertensive patients to lower their blood pressure or reduce their use of medication through practicing deep relaxation).

Several of those I interviewed meditate regularly.

"Meditation helps me relax, even when stressful changes are taking place in my life," says former Sacramento Mayor Ann Rudin. "Because of meditation I've kept my blood pressure at a very normal level, which many people in my position have not been able to do. It also has an energizing effect.

"Meditation has also helped me to reduce my anger level. I was a very volatile person before. Now I don't feel angry very often."

Rudin also reports that, since beginning to meditate, she drinks less coffee and eats a more balanced diet.

Deep relaxation and meditation are relatively easy to learn. One of the most widely used techniques is the Relaxation Response, a simple relaxation exercise devised by Boston cardiologist and Harvard University professor Herbert Benson, author of *The Relaxation Response*.

To practice the Relaxation Response, first find a quiet place where you can be alone. You may need to unplug the phone, put a sign on the door, and/or tell family or friends you will be taking some time by yourself. If you explain briefly what you're doing, people will generally be understanding—they may actually go out of their way to help you get your quiet time.

To practice the Relaxation Response:

1. Use a kitchen timer (set in another room), a clock radio, or the hourly chime on an alarm watch to remind you when to stop. Make sure your alarm or other reminder is not too loud.
2. Sit quietly in a comfortable position and close your eyes.

3. Deeply relax all your muscles, beginning at your feet and progressing up to the face. You might say to yourself, "My feet are warm and relaxed, my ankles are relaxed, my calves are loose and relaxed." After you've finished relaxing your body (just take a few minutes), begin to focus on your breathing.
4. Breathe in through your nose. Then, as you breathe out, say the word "one" silently to yourself. Continue, IN . . . OUT, "ONE"; etc. Breathe easily and naturally. (Recent research shows this step is even more effective if, instead of the word "one," you use a word that has special meaning for you. It could be a word from a religious or spiritual tradition, or any other word. Some possibilities: *peace, joy, relax, calm.*)
5. Continue for fifteen to twenty minutes. When finished, sit quietly for several minutes, at first with eyes closed, and later with them open.
6. Don't worry about whether you are successful in achieving a deep level of relaxation. Maintain a passive attitude and permit relaxation to occur at its own pace. When distracting thoughts occur (and they do for everyone), gently return your attention to your breathing and the key word.
7. With practice, the Relaxation Response will come more and more easily. Practice the technique once or twice daily, but not within two hours after any meal, since digestion interferes with the process.

Many people find their minds wandering when they first try this technique. Others notice that they're restless. It's fine to feel either or both. Distractions will lessen as you become more experienced. In fact, after becoming skilled at relaxation, you'll be able to practice it even in noisy environments, such as on buses, trains, and in airports.

Feeling Good

Some report experiencing strong emotions, both positive and negative, during deep relaxation. That's fine. In fact, experiencing a negative emotion while relaxed can be helpful. By so doing, you desensitize yourself to it.

Several years ago, I was giving a change management seminar for a government organization. When we discussed the benefits of deep relaxation, a woman I'll call Kate told of how she had used it to recover from grief.

Kate's son had died about a year before, and she was overcome with grief. To deal with the pain, Kate decided to keep busy. She took a second job and spent almost eighty hours a week working. Still she felt terrible.

So Kate bought a relaxation tape and listened to it, hoping it would help. But when she played the tape, Kate felt even more grief than before, so she decided not to use it. Finally, though, when she continued to feel worse, Kate tried the tape again and spent several hours listening to it over and over.

At first, her grief was very strong. Kate was afraid it would overwhelm her. It didn't. As she continued to experience her feelings in a relaxed state, she discovered that they were passing. Soon she began feeling better.

Even after she stopped listening to the tape, Kate felt much better. She still felt sad about her son's death, but the overwhelming, debilitating grief was gone.

Most people don't have a relaxation experience as strong as Kate's. And, of course, if negative feelings continue or build in intensity in spite of your relaxation, it's best to seek professional help. But the vast majority of people who try deep relaxation report that it helps them handle change more effectively.

If you'd prefer to have help getting relaxed, relaxation tapes are available. People have told me that one of the tapes my company produces, *Stress Release: The Thirty-Minute Vacation*, has helped them learn to relax. Insomniacs say it puts them to sleep. I assume that's a compliment. (The tape is available from Olesen and Associates, at the address listed in the back of this book.)

To benefit from deep relaxation, practice is essential. Most people find it easiest to do first thing in the morning. It's helpful to have a reminder when starting something new, so you may want to make a chart to keep track of when you practice. Then, after a while, most find that the benefits are so significant that they look forward each day to relaxation.

SIX STRATEGIES FOR TAKING TIME OUT

STRATEGY 1

Get Natural

Waiting for a client who was late for his counseling appointment, I moved my chair outside my office. I planned to update my calendar while waiting. Instead, I just sat. The warm sun soothed me as I looked at the trees and grass, felt the breeze, heard the birds singing.

When my client arrived, I felt refreshed, relaxed, and full of energy. We had a great session.

Researchers have discovered that nature reduces stress and helps people feel better. And when we feel positive and relaxed, changes (even negative ones) seem easier to handle.

In 1987, Roger Ulrich, then a geography professor at the University of Delaware, studied the reactions of college students who had just viewed a stressful film about workshop accidents.

After the film, some students watched films of nature, while others looked at videos of traffic and urban environments. Those who looked at the natural scenes began feeling calmer within three minutes.

As Ulrich reported: "We found that subjects recovered faster and much more completely from stress when they were exposed to nature as opposed to either the pedestrian mall or traffic settings."

Ulrich also found that surgical patients who look at greenery outside their windows recover faster and feel less discomfort.

Luckily, you don't have to go far to benefit from greenery. Even if you live in the city, a nearby park can help. Just find a place where you can see more of nature than you can of man. Then, when you return to your office or home, you'll be better able to cope with the stress and change in your life.

STRATEGY 2

Ship Out

One way to lose sight of other people is on the water. Several I interviewed told me about the sense of renewal they get from sailing. And though some sail good-sized yachts, you can derive similar benefits by taking the helm of a smaller boat. Concessions at most water recreation areas rent small sailboats for a modest hourly or daily fee. These boats deliver the fun of sailing without the sometimes significant headaches of ownership.

For those I interviewed, sailing is more popular than motorboating. Perhaps it's because it's one of the few places away from internal combustion engines. And, when sailing, we get a chance to use all the three C's: **Challenge,** in dealing with the ever changing environment. **Commitment,** to handling the boat properly. And **Control,** as you pilot the craft safely out and back.

One of my clients, Dave, decided he wanted two things: a hobby and something to bring his family closer together. So he searched the want ads and finally bought a small used sailboat. The price, including trailer, was $1500. Dave hooked up the boat, gathered the family, and drove to a nearby lake. It took him a couple of weekends to make the boat go where he wanted it to. But soon Dave and his family were sailing fanatics. He reported that the money spent on the boat was one of his best investments ever.

Boating provides a great break. And, in many places, it can be done inexpensively. If you don't know how to sail, lessons are usually available wherever boats are sold or rented. But if sailing doesn't appeal to you, there are many more ways to change pace.

STRATEGY 3

Exercise

Exercise helps reduce stress, improve health, and raise self-confidence. It's also a great way to take a break. (See Step 10 for more information.)

STRATEGY 4

Watch (Out for) TV

Television is America's favorite form of relaxation. Does it relieve tension? Yes, but only in limited doses. The top achievers we surveyed watch, on average, less than eight hours of television per week—a little over one hour per day.

According to the Nielson ratings, the average American watches 29.4 hours per week, over four hours per day. Many teenagers and kids watch even more. And 34 percent of all households are now "total TV" homes. The television is on every minute that anyone is home.

In a recent study at Auburn University, researchers found that men who spent more than three hours a day watching TV had a tendency to be overweight. When compared to those who watched less than an hour, they were two times as likely to be obese.

It takes courage to watch less TV. By carefully choosing programs, we reap the relaxation benefits of TV, without getting stuck in the prime-time doldrums.

──────────────── **S T R A T E G Y 5** ────────────────

Time Out with Massage

It's tough to stay tense when we're touched and rubbed. Unfortunately, massage has a sexual connotation in the minds of many. But therapeutic massage can provide a tremendous time out that's sensual, not sexual.

In one study, reported in the *Journal of Psychosomatic Research*, a group of patients with chronic anxiety and muscular tension received ten sessions of deep massage. Previously these folks hadn't responded to relaxation training or medication. After the massages, they reported less tension and pain and reduced need for medication. They also talked more freely.

One good place to get a massage is from a spouse or friend. It's a great way to build closeness and have fun together. Some colleges and universities have courses available through their adult education departments. And in many cities, independent adult learning centers give regular courses on massage for couples.

Therapeutic massages are also available from professional masseurs in health clubs, chiropractic officers, and sometimes at wellness centers. In advertisements, "straight" massage is usually called *therapeutic* or *nonsexual.*

──────────────── **S T R A T E G Y 6** ────────────────

Get a Lot of the Breaks

There are many other ways to take time out: sex, music (a study at Stanford University found that some get a bigger thrill from music than from sex), and hobbies. Perhaps music or sex *is* your hobby. Indeed, *74 percent of our survey group reported that hobbies help them relax and recharge.*

Gertrude Crain practiced perhaps the most innovative way of taking a break several years ago, at the age of seventy-five.

Leon Mandel, then editor of the Crain magazine *AutoWeek*, asked his boss if she'd like to go two hundred miles per hour in a stock car. "Sure," she said. "I think that would be fun." So Mandel arranged for Crain to fly to North Carolina to ride around the Charlotte Speedway with professional driver Tim Richmond at the wheel.

Mandel still talks about what happened that day. "Her administrative vice-president, Jim Franklin, called, and said, 'Please, can't you talk her out of it?' I told him that no guy as experienced as Tim Richmond was going to put a Gertrude Crain in any kind of peril. Well, as it turned out, she jacked him up to the point where he came within one mile an hour of the track speed record."

"The ride was tremendously exciting," Crain says now, with a laugh. "At one point we came so close to the wall that I could have touched it with my hand. And that was at 185 miles per hour."

After her stock car ride, *Working Woman* magazine wrote that Crain held the "publishing-magnate land-speed record," and Chicago's "PM Magazine" aired a segment on the board chairman entitled "Gutsy Grandma." Good publicity for Crain Communications—and fun, too.

- As Gertrude Crain knows, there are few limits when it comes to taking time out. To pinpoint those that are best for you, make a list of the things you like to do most. Note how often you actually do each one. Most people find that the great joys of their life are, unfortunately, practiced infrequently.
- You might choose *just one* activity that you love (or think you *might* love) and resolve to do it more often. Set a goal for the number of times you'd like to do it each week, or each month.

When you do the things you love more often, you'll give yourself a change in perspective.

SUMMARY: PERSPECTIVE IS...

Perspective is the essence of change management. Without it, every change is a big deal. With it, events occupy a place relative to their true importance.

Fresh perspective is available through spirituality, helicopter rides, drives in the country, and trips to the moon. You'll discover it in vacations, naps, weekends, evenings, and days. You can prime perspective by thinking, meditating, and relaxing.

You'll also find perspective through looking at trees, TV, books, and waves. And you can change your pace through sex, saunas, massages, music, and hobbies.

But most important, a healthy perspective is found where love is—love, not just of other people, but of the little things in life. We gain perspective through living our lives moment by moment. Planning, of course, but then letting the plan be a framework as we savor each bit of time for itself. This way of living lends hope, health, and serenity.

NOTES

Julia Child made her statement about love and God on "The Class of the 20th Century," a series that appeared on the Arts and Entertainment television cable channel in 1992.

The survey on prayer appeared in *Psychology Today*, January/February 1992 (excerpted from *The Great Divide*, by Daniel Evan Weiss, Poseidon Press/Simon & Schuster, Inc., 1991).

The research on active Christians is from "A Healthy Dose of Religion," by Jamie Talan, in *Psychology Today*, November 1988.

The leisure survey was summarized in "Americans Work More, Play Less," by Patricia McCormack of UPI, in the *Auburn Journal*, April 23, 1989.

The Hilton Hotels Corporation survey was summarized in a *New York Times* article, "Weary 90's Workers Yearn for Time More Than Money," by Peter Kerr, reprinted in the *Sacramento Bee*, October 27, 1991.

The quote about the reduction in stress as a result of vacations is from *Healthy Pleasures*, by Robert Ornstein and David Sobel, Addison-Wesley, 1989.

Nap research was quoted in "An Afternoon Nap Is Only Natural," by Daniel Goleman, in the *Sacramento Bee*, September 26, 1989.

Immunity and sleep information is from "Get a Good Night's Rest," by Anne Moffat, from *American Health*, August 1988.

The value of naps for the heart was covered in "What a Difference a Nap Makes," by Morton Hunt, in *Parade* magazine, January 29, 1989.

Benefits of meditation are summarized in *Mind as Healer, Mind as Slayer*, by Ken Pelletier, Dell Publishing Company, 1977.

The study about hypertension and relaxation was reported in "The Healing Power of Positive Thinking," in *Better Homes and Gardens*, November 1991.

The findings on the benefits of nature were reported in "Research Shows Greenery Helps to Reduce Stress," by Thomas F. Troy, Jr., in *The Auburn Journal* (UPI story), April 3, 1987.

The television statistics are from the *Information Please Almanac*, Houghton-Mifflin, 1989.

The data on obesity and television was reported in *American Health*, November 1989.

The research on massages was covered in *Healthy Pleasures*, cited above.

The information on musical thrills was reported in *Healthy Pleasures*, cited above.

The Leon Mandel quote is from "The Keeper (and Stoker) of the Company Flame," by Stephan Wilkinson, in *Working Woman* magazine, October 1987.

13

STEP TEN

Tuning the Body

Imagine you've just been to see your family doctor. He told you about a new drug—one with tremendous benefits. The drug provides renewed perspective, improves appearance, extends life, reduces stress, boosts energy, creates happiness, improves immune system functioning, and raises sexual satisfaction. Would you be interested?

The miracle product that can do all these things is available today. But it isn't a pill, powder, or potion. That miracle is exercise. Many would pay huge sums of money for a medication that provided all these benefits. But we don't need to. The only investment required for exercise is time—an hour or more per week.

Almost all the top achievers I interviewed work out regularly, many every day. And 91.5 percent of our survey group exercise regularly—an average of 4.7 hours per week. Yet the President's Council on Physical Fitness estimates that less than 50 percent of all Americans get regular exercise. And only about 10 percent of U.S. adults follow the Surgeon General's guidelines: twenty minutes of vigorous exercise, three times per week.

Does physical fitness have anything to do with handling pressure-packed change? When asked, those I interviewed replied with a resounding "yes."

HOW EXERCISE HELPS US MANAGE CHANGE AND STRESS

Exercise Reduces Anxiety and Stress

A recent *American Health*/Gallup survey found that regular exercisers list relaxation as the number one benefit of working out. (Paradoxically, it also boosts energy—but more on that later.)

A study at the University of San Francisco's Human Performance Laboratory found that physically fit people control their reactions to stress better than the nonfit. When given an unsolvable verbal ability test, a physically fit group handled the stressful situation with minimal jumps in anxiety, muscle tension, and blood pressure. The nonfit control group showed big rises in all three measures.

Fitness Boosts Our Confidence

Exercise boosts confidence. And when we're confident, we're better able to master life's changes.

California psychologist M. G. Saipe studied college students, finding that their self-confidence rose as they became more fit. Using the Tennessee Self-Concept Scale, which rates self-confidence, other researchers have also pinpointed the confidence-boosting benefits of exercise.

Exercise Increases Optimism and Positive Moods

Creating an exercise habit also leads to increased optimism and reduced depression. In a recent *American Health*/Gallup survey comparing the fit and nonfit, folks who worked out regularly were two and a half times more likely to say they were happy.

Other research studies reinforce the value of exercise in banishing low moods. In fact, several studies have found regular exercise more effective than therapy in curing depression, though a combination of working out *and* counseling yields the best results of all. In eight other studies, summarized in the *Journal of Coun-*

seling and Development, researchers agreed that exercise elevates mood and reduces depression.

Exercise Clarifies Thinking

Exercise also makes our brains work better, enabling us to negotiate transitions more easily. Researchers at Scripps College studied a group of adults aged fifty-five to ninety-one, testing their memory, reaction time, and reasoning abilities. The physically fit men and women performed significantly better than those who didn't exercise.

Physical Activity Boosts Energy

When we don't have enough energy, it's difficult to stay on top, especially when change buffets us. Exercise actually *boosts* energy, partly because it reduces tension.

Dr. William Friedewald, associate director of the National Institutes of Health, says that people who exercise regularly feel more energy after working out, even if they were tired before starting.

Psychologist Robert Thayer, of California State University at Long Beach, recently completed research on the energy-raising value of a brisk walk. He compared two groups of students. In one group each member ate a candy bar. In the other, the subjects took a brisk ten-minute walk. The students then rated their energy, tension, and fatigue twenty minutes, one hour, and two hours later.

Thayer found that the walkers had more energy and less tension than the candy eaters. Those who ate candy bars reported increased energy for about twenty minutes, but found that it dropped fast after that. They also reported increased tension.

Other Fitness Benefits

The benefits of regular exercise are countless. Here are a few more:

- **Improves physical appearance** by tightening skin, improving muscle tone, and reducing excess weight. CEO Lillian Vernon told me that she met her ex-husband on the street some time after she'd begun exercising. "He didn't recognize me," she said with a laugh. "Exercising has toned me up and helped me feel better about my body."
- **Burns calories.** Vigorous exercise burns over 300 calories per

hour. Watching TV for an hour uses only about 80. More importantly, *when people exercise regularly, their bodies burn more calories twenty-four hours per day.*

But you don't have to exercise hard to lose weight. Researchers at the Institute for Aerobics Research in Dallas found that low-intensity exercise (50 to 60 percent of maximum heart rate) burns fat as effectively as more vigorous exercise.

Actress Jill Eikenberry experienced firsthand the power of exercise for weight loss. Eikenberry was overweight when she began attending Yale Drama School. During one summer vacation she started a diet and began exercising every night before going to bed. She lost thirty-five pounds. Today she believes that exercising changed her metabolism. She still works out regularly but hasn't had to struggle with her weight since college.

- **Increases longevity.** A study of Harvard University graduates found that those who exercised regularly lived longer, healthier lives. They received, on the average, two hours of extended life for every hour of exercise. For instance, participants who walked at least nine miles each week, had a risk of death 21 percent lower than those who hiked fewer than three miles per week.

  As Lillian Vernon says about her exercising, "If I'm going to get old, I'm going to get old healthy and strong."

- **Improves sexual drive and satisfaction.** Researchers at the University of California, San Diego, followed a group of people on a nine-month exercise program. The participants reported more frequent sexual intercourse, kissing, and caressing. (They love researching this kind of thing in San Diego.)

- **Triggers the release of endorphins,** the body's natural opiatelike pain killers. Endorphins give exercisers the often reported "natural high." Lee Berk, an immunologist at Loma Linda University Medical Center, says, "Regular exercisers have frequent practice in releasing endorphins in the proper amount and in the proper patterns to handle stress. When a well-conditioned individual is then exposed to distress, the body responds with practiced efficiency."

- **Boosts immune system functioning.** Loma Linda's Lee Berk, mentioned above, also reports that physically fit people have more highly functioning immune systems.

- **Reduces jet lag.** Researchers at Stanford University report

that exercise helps jet-lagged travelers reset their body's sleep cycle.
- **Improves brain functioning.** In a study at the University of Illinois, neuropsychologist William Greenough found that rats who exercised aerobically for four weeks showed a 20 percent increase in the number of blood vessels nourishing the cerebellum, the region of the brain that coordinates movement.
- **Reduces risk of cancer and coronary heart disease,** according to a recent study by the Institute for Aerobics Research and the Cooper Clinic in Dallas.

CAN EXERCISE HURT?

"What about Jim Fixx?" people often ask me. Fixx, author of several books on running and an accomplished jogger himself, died of a heart attack several years ago while running. Many use this as an excuse to avoid exercising.

What most don't know is that Fixx didn't do enough. He got plenty of exercise but lacked a well-rounded stress management program. He came from a family with a history of heart disease, so his own risk was much higher. Fixx was also a "Type A" individual who found it difficult to relax—another risk factor for heart disease. Rather than hurting, his jogging undoubtedly helped him live longer than he would have otherwise.

Jim Fixx is an anomaly. Most people find only pluses from an exercise program. However a few tips will help you reap the benefits and avoid the problems:

- If you haven't been exercising regularly, check with your physician before embarking on a new program.
- Start slowly and work up. If you've been sedentary, don't make your first run a marathon or your first round of tennis a day-long battle.
- If you suffer an injury, back off on the duration, frequency, and intensity of your exercising.
- Don't overdo it. Too much exercise ceases to help. Research shows that people who run farther than ten miles per day may be doing their bodies more harm than good. That, of course, is not a concern for most of us. The majority of people

have the opposite problem—too little exercise. Balance is the key.

TYPES OF EXERCISE

There are three basic kinds of exercise: aerobic, strength building, and stretching. Some activities emphasize one or two, others incorporate all three.

Aerobic exercise conditions the cardiovascular system. Until recently, experts thought that only vigorous exercise like running, jumping rope, and cross country skiing helped strengthen and tone the heart muscle. However, experts now believe that less vigorous activities like walking, tennis, golf (without a motorized cart), and even yard work can be beneficial to the heart.

Strength building exercises build muscle mass and definition. Examples include weight lifting (using either free weights or weight machines), rowing isometrics, floor work in aerobics classes, and chopping wood.

After the age of twenty-five, we lose approximately one-half pound of muscle mass each year unless we practice some kind of strength-building exercise. Thus the American College of Sports Medicine recently amended their "Fitness Prescription for Healthy Adults" to add a strength training component. More about this in the "Strength Training" section later in this chapter.

Stretching builds flexibility and coordination. It is an important beginning to other kinds of workouts. Most aerobics classes emphasize prolonged stretching at the beginning and end of the class. Yoga is one of the most effective ways to stretch.

Before stretching, take a few minutes to warm up by jogging in place, doing jumping jacks, calisthenics, or some other light aerobic activity. This increases blood flow to joints and muscles, and also helps to lubricate the joints. When you stretch, do it gently. Forcing the stretch by bouncing or lunging can injure your muscles. Instead, just stretch to the point of tension, then hold that position for about twenty seconds. After 20 seconds, muscle tissue relaxes, and you'll be able to stretch a bit farther.

The top achievers I interviewed run the exercise gamut from the most vigorous activities to the most mellow. Most of them have chosen something they like to do. But no one enjoys working out all the time. Sometimes getting started requires a self-inflicted kick in the backside.

To achieve good cardiovascular conditioning, most experts recommend working out at least three times per week, for twenty minutes each time. This is the *minimum* required. Exercising longer provides more benefits, within the limits outlined in the section above. A less vigorous activity requires more time for good conditioning.

GETTING MOTIVATED TO WORK OUT

If you've decided to begin or expand a fitness regimen, you *can* do it. This section covers some of the self-motivation strategies useful in starting, and sustaining, an exercise program.

STRATEGY 1
Imagine Alternate Futures

What follows is an effective technique for weighing the benefits of any activity. The process is simple:

First, sit in a comfortable place and allow your eyes to close. Imagine yourself ten years from today. Imagine that you haven't exercised for the past decade. Then ask yourself these questions. (If you aren't able to experience all the sights, sounds, and feelings, that's okay. One or two are enough.)

- What do you look like?
- What do things look like to you?
- How do you sound?
- How do things sound to you?
- How do you feel?
- How does your body feel?
- What emotions are you experiencing?
- How do you feel about your life?

When finished, open your eyes for a moment. Then close them and again imagine yourself in ten years. This time, suppose you've been exercising regularly for the past decade. Ask yourself the same questions:

- What do you look like?
- What do things look like to you?
- How do you sound?
- How do things sound to you?
- How do you feel?

- How does your body feel?
- What emotions are you experiencing?
- How do you feel about your life?

Most people discover there's a graphic difference between these two futures. Which would you rather have? What are you willing to do to achieve the future you want?

STRATEGY 2

Do Something You Really Enjoy

When choosing a sport or exercise, pick something you like, rather than something you "should" do.

While writing this book, I boosted the frequency of my own workouts when I began playing racquetball. I enjoy playing so much that I actually look forward to doing it. While I'm playing, I lose track of time because I'm having fun. That makes exercising easier.

But don't expect that you'll always want to exercise, or that you'll always enjoy it while you do it. I never walk into the weight room at the gym saying to myself, "Oh boy, now I get to work out." Many times I'd rather not. Sometimes I try to talk myself into going home halfway through my routine. But I focus my mind on the benefits the workout provides. And by the time I finish, I'm always glad I continued, because I feel great.

STRATEGY 3

Do It with Someone Else or Do It Alone

Peer pressure and support are powerful motivators. A surprising number of people exercise with a friend or family member. This helps them get up and go, even when they don't want to. Most of us don't want to disappoint, let down, or disillusion a friend we've agreed to work out with.

Researchers at Saint Francis Medical Center in Peoria, Illinois, found that couples who joined an exercise program together were more likely to complete it than those who started alone.

I presented a day-and-a-half stress management seminar for one organization. Two weeks separated the first day from the second half day. During that time, one group of eight employees who had been through the first day began walking together during their lunch break. They divided into two groups—the fast and the slow walkers. When they returned to the seminar, all reported that it was easier to exercise, because the group provided motivation. Since then they've continued their new walking program and even added a few new participants.

You can join an existing walking group. Many malls have walking clubs whose members stride through the mall together. The business office of your local mall can tell you if one of these groups is available nearby.

STRATEGY 4

Avoid Mind Traps

There are several ways we talk ourselves out of exercising. Here are a few, and some answers to each.

- "I'm too tired."
  Exercise actually provides extra energy and helps clear mind and body of stress.
- "I'm too fat."
  Start slowly, perhaps just by walking around the block. Build from there.
- "Exercise is boring."
  Most activities are boring sometimes. But pick something you enjoy, and you'll find eventually that you look forward to exercising.
- "My family/spouse doesn't want to do it."
  If you want to work out with someone, ask a friend, or put up a notice at a health club. Eventually, when your family sees that exercise helps you, they may come around themselves.
- "I always feel sore after exercising."
  Start slowly and work up. That way your body adjusts gradually.
- "I've tried exercising more before, but I always quit."
  The motivation strategies in this chapter will help if you use them. Make exercise a priority. Eventually it becomes a positive habit.

When your mind begins to find excuses to avoid exercise, don't play the game. Instead, find ways to do what will help you become more successful and healthy.

STRATEGY 5

Fit It into Your Life

Being physically fit also helps top achievers relate positively to their friends and families because *they're feeling good about themselves*. If your reserve of good feelings is empty, how will you give any to others, even those you love?

- Structure exercise and your life so that they fit together. Do you travel a lot? Figure out how to work out wherever you'll be. Steve Allen exercises by jogging back and forth in his hotel room when he's on the road. When I'm traveling, I usually go for a walk after checking into my room. That helps me relax and reduces jet lag.
- Does your schedule change frequently? Discover how to include exercise even when changes occur. I used to put everything else before exercise. Now I write workouts in my appointment book and *do* them because it's part of my schedule.
- If you don't get enough time with your family, ask them to walk with you or play a sport you enjoy together. They may resist the idea at first, but keep trying and they'll probably join in, particularly if it's fun.
- At home, or at work, you can schedule a walking meeting. Most people think better when they're walking. Why not walk as you talk, or double the benefits? At several companies where I consult, walking meetings take the place of some sit-down meetings. The moving meetings are shorter, more efficient, and leave the participants feeling energized.

STRATEGY 6

Make Exercise a Habit

Almost every peak performer I surveyed or talked to practiced their sport or exercise on a regular basis, many every day.

I worked with one single mother, Sandy, who complained of begin overweight. She began attending Overeaters Anonymous but wanted to do more. We set up an exercise program for her. But Sandy didn't follow it—she said it took too much time away from her two children. We adjusted Sandy's program so she could do it with her kids. Every evening after work, if it wasn't raining, Sandy agreed to take a half-hour walk with her kids and the family dog.

At first her children thought the idea was "dumb." So Sandy and the dog went by themselves. After a few days, Sandy's daughter joined her, and about a week later, her son said he thought he'd try, too, even though he said it was "nerdy."

At first, Sandy missed some days. She found excuses for skipping her walk. But she kept reminding herself of how much better she'd feel and look if she exercised regularly. She began using a chart, writing the days of the week on it and checking them off after she had taken her walk. That helped.

After a few weeks, the evening walk had become a positive habit. Eventually, the family walked together three or four days a week. Sandy went out with the dog on the other days, except Sunday, which she chose as a day off. Within six months she'd lost thirty-five pounds and felt much better. Exercise became a regular part of her evening.

- Think of a positive habit you already have. How did you make it a regular part of your life? Chances are you pushed yourself to do it, day after day, until it became automatic. After that, you didn't have to think about it, you just did it.

SUMMARY: JUST DO IT

Exercise makes us healthier, happier, more relaxed, more energetic, and sexier. And the peak performers I interviewed say it contributes greatly to their success and ability to handle change.

Dozens of sports and workout routines beckon, from aerobics to golf to cross-training. To sustain motivation:

1. Imagine what you'll be like in ten years—with and without exercising.
2. Find an activity you enjoy. But realize that sometimes exercising will require commitment.
3. If it helps you to stay motivated, exercise with a partner or a group.
4. Avoid mind traps (all the reasons you say you can't exercise).

5. Fit exercise into your life by planning and prioritizing.
6. Make it a positive habit.

Before writing this chapter, I exercised two to three times a week. After reevaluating the benefits of physical activity, I began working out five or more times per week. I quickly noticed a marked increase in my energy, optimism, and confidence.

The next step is yours.

NOTES

Recommendations from the U.S. Surgeon General were covered in "How Execs Get Fit," by Faye Rice, in *Fortune* magazine, October 22, 1990.

The *American Health*/Gallup survey was mentioned in "The Performance Plus," by James Rippe, in *Psychology Today*, May 1989.

Research on controlling stress through exercise was reported in "Fit Folks Handle Stress Better Than the Non-fit," from the Health and Fitness News Service, Rodale Press, 1982.

Dienstbier and Landers's research was surveyed in "The Anti-Stress Power of Exercise," in *Self* magazine, November 1989.

Research on self-confidence in fit college students appeared in "A Morphological Investigation of Physiological-Psychological Change," by M. G. Saipe, in *Dissertation Abstracts International*, 38, 3905B.

Other studies on exercise and confidence are surveyed in "The Therapeutic Effect of Physical Fitness on Measures of Personality," by Rob Doan and Avraham Scherman, in the *Journal of Counseling and Development*, September 1987.

The literature search on depression and exercise is from "The Therapeutic Effect of Physical Fitness on Measures of Personality," cited above.

The Scripps College study on reasoning ability was summarized in *Prevention* magazine, April 1991.

Greenough's research was summarized in "Annual Check-Up," by Rebecca Boyd, in the *Sacramento Bee*, December 17, 1990.

Thayer's research on walking vs. candy appeared in "Tired? Take a Walk," by Holly Hall, in *Psychology Today*, May 1987.

The Harvard study on longevity was reported in an Associated Press story, "Harvard Study Supports Exercise-Longevity Concept," in the *Sacramento Union*, March 9, 1986.

The Lillian Vernon quote about growing old is from "Lillian Vernon," by Russell Shaw, in *Sky* magazine, June 1991.

The sex and exercise survey was reported in "Jogging Makes You Sexier," *Medical Self-Care*, Spring 1983.

Lee Berk's observations on endorphins are from "Future Fitness? Mind Health," by Sherwin Nuland, in *Self* magazine, March 1989.

The information on exercise and immunity is from "Diet, Exercise, and Immunity," by Jeanine Barone, in *American Health*, December 1987.

The research on jet lag was reported in "Jet Lag? Do Some Push-ups," by Deborah Blum, in the *Sacramento Bee*, January 17, 1989.

14

Building Confidence

He drives briskly down Michigan Avenue. A sliver of sun shows itself over Chicago's Soldier Field, as the car turns into a private driveway leading into a large building.

He leaves his car and climbs aboard an elevator that silently carries him to his lake-view suite on the eleventh floor. There lie his offices, an exercise room, a private apartment, dining room, and kitchen. Even a barber's chair. The previous evening he was in Hollywood rubbing elbows with the elite of the entertainment world. Now he's back on the job . . . early.

The early riser is John Johnson, owner of Ebony-Johnson Publishing Company and one of the four hundred richest men in America. But Johnson wasn't always wealthy. He grew up poor and black in Arkansas. At one time his family was on welfare. And as a youth, Johnson struggled with tremendous change and low self-esteem.

How did Johnson rise to the heights of Michigan Avenue? How did he marshal the self-esteem to fuel his rise? How does he handle the pressure and change inherent in running a multi-million-dollar publishing and merchandising empire?

YOUR CONFIDENCE IS SHOWING

John Johnson, like others I interviewed, boosted his self-confidence as he grew and prospered. As confidence grew, so did his ability to handle change and pressure. You'll learn about his techniques later in this chapter. In our survey, 82 percent of the peak performers agreed with the statement "I am a self-confident person." And in our interviews, they emphasized the importance of self-confidence.

As *One Minute Manager* coauthor Ken Blanchard told me, "I'm convinced that dealing effectively with change and stress starts with your own self-esteem."

Researchers at the University of Illinois, who studied mothers giving birth, agree. Mothers who were confident that they could handle the pain reported that they experienced *less* pain. In fact, confidence was a better predictor of ability to handle pain, even compared with factors like earlier childbirth experience, preparation, and age.

Nancy Lowe, head researcher in the study, said, "We need to recognize that psychological factors that contribute to confidence are extremely powerful in a woman's perception of pain."

If confidence can reduce pain in childbirth, certainly it can help when dealing with other situations where other kinds of change bring pain.

SELF-EFFICACY: BELIEVING WE CAN ACHIEVE SUCCESS

Self-confidence is an individual's concept of *general* worth and ability. **Self-efficacy,** on the other hand, is the perception of the ability to do a *specific* task—giving a speech, following an exercise program, or completing a report. We're more likely to reach a goal, especially when dealing with change, if we have a strong belief in our ability to do so. That's self-efficacy. Confidence in our abilities makes us handle change more effectively. Self-doubt creates anxiety and tension and blocks productivity.

Psychologist Albert Bandura of Stanford University has done ground-breaking research on self-efficacy. Bandura says, "When beset with difficulties, people who entertain serious doubts about their capabilities slacken their efforts or give up altogether, whereas those who have a strong sense of efficacy exert great effort to master the challenges."

Thus, if you have *self-efficacy* in specific areas, you'll have higher self-confidence in general. Several factors contribute to self-efficacy:

- Encouragement from others
- Past successes
- Having successful role models who have done what you want to do

As self-efficacy grows, the fear and stress of difficult situations and transitions diminish. But feeling fear doesn't mean you're not confident. Most of the peak performers I interviewed get scared, even in situations where they have experience. But as we gain mastery, the anxiety becomes more controllable. Then we handle change much bettter.

ACHIEVING MASTERY

Researchers believe that experts in any given field are good at what they do because their experience enables them to comprehend information differently from the way others do. They can perceive large meaningful patterns rapidly. This process happens so quickly, it seems intuitive.

For instance, chess masters can identify 100,000 or more board positions and make the best response to each. Rather than thinking deeply about moves to come, the chess master recognizes chunks of information, perceives problem situations, and takes the appropriate action(s).

Studies show that expert cab drivers do the same. They have superior visual knowledge of the city, so when they see a given intersection, they can instantly assess the best route from that point to where they want to go.

After working at something for years, we come to recognize, almost instantly, patterns experienced before. We know what action led to success and can re-create it without thinking. And as we gain mastery, a unique phenomenon occurs. Because of increasing ability to recognize and organize information, time seems to slow down when we're in the midst of an activity we're good at.

Baseball great Ted Williams said that he could sometimes see the seams on the baseball as the pitcher threw it toward him. For him, the ball seemed to take longer to reach the plate than it did for less expert hitters.

Sound strange? According to modern physics, speed and time are relative phenomena. They are functions of the way we perceive them. So, very literally, as we gain expertise, confidence rises, because we have more "time" during which to act.

Practice Makes Mastery

Achieving mastery takes much time and practice. And in our instant society, people often don't want to invest the time necessary for mastery. Yet there are no short cuts.

Famed attorney F. Lee Bailey told me he memorizes huge volumes of information to use during cross-examination in a trial. "When I prepare for a case, I spend a lot of time memorizing, while other lawyers spend their time putting notes in order so they can find them if they need them. You can never find notes fast enough to use them in an effective cross-examination. Speed is a critical ingredient. If you don't trust your memory, you keep reaching for the notes. I call them crutches. And a person on crutches will never be able to outrun someone who doesn't need them."

I asked Bailey how he memorizes such large amounts of information.

"It's just like your muscles," he said. "If you train them and work them, you can become a weight lifter, a runner—whatever you want, unless you have a chronic disability. You may not win the gold medal, but you can become much better at it than the average person. The same is true with the memory. You must practice to gain increased ability."

John Johnson agrees that practice is the key. "Everything gets better with practice. Musicians rehearse. People taking an examination cram. Concentrate and practice. There's no way to do it without practicing, trying and failing and trying again."

CONFIDENCE GROWS AS YOU DO

Over ten years ago I presented my first day-long stress management seminar. Before that, I'd led several weekly classes but had never spoken in front of a group for a full day.

I flew down to San Diego, where the seminar was to take place, and checked into a hotel. I was so nervous I didn't fall asleep until 3 A.M. My wake-up call came at 6.

Though I was bleary-eyed and tired, my adrenaline was pumping full blast as I drove to the company where I was to speak. When I got up in front of the group my hands shook, I spoke too fast, and my knee developed a twitch. I wasn't much of a model for good stress management. Luckily, no one seemed to notice, and the seminar went well, though I made some mistakes I wasn't proud of.

Since then, I've given hundreds of speeches and seminars. And, over time, I've become more confident and relaxed. These days I still feel myself get "up" for a presentation, but just enough to do a good job. Doing what I feared, over and over, taught me to master the pressure.

And sometimes the circumstances of my presentations change. For instance, I may be asked to alter my topic, cope with a particularly difficult group, or present a one-hour speech in twenty minutes (because a previous speaker talked too long). I'm now able to stay on top of these situations because I've built my confidence through practice and experience.

Fear is natural. And it's always strongest when we're doing something new. That's why so many people give up at the start of a new endeavor.

As we gain skill and experience, fear diminishes. In 1982, William Morrow and Company released Ken Blanchard's book *The One-Minute Manager*. It was a runaway hit. Blanchard and his coauthor, Spencer Johnson, appeared on the "Today Show"—Blanchard's first time on television. He told me what it was like.

"They said 'We're on,' and my throat was dry—I was nervous. I called my mom after the show and said, 'How do you think it went?'

"She said, 'Spencer talked too long.' That happened because I couldn't get anything out. Spencer had already been on three hundred television shows promoting his children's books, so it was easier for him."

Today, Blanchard is one of the most self-assured speakers I've seen. He appears frequently on television and often speaks before thousands of people at a time. He's become more confident through experience.

Another peak performer, U.S. Senator Barbara Boxer, gained increased confidence through losing. "I ran for supervisor [in Marin County, California] in 1972 and lost. After something like that, a lot of people would say, 'It's too painful. I can't face doing that again.' But I decided that in politics you shouldn't take it personally if you lose. It's because you stand for certain things that not everyone likes. If everyone loved you, you wouldn't be doing anything important."

So Boxer waited four years and ran again. This time she won. Later she was elected president of the board of supervisors, the first woman in the county's history to gain that position. From there she went on to a seat in the U.S. House of Representatives. Finally, in 1992, she ran for the United States Senate, winning a fiercely fought battle with columnist Bruce Herschensohn to become one of the few women in the male-dominated Senate.

"I've lived through political loss and personal losses, and I know I can get beyond the pain and be okay," Boxer told me. "Having dealt with a loss gives you the confidence to move ahead."

It's a paradox. To handle change more effectively, we must build self-confidence. But raising confidence can be tough, because it means taking risks. It's a matter of putting up with temporary discomfort for future gains.

Like several peak performers I interviewed, Steve Allen struggled with shyness as a child and young adult. He told me how scared he was the first time he made a speech. "I had an acute case of stage fright the first time I made a speech. I was nine or ten years old, and all I had to do was go across the hall and address the children in another room. It was a horrifying experience, but mostly in anticipation. Once the thing started, it turned out to be not nearly as bad as I thought it would be.

"I was never that afraid again. A few years after I got into show business, my anxiety was very close to the bottom of the charts and it almost never bothers me now. In fact, I can be more socially at ease in front of ten thousand people in an auditorium someplace than in front of ten strangers at a cocktail party or dinner setting where I don't know anyone."

Allen met his wife, Jayne Meadows, at a dinner party in 1952. She describes what it was like.

"He sat down beside me and didn't say one word to me. At the end of the evening, I turned and said, 'Mr. Allen, you're either the rudest man I ever met or the shyest.' His face turned beet red and his head slumped. I had my answer."

I asked Allen about his shyness.

"There is a certain element of social shyness that I don't think I will ever lose," he said. "It's much less now, and it affects my behavior in a social setting much less now than it did thirty years ago.

"A few months ago, Jayne and I were looking at a tape of an interview we did with Edward R. Murrow on his old show, where he sent cameras to people's homes. My God, I was shy. It was incredible. I didn't see it then. I knew I was shy but I didn't think it was any big deal. But as I look back now, I am embarrassed at how shy I was thirty years ago. Today I feel relaxed. I know what I am and what I'm not."

Steve Allen became more confident with time, and that helped him handle change more effectively. He boosted his self-confidence by getting out and *doing* what he was frightened of. Then, as he gained experience, his sense of self-efficacy and self-confidence rose.

Like most of the people I interviewed, Allen isn't totally confident all the time. Yet he has a happy life, filled with success, and he handles change beautifully. Total self-confidence is unusual. But self-esteem can be built little by little.

CAN YOU BE TOO CONFIDENT?

Researchers are discovering that we can all benefit from a *bit* of overconfidence—that good mental health sometimes involves stretching the facts a bit.

Not long ago, psychiatrists believed that a sense of utter realism, no matter how unpleasant, was required for an individual to be mentally healthy. But this approach stemmed from research with patients who had severe mental problems. For such people, stronger contact with reality *is* necessary.

But those who don't suffer from a major mental disorder can actually benefit from holding some illusions about themselves. Most of us fool ourselves, whether we know it or not. Researchers have found that most people believe that they are more content, more mentally healthy, and more talented than other people, despite impartial appraisals that show they are not.

Most people also tend to remember their strong points and successes and forget their weaknesses and mistakes. People often excuse their shortcomings as trivial and see themselves as being better than others see them.

In one study, researchers asked a group of men to rate their ability to get along with others. One hundred percent—all of the subjects—said they were in the top half of the population at large. Sixty percent of the group believed they were in the top 10 percent of the population. And 25 percent claimed they were where destiny evidently placed them—in the top 1 percent. In another study, 60 percent of the men surveyed said they were in the top 25 percent of the population in athletic ability. And 70 percent said they were in the top 25 percent as leaders. Obviously, most of us, especially men, bend the data.

But refracting the facts, in this case, isn't so bad. Shelley Taylor, a UCLA psychologist, did a thorough review of hundreds of experiments on the issue of confidence and self-image. In talking about the way people tend to overrate their abilities, she said, "Such illusions put a kind of positive twist on information about yourself. Negative facts are not experienced as so negative, and positive ones as even more positive.

"For instance," Taylor continued, "you explain away social rebuffs, or alibi yourself on work poorly done, by telling yourself that some extenuating reason was to blame, instead of just admitting that the other person doesn't like you, or that you did a terrible job."

As you discovered in the chapter on optimism, a bias toward the positive can be beneficial for performance, health, and happiness. Thus, for most people, it doesn't hurt to think a bit more favorably of yourself than may be realistic. And for those who are very hard on themselves, some extra self-lenience and self-love are certainly in order.

AVOID GOING OVERBOARD: RETAIN SOME HUMILITY

> *"Hooray, boys, we've got 'em!"*
> —The first words uttered by General George Custer
> after spotting the Indians at Little Big Horn.

But there's a delicate balance between healthy self-confidence and unhealthy denial or egotism. Humility must accompany confidence. Overconfidence alienates others and may lead to failure as we neglect proper preparation for important events.

Most of the successful people I interviewed had a delightful quality. While obviously confident, they weren't smug. During the interview, many said things like, "Now, I don't mean to sound overconfident when I say . . ." or "Well, I've certainly screwed quite a few things up along the way . . ." Most were careful to avoid taking a "one-up" position. Their statements showed humility, and that quality made me admire them more.

Walter Cronkite has enough humility to tell of a time he was sailing with his wife on the Mystic River in Connecticut, following the tricky turns of a channel surrounded by shallow water. As a motorboat shot by them, the young people aboard it waved their arms and shouted. Cronkite waved back in greeting.

"Do you know what they were shouting?" Cronkite's wife asked.

"Why, it was 'Hello, Walter,'" he answered.

"No," she said. "They were shouting, 'Low water, low water.'"

Cronkite chuckles at himself as he tells this story. He's able to maintain that crucial balance between self-confidence and ego.

One of the primary tasks of a coach in any sport is to help the players be confident, but not overconfident. They have to believe in their ability to win but still put in the necessary effort to make certain they do, without getting smug and letting down.

Sometimes, overconfidence can cause problems. When Muhammad Ali was world heavyweight boxing champion, he frequently flew to speaking engagements and business meetings throughout the United States. On one flight, the stewardess came down the aisle before takeoff and reminded the champ to fasten his seatbelt.

"Superman don't need no seat belt," said Ali, with a grin.

"Superman don't need no airplane, either," replied the stewardess. Ali buckled the belt.

It's healthy to have a bit of overconfidence. That can help you keep going when things are rough. But few of us are Superman or Superwoman. There are limits to what we can accomplish. Yet if we plan well, choose our battles, and remain confident, we can do the things that are truly important.

WHAT YOU THINK OF ME IS NONE OF MY BUSINESS

> *I don't know the key to success, but the key to failure is trying to please everybody.*
> —BILL COSBY

President Calvin Coolidge once invited friends from his hometown to dine at the White House. Worried about their table manners, the guests decided to do everything that Coolidge did. This strategy succeeded, until coffee was served. The president poured his coffee into the saucer. The guests did the same. Coolidge added sugar and cream. His guests did, too. Then Coolidge bent over and put his saucer on the floor for the cat.

It's important to get along with others. But in trying to please everyone, we may get in the kind of trouble Cal Coolidge's guests did. Many of us worry too much about what other people think. We plan our lives to fit the expectations of those around us. In so doing, we stifle self-confidence and make change more difficult to handle.

Making everyone happy is an impossible task anyway. Some people are perpetually unhappy. If you believe you must please them, you'll be unhappy yourself, and your confidence will plummet.

PREPARE FOR CONFIDENCE

One of the best ways to handle change is to start planning before it happens. *Prepare.*

What I discovered about preparation as I interviewed top achievers was a surprise to me. When I began the interviews, I hadn't thought of preparation as a change management tool. But as I interviewed people, most recommended it. They said it helped them to relax. Several even said that preparation was *the most important* strategy for handling change.

"It's essential to prepare yourself for change," weight-loss executive Jenny Craig told me. "When you anticipate change, you reduce the amount of negative stress you'll encounter."

Tootsie Roll Industries, Inc., president Ellen Gordon helped her company remain independent by anticipating and preparing for change. Initially, Gordon inherited control of The Sweets Company of America (SCA) and the Tootsie Roll trademark from her parents, who had been investing in the company for years.

When Ellen Gordon joined the renamed Tootsie Roll Industries as a director in 1968, she focused on increasing her family's percentage of stock ownership so that the company wouldn't become a takeover target. In 1978, Gordon was elected president of Tootsie Roll, becoming the second woman president of a company listed on the New York Stock Exchange.

As her husband and Tootsie Roll CEO Melvin Gordon says today, "We're very near to [owning] 50 percent of all the stock, and certainly a higher percentage of the voting stock, because Ellen was primarily interested in making sure nobody wrested control of Tootsie Roll from the family. This was *years* ago, way before takeovers became common. It was back when people with 20, 25 percent of a company felt very secure. Ellen didn't."

Analysts say that if the Gordons hadn't kept such a large share of stock, the company probably *would* have been taken over, because it's at least twice as profitable as the average Standard & Poor's 400 company. By anticipating change and preparing for it, Ellen Gordon stayed on top when merger mania swept the country in the 1980s.

Ellen Gordon also prepared for and initiated change by spearheading extensive automation and computerization at Tootsie Roll in the 1980s. Thus the company avoided the problems encountered by other industries that didn't invest in the latest equipment and methods. "Looking at the [U.S.] steel and automotive industries, we decided we must never be like that," she says. "We must be sure that we're state-of-art."

To assess the importance of preparation for yourself:

- Take a moment and think of a time when you didn't prepare properly for a situation—perhaps a meeting or speech. How did you feel? Was your confidence level high or low?
- Next, think of a time when you were well prepared for a task. Were your feelings different from those you had in the first situation. Was your confidence higher?

Books on stress and change rarely mention preparation. But without it you won't achieve what you want. For instance, many of us make a telephone call before we have all the information needed to communicate effectively. Or we go to a meeting without knowing enough about the topic or about the people who will be attending. Lack of preparation adds to our stress level and makes challenges more difficult to handle.

HOW ONE MAN CREATED POSITIVE CHANGE THROUGH PREPARATION

The Early Years

John Johnson is a self-made man. Every step in his journey he has prepared to win. And along the way, he's learned to handle enormous change with confidence and grace.

Johnson was born in 1918, in Arkansas City, Arkansas, a small town on the banks of the Mississippi River. His father died in an accident when John was six. The boy's mother, who had never gotten past the third grade, made a living washing clothes and cooking for the men who worked the levees along the Mississippi.

When he was fourteen, Johnson's mother moved the family to Chicago, where she got a job as a maid. But in the aftermath of the Great Depression, she lost her job and couldn't find another. The family went on welfare.

In Chicago, Johnson attended all-black Du Sable High School. He was shy, insecure, and inarticulate. The other kids made fun of him for his bow-legs and "mammy-made" clothes. They also teased him about his "hick" southern accent. Often he ran home from school crying.

But Johnson didn't give up. Johnson *prepared* to succeed and to cope effectively with the changes in his life. He began reading self-help books, particularly those of Dale Carnegie.

He began speaking in front of the mirror for hours at a time. He rehearsed speeches, and practiced approaches to the girls he couldn't afford to take out on dates. Then he forced himself to speak up in class. At first the other children laughed. Eventually though, as Johnson got better and better, they began to applaud.

When he was a high school junior, Johnson's class met to organize. The sponsoring teacher asked the students for input, but no one said a word. Finally Johnson rose, and put his preparation to work. He thanked the teacher and talked about how his class would work hard to succeed. Johnson seemed relaxed and articulate—his fellow students elected him class president.

The following year he was elected senior class president and became editor of the school newspaper. The shy, insecure, bow-legged kid had, through preparation and commitment, elevated himself to the top of his class. John Johnson was on his way.

Negro Digest

After high school, Johnson began working at Supreme Liberty Life Insurance Company, the largest black-owned business in Chicago. There Johnson prepared for a new challenge.

At that time, there were no successful black commercial magazines. Johnson's dream was to start one. He even knew the name—*Negro Digest*. He visualized it having a format similar to *Reader's Digest*, with an emphasis on the positive accomplishments of blacks in America.

But Johnson had a problem. No one wanted to invest money in the dream of a twenty-four-year-old kid who worked for an insurance company. So Johnson decided to do it himself. Supreme Insurance had a machine called a "Speedaumat," which addressed letters to the twenty thousand company subscribers. Johnson figured he'd send a letter to each person on the list, offering them a $2.00 prepaid subscription to *Negro Digest*.

Johnson got permission to use the Speedaumat to send a letter, but that created a new problem. He needed $500 for postage, and no one he'd spoken to would lend it to him. So he went to a major Chicago bank, meeting there with a man Johnson says was the "assistant to an assistant." When Johnson made his request, the bank employee laughed in his face. "Boy," the man said, "we don't make loans to colored people."

Johnson was humiliated and angry. But he remembered what the self-help books said, "Don't get mad, get smart." He asked the man who *would* make him a loan. The assistant to the assistant looked surprised and suggested the Citizens Loan Corporation.

Citizens Loan agreed to lend the money, but only with collateral. Johnson's mother, by now working again, had just purchased the first new furniture of her life. Johnson asked if she'd let him use the furniture for collateral. She prayed about it, thought about it, and finally agreed.

So John Johnson sent out his twenty thousand letters, and got 6,000 prepaid subscriptions to *Negro Digest*. But there was another roadblock. He had taken in just enough to publish the first issue. If there was to be a second, he'd have to sell copies of *Negro Digest* on the street.

So Johnson contacted the Charles Levy Circulating Company, the largest magazine distributor in the area, and asked Levy to handle newsstand distribution. Levy declined, saying that black publications didn't sell. Johnson knew he'd have to prove Levy wrong. He convinced thirty of his friends to begin asking for the magazine at newsstands.

Soon after, Levy called and said he'd take 500 copies of *Negro Digest* after all. Johnson convinced him to double his order. Then, when the magazine came out, Johnson used the last of his money to have his friends buy all the copies available. Levy ordered a thousand more. Copies began to sell briskly on their own. Within a year, *Negro Digest* was selling 50,000 copies a month. Circulation later rose to over 100,000.

As circulation rose, so did John Johnson's confidence. And, as he became more confident, he became better able to handle the increasing pressure of his changing circumstances.

The *Ebony* Challenge

The next big change in Johnson's life was the start of another new magazine. In 1945 he launched a big, slick publication called *Ebony,* filled with pictures and prose celebrating black achievement in America. The first press run sold out in hours.

Unfortunately, as *Ebony*'s circulation climbed, advertising revenues didn't follow. Big companies wouldn't advertise in a black magazine. Cash flow became a problem. The revenues from solid, dependable *Negro Digest* were drained by its newer, flashier sister. Things got so bad that Johnson had trouble paying the bills.

The tenacious young publisher redoubled his efforts. He realized that if he were to succeed, he'd have to sell himself. Johnson began calling and writing to CEO's and presidents of the companies he'd targeted for ads. He called one CEO four hundred times.

The big break in *Ebony*'s fight for survival came in 1947, when Johnson decided to center his efforts on companies selling in the black community. His first quarry was Zenith Radio Company.

After Zenith's advertising manager turned him down, Johnson went straight to the top. He wrote to Commander Eugene F. McDonald, Zenith's CEO—an astute, hard-nosed executive who ran Zenith with the same dedication and control he'd shown as a U.S. naval commander. When Johnson wrote him, asking for an interview, McDonald replied that he didn't handle advertising.

Johnson wrote again, asking if he might speak to McDonald about advertising *policy*. The Zenith CEO, recognizing true persistence when he saw it, agreed to the interview, on one condition. If Johnson discussed advertising in *Ebony,* McDonald would end the interview.

"I had to find a way," Johnson told me, "to keep up the conversation until, hopefully, I could bring it around to *Ebony.*"

The young publisher knew that preparation was the key to success. "I looked McDonald up in *Who's Who in America*," Johnson said, "and discovered that he had been an Arctic explorer."

Johnson already knew that a black man named Matthew Henson was part of Commodore Robert Peary's historic Arctic expedition in 1909. After further research, Johnson discovered that

Henson was living in Harlem, and that he'd written a book about his adventures.

"I had my editor look Henson up," Johnson said. "I got him to autograph a copy of his book to Commander McDonald. I also had enough time between then and the interview to do a story on Henson." Johnson ran the piece in *Ebony*.

"When I went to see the commander I felt quite confident," Johnson said. "I had two important things to talk about that he could relate to."

When Johnson arrived at McDonald's huge office, the commander greeted him, then pointed to the wall. "Young man," he said, "do you see those snowshoes? They were given to me by Matthew Henson. He is worth any two white men I have ever known, and if you are smart, you will emulate him.

"I understand," McDonald continued, "that Matthew wrote some kind of book."

"It just so happens that I have a copy here," said Johnson, "autographed to you, Commander."

McDonald paged through the book, smiling. Johnson had broken the ice.

"Well, Johnson, if you have any kind of magazine, it seems to me you would have done a story on a man like Matt," McDonald said.

Johnson pulled out the recent *Ebony* article. The commander looked at it and smiled again. With a nod in Johnson's direction he said, "I don't know why we shouldn't be advertising in this magazine."

Turning away for a moment, McDonald hit the intercom button on his desk and called in Zenith's advertising manager.

"Mackey, why aren't we advertising in *Ebony*?" McDonald said.

"We're considering it, Commander," came the reply.

"By God," McDonald thundered, "we ought to do it."

Then, before Johnson left his office, McDonald telephoned the chairmen of Armour Foods, Quaker Oats, Swift Packing Company, and Elgin Watch. All agreed to see Johnson. Later each bought ads in *Ebony*.

From then on, the magazine was a financial success. And, in the years that followed, Johnson's empire expanded to include more magazines, several radio stations, and companies selling cosmetics and beauty products. Today, *Ebony* magazine is read by 45 percent of the black adults in America. Because Johnson prepared carefully to meet his challenges, he handled change with confidence and aplomb.

Though he's small in size, Johnson's energy is enough to change the face of America. In his mid-seventies now, Johnson still believes in hard work and preparation. He personally interviewed each of the three hundred-plus employees who work at Johnson headquarters.

"Preparation is essential," he told me. "When going into a situation, take time to prepare yourself to deal with it. Preparation provides confidence and makes changes and challenges less stressful."

As young John Johnson discovered, when we reach for a dream, dramatic change often accompanies the quest. And though most of us don't stretch as high as Johnson did, managing *any* transition is easier when we've laid the groundwork for success. Whatever the goal, **proper preparation creates confidence.** And John Johnson isn't the only peak performer who believes in it.

PREPARE WITH INFORMATION

Fortune magazine once called Harvey Mackay "Mr. Make-Things-Happen." CEO and author Mackay makes things happen because he's prepared. "If you're a super organizer, you can mitigate the effects of stress and change," he says.

For years, Mackay has used a sales tool called "the Mackay 66." It's a sixty-six-question profile his salespeople complete on each of their customers. The profile contains information on everything from the customer's home town to his or her vacation habits.

In his best-selling book, *Swim with the Sharks Without Being Eaten Alive,* Mackay talks about how these sixty-six bits of data have helped his company survive and thrive. He says "the Mackay 66" aids his people in getting closer to the customers. And what envelope buyer wouldn't appreciate getting a birthday card, clippings from his hometown newspaper, or tickets to a favorite football team's home game?

And Mackay prepares in other ways. "Wherever I go, I'm always ten minutes to a half hour early. If I've got a big appointment at three o'clock, I'll get there at two thirty-five and just do nothing. You don't have to drive eighty miles an hour if you're well organized."

When he gives a speech, Mackay gets all the information he can in advance. "When I make a speech, I want to know the answer to fifteen, twenty different questions," he says. "I just did this an hour and a half ago. I'm flying to Memphis. So I asked the person who had booked my speech, 'What speakers have you had the last five years?' He told me, and they were all name people. I said, 'Give me a ranking, one to ten, of how well you thought they did.'

"Then I ask, 'Why were they a six, why were they a seven?'

By asking all these questions, I gain confidence. I have superior information."

Superior information leads to confidence, even when pressure-packed change occurs. Mackay *knows* the value of proper preparation, and uses it regularly.

HOW TO PREPARE FOR THE SPOTLIGHT

Another peak performer, Geraldine Ferraro, the first woman vice-presidential candidate, used preparation to sail through one of her toughest challenges—when her family's finances came under scrutiny after Walter Mondale nominated her as his running mate on the Democratic ticket in 1984.

On August 21, Ferraro spent a two-hour press conference answering questions about various aspects of her financial situation. I asked how she handled the scrutiny.

"I spent the entire weekend preparing for that press conference," she said. "Preparation is how I deal with something that's going to be tense. I went over the answers again and again with the lawyers and accountants.

"We went through everything that we thought could be questioned. And so I knew the answers, and I said, 'If I don't, I'm going to call on one of you guys.'

"Then, before I went to the press conference, I called my mother and asked her to pray for me. Usually at this kind of press conferences, they have a box where they hook in all the microphones from the various television people, so you end up with just one microphone in front of you. I asked that they not use the box. I said, 'Let all the microphones be there. I want people to see what I'm going through.' I kind of made the world share my tension by putting the microphones there."

Most critics complimented Ferraro's calm, confident bearing during that press conference. She passed a crucial test.

Ferraro and I also talked about how she handled her debate with George Bush during the '84 campaign. "Lots of preparation. Which is what George Bush was doing, too. Everybody does in that kind of situation. Over and over, I practiced answering the questions that we thought I'd be asked."

"When I got there I knew what to expect, but I was an absolute wreck. I wrote my closing remarks in my own words and memorized them, because I wanted to be able to speak directly and not be afraid of leaving something out.

"The way I dealt with the nerves was preparation, preparation, preparation. It could not have been a more difficult situation I was walking into. One way to reduce the pressure of change is by preparing as much as you can for what's coming. And for me, it works."

PREPARE TO PREPARE

When a potentially stressful change or situation is on the horizon, get ready early. Whether it's a speaking engagement, meeting, family gathering, wedding, or an important project—sit down and analyze what needs to be done, and when.

In the past, I sometimes didn't prepare properly for important events. Because I took on too many projects, I'd rush through some of them. I didn't allow myself time to complete them the way I knew I should.

Then, while interviewing people for this book, I came to believe what they said—that preparation builds confidence. I began spending more time getting ready for important events. Before writing this book I spent almost forty hours planning the steps necessary to complete it. I wrote a timeline, which included everything from determining my goals, to writing a chapter outline, to planning my publicity tour. I wrote a "due date" for each item on the list.

This part of the preparation process is much like the goal-setting plan in Chapter 5. After you've analyzed what needs to be done and written (or mentally noted) your timeline, build in extra space for the inevitable roadblocks and problems. Your schedule won't run perfectly—why not prepare for that to happen? Then follow the schedule as best you can. If you get off track, don't despair. Make necessary adjustments, and keep plugging away.

I also learned to spend more time on preparation in other areas, once taking more than fifty hours to prepare a twenty-minute speech. When I gave the talk, I felt relaxed and confident. I received a standing ovation and the best overall response I'd ever had. The speech was successful beause I prepared it carefully.

But how do you find the time to do all this preparation? Selectivity is the answer. The peak performers I interviewed choose their projects carefully. If they think they can't devote the time necessary to do a good job on something, they won't agree to do it. They use the word "no" . . . liberally.

Since I began reemphasizing preparation in my own life, I, too, have had to say "no" more often. I give fewer speeches and seminars, but those I do are better received. Thus I now earn more from each presentation. And in my counseling practice, I accept fewer clients, but the ones I work with feel better faster.

Prepare to prepare. When you do, confidence will rise. You'll walk into situations *knowing* that you know, and can do, what needs to be done.

PUT OFF YOUR IMPORTANT DECISIONS

Sometimes a bit of procrastination can be a confidence builder. But just a bit. Many of the peak performers I interviewed said they avoided rushing into an important decision. They take awhile to mull it over. By taking extra time, when possible, they reduce stress and boost the chance they'll make the best decision during a time of change. That helps them be more confident.

Ellen Gordon, president of Tootsie Roll Industries, Inc., says, "I like to take time when I'm dealing with stress and change. I think about a problem a lot, and talk about it with people. One of my rules is that if there's time, I've got to sleep on it. Something happens at night when you sleep and dream. Often the next day you look at the problem with fresh insight and ideas.

"I weigh all the pros and cons. Sometimes I make a chart with the pluses and minuses of each course of action."

Gordon generally makes good decisions, partly because she doesn't rush into them. Instead, she builds internal confidence by giving herself time to make the correct choice. In the process, she inspires confidence in those who work for her.

HOW CHILDREN BECOME CONFIDENT

Some people grow up feeling confident, while others have to learn self-esteem for themselves. As we discussed in Step 6, family environment is the most important key in determining confidence later in life.

In our interviews, several peak performers talked about the unconditional love they received from their parents. It seems to have made their life's journey easier. Of course, even though we love our children as they are, we still set limits for them. But ideally, the discipline we provide always arrives along with a healthy dose of love and respect.

Another peak performer with high self-confidence is modeling agency executive Eileen Ford. I asked Ford about her family. "I was born after my mother and father had been married nine years. So this little bundle of perfection arrived on their doorstep," she said, laughing. "I was the apple of their eye, and I always got a lot of praise as I grew up. That's probably why I'm so confident today."

When I interviewed Jenny Craig, I was amazed at her ability to remain confident and optimistic, even in the most difficult situations. As you may remember from Step 6, Craig and her husband, Sid, started Jenny Craig International in Australia in 1983. In those first years, the company often teetered on the edge of failure, but Jenny says, "I always knew that we would make it. I used to tell Sid every day, 'It's going to work, it's going to work.'"

Later, when the company *did* become successful in Australia, the Craigs began opening centers in the United States. Again, success came slowly, especially because competition with other weight loss companies was fierce. But Craig says, "I don't remember ever feeling, deep in my heart, that it wasn't going to work. I believed we'd make it."

Craig's confidence helped her make a vital change in her approach—introducing frozen meals at each diet center. And make it they did, with Jenny Craig International becoming one of the largest weight loss programs in the U.S., and the world.

Fascinated by Craig's ability to remain confident, even when surrounded by problems, I asked her, "When you were growing up, did your parents help you become confident in yourself?"

Craig responded immediately. "My dad used to say to me all the time, 'You can do anything or be anything you want.' When I came home from school, he would always tell me how smart I was, how good I was, how pretty I was. I never had to work at having high self-esteem. Those seeds were planted as I grew up."

As an adult, whenever Craig encounters pressure-packed change, she has the positive messages she learned from her father to counteract it. His loving words, "You can do anything or be anything you want," echo in her head, helping Craig remain confident, whatever the circumstances.

But many of us don't learn that kind of self-esteem at home. Instead, we must build it later in life. That's the way it was for Maureen DiMarco, now California's secretary of child development and education.

"I grew up in a very stressful household," she told me. "Eventually my parents divorced. And I grew up with a fear of not being enough. I often thought to myself, 'I can't.'"

Because DiMarco felt that she didn't receive unconditional love as a child, she had to learn to give it to herself.

"I finally learned that approval doesn't come from anyone else," she says, "it comes from you, and that has to be enough. That was a hard lesson to learn, and I don't think I really started learning it until I had children of my own. I realized that I could be okay just by being me."

I asked DiMarco how she began to turn her low self-esteem around. "First, I realized that we have a choice about how to view ourselves—positively or negatively. Second, there were some close friends who took an interest in me. They helped me to learn to accept myself as I was."

Actor LeVar Burton also had to shed negative images of himself that he learned as a child. "Much of my childhood I was given messages that I was not okay. I bought into that belief system—I adopted it as mine."

Later, after he starred in "Roots," Burton began the difficult process of increasing his self-esteem. "I really had to learn how to accept myself and learn that everything was okay. Even those aspects of me that I loathed, that I had no desire to look at and deal with, it was all okay. And that was the beginning of what I'm experiencing now, which is acceptance of myself, as I am."

Neither DiMarco nor Burton has had an easy journey. They've had to struggle to learn self-confidence. But through hard work and commitment, they did it.

SIX EFFECTIVE WAYS TO BUILD YOUR CONFIDENCE

STRATEGY 1

Learn to Love Yourself More

Loving yourself creates self-confidence. In this section you'll learn to love yourself more, even when negative change or stress occurs. We'll start with the following exercise:

- Think of someone or something you love unconditionally. This is often easiest if that individual is someone you're not *too* close to—perhaps a grandparent, a good friend, or a child. If it's difficult to identify the right person, think instead of a *pet*, or even an *activity* you truly enjoy.
- Close your eyes and think about the person or thing you love. Notice the feeling in your body as you think about it. This feeling varies from person to person; many describe it as a sensation of an opening up in their chest, others talk about a feeling of warmth and comfort throughout their body or in one specific area. However the feelings of love manifest themselves for you, just observe them.

If you have difficulty feeling anything, try noticing the general feelings in your body as you go through the day. As your powers of observation grow, so will your ability to notice the sensations of love.

- Now, imagine turning that loving feeling onto yourself. Some people think of small doors in their chest opening *inward* rather than outward, others think of the way they feel when someone really loves them.
- If you try this and it doesn't seem to work, you might try another approach. For instance, approach it through self-talk. Say to yourself, "I love myself for having trouble with this." Even if you don't believe what you're saying, say it anyway. It will still have a positive effect on you.

When people get unconditional love as they grow up, it's as though they live in a constant shower of acceptance. Even when they make mistakes or when they're frightened, they know they're loved. You can now begin to create that warm shower of love for yourself.

I counseled a woman named Joyce, who worked as an accountant for a large manufacturer. Joyce had a supervisor who treated her poorly, often saying negative things to Joyce in front of other employees. Joyce's response was to work harder and harder, trying to avoid giving her boss anything to criticize. She often came to work on weekends to make sure nothing was undone.

When Joyce first came to see me, she was feeling anxious and depressed. She didn't know if she could stay at the job. We talked about self-acceptance, and Joyce said she'd grown up in a family where she received a great deal of criticism. She expected the same as an adult.

Over the course of several sessions, I helped Joyce learn to love herself, starting by using the exercise I've just described. The more she accepted herself, the more Joyce learned to stand her ground with her boss, politely but firmly. Eventually her boss began treating Joyce with more respect. As Joyce learned, when we become more confident, other people tend to treat us better, too.

STRATEGY 2

Think Confidently

When it appeared *Ebony* magazine might fail, publisher John Johnson channeled his thoughts toward success. He sometimes locked himself in his office, fighting to keep his confidence up. He repeated the word "success" out loud, over and over again. He did it, he said, like a monk chanting. The young publisher chanted another phrase, too: "John Johnson, you can make it. John Johnson, you can make it. John Johnson, you can and must make it." The positive self-talk helped Johnson handle the stressful changes in his business and keep going.

It wasn't long after this that the tide began to turn, and *Ebony* became a success. As Johnson focused his mind on success, he was able to change the outer world, too. Johnson followed a path Plato pointed out centuries ago, when the Greek philosopher said, "Take charge of your thoughts. You can do what you will with them."

Developing positive self-talk is an essential key to self-confidence. If you have difficulty hearing your inner dialogue, try focusing in on it every now and then, especially when experiencing negative emotions. Psychologist Harriet Braiker, writing in *Psychology Today*, suggests asking yourself, "What am I saying to myself right now?"

Here's a simple strategy designed to help you become more confident. I call it the 1–2 Punch for Negative Thinking. It's best to write the exercise at first. Later, after you've mastered it, you can practice the technique in your head.

A secretary named JoAnne, who attended one of my seminars, told me she had trouble being confident, particularly on the job. I encouraged JoAnne to pinpoint her negative thoughts by using the 1–2 Punch. Here's what JoAnne wrote for Part One:

1. I can't perform as well as the others in my department.
2. I made a mistake on the report I just turned in. My boss will be furious.
3. I can't stand this job anymore

Next, I asked JoAnne to challenge the negative statements. When doing this for yourself, there's no need to be a Pollyanna. Acknowledge the truth in the negative statement, then look for a way to make it more positive. JoAnne challenged her negative thoughts in Part Two:

1. Nonsense. I've done a good job on many projects in my department and have been told so by my boss and others.
2. Not true. I did make a mistake, but it was minor. The rest of the report was excellent.
3. There *are* aspects of this job I dislike very much. But I enjoy other parts of my work. And as I become more confident, I'll probably enjoy the job more.

Through completing this exercise, JoAnne analyzed and changed her negative thinking. Of course, doing this exercise once isn't going to make a major difference in your life. Try practicing it on a daily basis, for several weeks. By so doing, you'll begin to permanently change the way you think.

The 1–2 Punch also works beautifully if you're feeling low, depressed, stressed, or overwhelmed by change. Many people with whom I've worked report that their mood shifts, sometimes dramatically, when they analyze it with this technique.

STRATEGY 3

Analyze Your Strengths and Weaknesses

Another form of self-analysis can also boost confidence and buffer the stress of change. It entails taking a realistic look at what you do well and what you don't.

Ex-IBM executive Buck Rodgers says, "I believe in continual self-appraisal. Periodically I step back and say, 'Okay, what should I do to strengthen myself, and what am I doing well that I could do better?' I focus on weaknesses, but also on strengths. When you do that, it's amazing what can happen, because you start to believe that you have a tremendous number of attributes."

- One way to analyze yourself is to write down your strengths and weaknesses.
- You can further refine the process by taking a daily inventory. Just write a " + " and a " – " at the top of a blank page. Then note the things you did that day and those you'd like to change in the future. For the items on the minus side, imagine (see, hear, and/or feel) yourself doing them differently next time.

STRATEGY 4

Take the Zig Approach

You can also *zig* your way to confidence. Zig Ziglar, one of the top professional speakers in the world, specializes in helping people boost their self-esteem. But he doesn't just talk about gaining it—he successfully raised his *own* confidence level while maintaining his humility.

Like many of those I interviewed, Ziglar blends confidence with humility. Zig and I talked about a few confidence boosters he recommends:

- Building vocabulary
- Reading positive literature
- Listening to confidence-building tapes

"In a study of 1,139 CEO's, the researchers found that 92 percent had outstanding vocabularies," Ziglar said. "You don't need to use a lot of big words, but with a good vocabulary you can understand whomever you are communicating with far more readily and easily.

"An International Paper Company study found there was a direct correlation between vocabulary and income. And a person just feels good when he or she can communicate and understand people."

Zig also recommends reading something educational or uplifting for at least twenty minutes each day. It could be a biography, information about business, or a spiritual text. Because the average person reads 220 words a minute, twenty minutes of reading each day enriches you by twenty average-size books each year. That's eighteen more than the average person reads.

"A third thing I recommend," Ziglar continues, "is to use the cassette recorder. For two years I was a visiting scholar at the University of Southern California. A study done there showed that if you drive twelve thousand miles a year, in three years time you can acquire the equivalent of two years of college education by listening to tapes in your automobile.

"When the typical person sees a traffic jam in front of him, he stomps his feet and gets really upset. What he really should do is say, 'It's going to take me thirty minutes to get out of this, and in thirty minutes time I can learn three new sales closes; I can learn five new words.'"

--- STRATEGY 5 ---

Visualize

There's another way you can use your mind to boost confidence, in the car or anywhere else: visualization.

In 1958, pianist Liu Chi Kung placed second to Van Cliburn in the Tchaikovsky competition, a yearly contest in which the finest young pianists in the world compete. A year later Liu Chi Kung was thrown into prison, as part of the Cultural Revolution in China. Liu was held captive for seven years. During that time, he was never allowed to play the piano. Yet upon his release, he went back on tour almost immediately. The critics said his playing was better than ever.

"How did you do this?" one critic asked. "You had no chance to practice for seven years."

"I practiced every day," Liu said. "I rehearsed every piece I had ever played, note by note, in my mind."

World famous flutist James Galway uses a similar strategy. "I get out my flute in my hotel room and imagine the situation as it's going to be," he told me. "Say I'm going to play in Carnegie Hall. I start cranking it out there, in the hotel room, like I'm on stage. Then, when I get to Carnegie Hall, it's not a problem."

Liu and Galway use visualization to build skill and confidence, and so do almost all star athletes. When psychologists Scot Machlus and Richard O'Brien of Hofstra University taught several groups of athletes to visualize themselves performing well in track and field events, all improved their performances significantly.

But what if you're not a musician or athlete? Can visualization work for you? You bet. In everything from business to child-rearing, more and more people are imagining themselves performing the way they'd like to.

- To try visualization, first find a comfortable place where you can be alone. Then close your eyes and take a few minutes to concentrate on your breathing. As you do, you may find yourself becoming more relaxed. Begin to imagine yourself in an upcoming situation in which you wish to perform well.
- Remember to use your three senses, as we discussed in the commitment chapter. *See* yourself doing the activity (as if you're watching a movie). Then shift your perspective, and imagine that you're seeing what's around you as you perform.
- *Hear* your environment and your own voice, if you're speaking in the situation you're imagining. *Feel* yourself going through the movements required for the activity. Imagine the emotions you'll be experiencing.

Remember that many people have difficulty imagining in one or more of the senses. That's okay. Just emphasize the ones that come to you naturally.

After you've practiced a few times, you'll no longer need a quiet environment. You can then practice visualization any place you have a moment or two.

STRATEGY 6

Try Another Confidence-Builder

If, by now, you haven't found a confidence-enhancing strategy you like, read on. During my interviews with them, the peak performers mentioned several other ways to gain confidence.

- *Public speaking and other communication skills.*

  Remember how John Johnson built his self-confidence during high school by learning to speak well? Zig Ziglar, Ann Rudin, Harvey Mackay, and Buck Rodgers, among others, agree that this is a great way to become more self-assured.

  Most colleges and junior colleges have public speaking courses available. In addition, the Dale Carnegie organization has good speaking courses, as does Zig Ziglar's company in Dallas.

  The Toastmasters organization, which is devoted to public speaking, has meetings in most cities and towns. When first attending the meetings, most people just sit and listen. Later, they get the chance to speak more and more. Thus, confidence builds gradually. To find a local Toastmasters chapter, check the telephone white pages.
- *Exercise.*

  Research studies, as we have noted, show that people who exercise regularly have higher self-esteem.

HOW TO PREPARE FOR PRESSURE-PACKED CHANGE

Sometimes, when a stressful event or change is on the horizon, self-confidence can plummet. This section is a quick guide to preparing yourself for confidence and peak performance, even when change occurs rapidly. Follow these steps, and you'll be more self-assured in almost any situation.

Know That Fear Is Natural

So you're scared. Almost everyone is afraid sometimes, whether willing to admit it or not. Courage isn't the absence of fear; it's feeling the fear and doing what you want anyway.

Most of the successful men and women I interviewed still become nervous when they're facing a particularly risky challenge.

Though actor George Peppard always appears self-assured on screen or stage, he feels frightened sometimes. That doesn't stop him.

"I just understand that I'm going to be a little anxious for awhile," he says, "and continue what I'm doing. I say to myself, 'I'm feeling anxious.' Then I concentrate on the task at hand. Your heart can race, you can sweat, you can worry, you can twitch, and still do a fine job."

Rate the Difficulty

Do this when you are faced with a task that seems insurmountable:

1. Measure the size of your challenge by writing about it. Do you really have to do *all* the paperwork on your desk? Must the speech be an hour long, or would a tight half hour be better? Is the upcoming meeting really going to be a bloodbath, or is "challenging" a better description of what you'll encounter?
2. Rate the difficulty on a scale of one to ten. Note what *absolutely* needs to be done, and what is optional.
3. Ask yourself an essential question: *What's the worst that can happen* if you're not successful in dealing with the challenge?

Maureen DiMarco, California's Secretary of Child Development and Education takes this last strategy one step farther. "Analyze the problem," she says. "Take a piece of paper, make four columns. Write down the problem in the first column. In the second column, write down the worst thing that could happen related to it. In the third column write down the *best* thing that could happen. And then do some brainstorming about what's the most *likely* thing to happen. And the fourth column is 'What am I going to do?.' Build an action plan."

Remember Past Successes

After you've evaluated your present situation, tune into what you've done well before. You may not have done something precisely like your upcoming challenge, but you've probably done something similar.

I recently consulted for a Fortune 500 company that was merging with another company it had purchased. The CEO, Glen, had never managed a takeover before, and he was anxious to do the job right.

After we discussed the situation Glen realized that, though he hadn't merged companies, he'd merged departments many times. And over the years he'd become very good at it. I asked him what he did when departments were brought together.

"First," he said, "I bring the department heads together, to discuss how things can be accomplished most effectively. Then I talk to the staff in both departments and let them know the benefits, and the difficulties, of the change.

"I give the employees an opportunity to talk about any negative feelings. That way, they'll be better able to buckle down and get back to work. And I ask the employees and the managers for their input on completing the merger as efficiently as possible."

Suddenly, Glen smiled. He realized that what he did to blend departments would be a good start in merging companies. By remembering past successes, he became more confident in the present.

- Remember your past successes. Write them down. Some people, like Peter Thigpen, president of Levi Strauss, actually keep a list of their significant accomplishments. Then, when they need a boost in self-confidence, they look back at past successes.

Visualize

We've already discussed the power of visualization. When you're going into a tough situation, imagine yourself doing what you want to do, the way you want to do it. Remember to use your senses: *sight, sound,* and *feeling.*

Let Your Unconscious Mind Work for You

Author, consultant, and former Waldenbooks CEO Harry Hoffman believes that his subconscious mind is always working to find the solution to problems. Yours is, too. As you prepare for a challenge, allow yourself slack time, perhaps overnight, for the subconscious mind to work.

Fake It

When the chips are down and you're feeling stressed by change . . . fake it. Almost everyone I interviewed said they sometimes put on a cool, relaxed front when deeply anxious inside.

When I asked Jack Lewis, CEO of computer mainframe manufacturer Amdahl, if he handled pressure well, he said: "From an external point of view, people view me as handling pressure very well. Sometimes internally I'm thinking differently, but externally I'm usually a very calm person."

And publisher John Johnson says, "I walk around here with great confidence. I issue edicts and statements and policy as though it were the final word and I'd gotten it from on high. But sometimes I'm trembling in my boots. I psych myself up and convince myself that I'm going to do it. I gain confidence from expressing confidence."

There are, of course, circumstances where it's best to admit feeling insecure. Those who never admit they're scared seem phony. But, in general, you don't have to broadcast your anxiety about pressure or change. Just *pretend* that you're feeling calm, even if you're not. You'll be in good company—*most peak performers do the very same thing.* You'll find that it helps.

SUMMARY: HOW TO BECOME A MORE CONFIDENT PERSON

As a counselor I've worked with hundreds who suffered from low self-esteem. Almost all made significant strides in boosting their confidence by using the exercises I've described.

Within this chapter lie the tools necessary to raise a sense of self-esteem, even where none has stood before. To use them, remember these key points:

- Some overconfidence can be good for you. But watch out for egotism.
- Be gentle. Beating yourself up won't help you accomplish more. It will only kill your confidence.
- Remember: What others think of you is none of your business.
- Use solid preparation to improve confidence and handle pressure-packed change.
- Pick a confidence-booster, and use it.

1. Learn to love yourself more.
2. Think confidently.
3. Analyze yourself.
4. Take the Zig approach (improve vocabulary, read positive literature, or listen to self-improvement tapes).
5. Visualize.
6. Practice confidence-building activities (improving communication skills, exercise, taking a risk).

Finally, follow these six strategies to prepare confidently for stressful changes and situations:

1. Know that fear is natural.
2. Rate the difficulty of the task.
3. Remember past successes.
4. Visualize (as you can note from its inclusion in both lists, this is an important strategy).
5. Let your unconscious mind work for you.
6. When all else fails . . . Fake it.

You *can* become more self-confident, even if your mind is full of negative self-talk. But you must decide to begin the process. It will not always be easy. Sometimes your mind will try to convince you that you aren't worth it, that you might as well give up. Pay no attention to this negative self-talk. Forge ahead. Make the choice, again and again, to believe in yourself.

As Eleanor Roosevelt said, "No one can make you feel inferior without your consent."

NOTES

The childbirth research cited was covered in "The Whys of Hard Labor," in *American Health*, June 1989.

The self-esteem research cited was reported in "Prejudicial Esteem," in *Psychology Today*, September 1986.

The Bandura quote was taken from the *Berkeley Wellness Newsletter*, May 1987.

Jayne Meadows, quoted in *Current Biography Yearbook*, 1982.

The studies where men rated themselves were condensed in "How Do I Love Me? Let Me Count the Ways," by David Myers, in *Psychology Today*, May 1980.

The Taylor quote is drawn from "Living on Cloud Nine," by Daniel Goleman, *New York Times* (reprinted in the *Sacramento Bee*), December 26, 1987.

The story about Ali and the plane is given in *The Little, Brown Book of Anecdotes*, edited by Clifton Fadiman, Little, Brown and Company, in 1985.

Melvin Gordon's quote about takeovers, and Ellen Gordon's quote about automation appeared in "The Practical Genius of Penny Candy," by Stephan Wilkinson, in *Working Woman* magazine, April 1989.

Research about the track teams appeared in "Relax, You'll Run Faster," in *Psychology Today*, December 1988.

The skiing story is from *The C Zone: Peak Performance Under Pressure*, by Robert Kriegel and Marilyn Kriegel, Anchor Press/Doubleday, 1984.

15

Communicating Effectively ... and Loving

Love is the medicine for the sickness of mankind. We can live if we have love.
— DR. KARL MENNINGER

When I began the interviews for this book, I knew that researchers claim that good support systems and communication skills enable people to handle change and stress effectively. My interviews confirmed this.

Most of the peak performers I spoke with are masters of networking and communication.

FRIENDS AND FAMILY HELP KEEP US HEALTHY

Being around people is usually good—for us and for them. James House, of the University of Michigan, researched the health benefits of social support. He reports that "The data indicates that social isolation affects mortality rates as much as smoking, high blood pressure, high cholesterol, obesity, and lack of physical exercise." House says, "It is as great or greater a mortality risk as smoking."

Researchers at Stanford University discovered that terminally ill cancer patients who participate in support groups lived almost twice as long as those who got medical treatment only.

TOUCH MAKES LIFE BETTER

People who are touched regularly are healthier and happier. Animals like to be stroked, too. Marion Diamond, Ph.D., of the University of California, Berkeley, discovered that laboratory rats touched frequently show greater brain growth than those who are not touched. "This," Diamond says "also holds true for humans."

Little humans grow faster when they're touched. In a Miami Medical School study, a group of premature infants gained weight 47 percent faster than others. The secret? They were massaged for fifteen minutes three times a day. These same babies became more active and responsive to their environment than were infants left alone. According to Tiffany Field, the psychologist who led the study, "The massaged infants did not eat more than the others. Their weight gain seems due to the effect of contact on their metabolism."

Months after discharge from the hospital, the massaged babies continued to do better than their lonely peers. They kept a weight advantage and performed better in tests of mental and motor ability. In another study, psychologist Seymour Levine, of Stanford University, found that physical contact with their mothers keeps infants calmer in stressful situations.

Dr. William Whitehead, of Johns Hopkins School of Medicine, reports that when adults are touched, their heart rate goes down. And the touch that soothes can be as minor as putting a hand on another's wrist. So touch helps reduce the stress of change, increases brain functioning, and just plain makes us feel better.

HOW WE TOUCH PEOPLE THROUGH EMOTIONS

Human beings also touch each other with their emotions. According to psychologist Elaine Hatfield, of the University of Hawaii, research shows that, "Emotional contagion happens within milliseconds, so quickly you can't control it, and so subtly that you're not really aware it's going on."

It appears that some people transmit emotions, while others are more likely to "catch" them. The emotional transfer process can take place, for instance, when one person unconsciously imitates the facial expressions on the face of another.

In one experiment, two volunteers—one emotionally expressive, the other less so—sat facing each other for two minutes, waiting for a researcher to come back to the room.

When the researcher returned, he had the two volunteers fill out an assessment of their moods. Through body language (and perhaps through some other mechanism not yet recognized), the less expressive person had taken on the mood of the more expressive one. And indeed, emotionally expressive people are more likely to transmit their moods to others.

Thus, if you're emotionally expressive, realize that other people may pick up your moods, both positive and negative. If you're less expressive, be careful who you spend time with. Your companion's moods may be catching, especially when he or she is dealing with stress or negative change.

How Bad Bosses Affect Us

Many people catch emotions on the job. Psychologist Suzanne Kobasa, who did the pioneering research on hardiness (Step 2), also looked into workplace relationships. She found that when employees felt they had the support of their boss they handled stress and change much better. In fact, they experienced half as much sickness in a year as those who believed their bosses weren't supportive.

William Hendrix, of Clemson University, who studied Defense Department employees at Midwest air force bases, discovered that rigid, authoritative bosses caused higher cholesterol, stress, and health problems in their employees.

Families Can Help ... or Hurt

But psychologist Suzanne Kobasa found that certain kinds of support can actually *hurt*, even in dealing with a bad boss. In studying the Illinois Bell employees, Kobasa found that those who said their families were most supportive actually had more stress-related illness—the highest rates found in the study.

Isn't support supposed to help? It does, but only *the right kind*. The *wrong kind* may make a worker bitter and self-pitying.

"If a family simply lets someone complain about how hard things are, that person is likely to retreat from dealing directly with his or her troubles," Kobasa said. "They won't walk into the boss's office and ask for help. They'll become increasingly alienated, and psychologically stay home from work."

So, for change and stress at work, the right kind of support is essential. And, to prove it, a good boss may be better than a family. Even if you don't have a supportive boss, research shows that you'll get more relief from talking about work problems with other employees than with a spouse or family. Family members can help if they don't encourage self-pity.

I worked with one man, Doug, whose wife, Lois, complained for hours each night about all the stressful changes taking place at her job. Doug listened and tried to support Lois, but her work situation didn't improve. Doug finally got fed up and began limiting the amount of listening he'd do when his wife complained. Soon, rather than complaining, Lois began dealing with the issues *on* the job. She talked to her boss and coworkers about the problems, and they agreed to work together on resolving them.

SUPPORT SYSTEMS WORK

Talking about problems *can* be helpful, as long as we don't overdo it. Sometimes, though, verbal communication is out of the question. It was, most of the time, for Commander Gerry Coffee when he was imprisoned in North Vietnam.

"We weren't allowed to communicate with the other prisoners," he told me. "So we worked out creative ways to communicate without being caught."

Coffee and the other prisoners devised an intricate code, tapped out on walls and pipes. They'd communicate news, technical advice, encouragement, and even poems. When prisoners were caught communicating, they were often tortured, but that didn't stop them. They went right back to tapping.

"The communication was really a godsend," Coffee said. POW's became close friends with other prisoners they didn't see for years. Communication and support helped them survive sustained and stressful change.

Archbishop Desmond Tutu helps build support systems wherever he goes. David Hochberg, vice-president of public affairs for the Lillian Vernon Corporation, told me about having lunch with Tutu when the archbishop received an honorary degree from the College of New Rochelle. Hochberg mentioned Tutu's warmth and graciousness, describing how the Nobel Prize winner greeted each of the forty guests in the room personally. Tutu created a support system on the spot.

Where Do You Stand?

How good is your support system? The following questionnaire, adapted from one created by the California Department of Mental

Health, can help you decide. (Copy it into a notebook if you don't want to write in this book.)

RATING THE STRENGTH OF YOUR SUPPORT SYSTEM

For each item, circle one response. Then add the scores of the items you circled and note the total.

1. When you have a job-related problem, do you discuss it with people at work? How many?

none (or not employed) (0)
one or two (3)
two or three (4)
four or more (5)

2. *Do you trade help with neighbors (e.g., loaning household items or tools, ride-sharing, babysitting, etc.?) How many?*

none (0)
one (1)
two or three (1)
four or more (3)

3. *Do you have a partner or spouse?*

no (0)
several different partners (2)
one steady partner (6)
married or living with someone (10)

4. *Do close family members or friends visit you at home? How often?*

rarely (0)
about once a month (1)
several times a month (4)
once a week or more (8)

5. *Do you talk with family members or friends about personal matters? How many?*

none (0)
one or two (6)
three to five (8)
six or more (10)

6. *Do you participate in a social, community, or sports group? How often?*

rarely (0)
about once a month (1)
several times a month (2)
once a week or more (4)

Next, compare your score to the levels below. If your Support System score is:

Less than 15: Your support system has *low strength* and probably does not offer much help. Consider making more social contacts.

15–29: Your support system has *moderate strength* and probably provides enough help except during periods of high stress and change.

30 or more: Your support system has *high strength* and will likely maintain your well-being even during periods of high stress and change.

If your score puts you in either of the first two groups, you might take a few minutes to think about how to build a stronger support system. Start by building support in the areas in which you scored lowest.

COMPETITION VS. COOPERATION

University of Texas psychologist Robert Helmreich has studied seven groups ranging from business people to grade-school children. In each group, highly competitive people usually performed less efficiently than those who cooperated.

David and Roger Johnson, of the University of Minnesota, recently surveyed 122 studies done over the past fifty years, looking at the effectiveness of competition versus cooperation in the classroom.

- Sixty-five studies showed that collaboration promotes greater success than competition.
- Only eight of the research projects showed that competition was more effective than cooperation.
- Thirty-six demonstrated no statistically significant difference.

Clearly, competition isn't a path to greatness. You can do a better job without trying to beat others.

LOVE AND ACCEPTANCE *DO* WORK

For years we've heard reports about Type A personalities—hurried, hard-driving, and highly competitive individuals. They're at higher risk for heart disease and stress-related ailments. Recently, researchers have pinpointed two components of Type A personality that cause problems: hostility and self-centeredness.

A study by Dr. Redford Williams, of Duke University, showed coronary arteries become more blocked in hostile people. In fact, Williams found that high hostility increases the risk of death from all causes. In one study, law school students took a test to assess their hostility level. In the twenty-five-year follow-up period, 20 percent of the attorneys with above average hostility scores died. The mortality rate for those with low or average hostility scores was 4 percent. A study of physicians found similar results.

When we feel hostile toward others, it's often because we don't really understand them. Several years ago, I was working as a consultant at a large northern California insurance company. My work brought me into the office several times each week. There, I'd greet the people I passed in the hall. One man, whom I saw frequently, would look away when he replied. At other times, he ignored me.

After a while, I got angry at his rude behavior. I made up all sorts of nasty scenarios about the man. Then one day I was using the copier after most of the staff had gone home. The man came in with some copying of his own. I introduced myself. Shyly he said hello, and I realized he had a speech impediment. I understood why he had sometimes avoided my greetings.

Forgiveness

If we know enough about someone, it's difficult to remain bitter. And even when people have done terrible things, forgiveness is important. Why? Because our anger hurts us more than it does them.

Archbishop Desmond Tutu demonstrates forgiveness every day, even as he continues battling injustice. For years some South African blacks worked as police informants, perpetuating government oppression. As a foe of apartheid, Tutu abhorred their actions. But his belief in forgiveness was stronger than his anger.

In 1985, one informant was captured by a mob of militant

blacks. They beat him, doused him with gasoline, and prepared to set him on fire. From the edge of the crowd, Tutu and Bishop Simeon Nkoane saw what was happening. The five-foot-three-inch Tutu and his fellow bishop pushed through the mob, grabbed the terrified informant, and carried him to safety.

Tutu risked his life for a man whose actions he despised. Why? Buti Thiagale, a Roman Catholic priest, states: "Tutu says, 'Love your enemy' . . . he believes in the Gospel literally." To help release your anger, don't dwell on the resentment. Analyze it, write about it, talk about it—then let it go. And if you find you can't let go, consider working with a counselor or spiritual guide to release the hostility. It'll make you, and those around you, feel better.

NETWORKING WORKS

People who reach out to people are richer not only in health and happiness, but in business. The concept is simple. When possible, we do business with those we feel close to. We feel safest with those we know. And today, because of society's increasing fragmentation, networking is more essential than ever.

Almost everyone I interviewed has an extensive network of personal and professional contacts. CEO and author Harvey Mackay is a friend of several others I interviewed. Mackay told me about maintaining his network.

"I've got enough telephone calls to make to last my lifetime," he said. "So I've got a little two-by-two piece of paper that I carry inside my checkbook and it's got two hundred names on it, the people I care most about. So if, all of a sudden, I'm at an airport and I hear, 'I'm sorry, we have a two-hour delay,' it's okay. I'm going to have nothing but fun, talking for two hours to people I care about."

Job Net

When Geraldine Ferraro served in Congress, she was known as a feminist, but also for her ability to get along with men. I asked her how she did it.

"I make an effort to get along with whomever I'm working with. To get a bill passed, you need votes. To get a position of leadership, you need votes. You need other people. I've reached out to other people my whole life."

U.S. Senator Barbara Boxer also believes in networking. When she was elected to the U.S. House of Representatives in the early 1980s, Boxer made a point of getting to know many members personally. And the networking worked, helping Boxer gain the presidency of the Democratic freshman caucus and posts on several committees.

How to Do It

The networkers I interviewed build contacts with people because they enjoy it. Sure, it helps business, but that's not their primary motive. Approaching networking with the thought "What can these people do for me?" dooms the effort to failure. Most people will respond to you only if they sense that you genuinely care—and show it through your actions.

To build your own network, try the following:

- Make a list of the people you know and what they do.
- Contact them on a regular basis, through cards, notes, or even a newsletter.
- Ask people if they'll help when you've got a project. Many will.
- Remember that one of the strengths of your network is not necessarily who's in it, but who the people in it *know*. Your friends may be able to connect you with the perfect person for a particular project.
- Expand your network by joining relevant professional, social, and charitable groups.

Maintain relationships with people, and business opportunities will present themselves. In the meantime, you'll be having fun and effectively managing change and stress.

DO UNTO OTHERS...

Gertrude Crain lives the philosophy of "do unto others as you would have them do unto you." She told me how she practices it at work.

"My husband [company founder, G. D. Crain, Jr.] always had an open door policy. Anybody could come in and see him. He felt very strongly about his employees, and wanted to protect them. When he died, we had five publications and now we have twenty-five. But I've tried to follow through with what he started, even though we have over one thousand employees now, and it's more difficult to keep up with what's going on with everyone."

In addition to excellent profit sharing and pension plans, Crain provides personal perks. "I always remember an employee's anniversary with the company. And if any unfortunate things happen to someone's family, I write them a note. They also know that they can come here and borrow the money from their profit sharing plan if they need to."

In celebrating the company's seventy-fifth anniversary, Crain Communications threw parties for all Crain employees. In addition, each received a day off on their company anniversary date.

Crain's philosophy of fostering good feelings with her employees returns to her. After employees had their day off for the company anniversary, many wrote to the chairman thanking her and describing how they spent the day.

Crain also keeps track of employees' weddings. "We always send them money when they get married," she says, "and we also send gifts when they have babies. Where possible, if I am invited, I go to the wedding. That's difficult because of so many employees now, but I always write them a note and attend the wedding if possible."

I asked Crain how she keeps on top of all the events in her employees' lives. She said that one employee at the company specializes in keeping up with changes in the other workers' lives. Crain's secretary also keeps her ears open for important events the chairman might like to recognize.

Michael Clowes, editor of Crain's *Pensions & Investment Age* magazine, says about Gertrude Crain, "She makes it a wonderful place to work . . . It makes people feel very good about the company. She takes the time to say 'hi' to the editors and to meet new people on staff. She's a fabulous woman."

It's not surprising that Clowes feels that way. Remembering Clowes' love for opera, Gertrude Crain calls him each year to find out when he'll be in Chicago. Then, when he's in town, she takes him to see the Lyric Opera.

PRAISE PEOPLE

Another part of doing unto others is letting people know when they've done something right.

Several years ago, after joining a health club, I decided to learn a new weightlifting program. Though I'd lifted before, I still considered myself a beginner.

The man scheduled to work with me was a muscle-bound fellow named Jack. He gave me directions in a flat monotone, looking around the room as he talked. He seemed bored. When we finished, I felt bored, too.

Several months later, Jack quit his job. I was feeling unmotivated in my workouts, and decided to get a new program. Jack's replacement was a man named Rick. He paid close attention when we worked together and listened to what I said. He gave me lots of positive feedback, saying, "Good work, good form," when I did something well.

Rick's feedback always seemed genuine, as if he really cared about what I was doing. I left feeling great. He helped me to accomplish more, feel better about myself, and become more relaxed. I stuck to my new program.

Ken Blanchard has spent years encouraging the world's managers to give their employees adequate feedback. His first bestseller, *The One-Minute Manager,* outlines simple, effective ways to tell people how they're doing on the job. Unfortunately, many managers still haven't gotten the message. They specialize in the wrong kind of feedback—criticism. Blanchard describes this approach as "seagull management."

"The seagull manager," Blanchard says, "flies in, makes a lot of noise, craps on everybody, and flies out again."

Researchers agree that feedback is essential. In one study, psychologist Robert Baron, of Rensselaer Polytechnic Institute, divided volunteers into two groups. He assigned a task to each: devise an advertising campaign for a new shampoo. Each group them received a critique of their work. For those in group one, it was specific and polite. But the members of group two received threatening, inconsiderate, and blaming criticism.

Naturally, those in group two became anxious and angry. But they also said that in the future they wouldn't cooperate with the person who had criticized them. Group one came through motivated and stimulated to excel.

In a later experiment, people who were harshly criticized stopped trying as hard at their jobs and began doubting their own abilities.

Researchers have also discovered that most managers criticize more often than they praise. Richard Huseman and John Hatfield, authors of *Managing the Equity Factor,* found in a survey that managers believe they "frequently" tell their employees that they're doing a good job. The workers themselves report *their bosses "seldom" praise them.*

How to Shape Behavior

When I cover praising in my seminars, someone often says, "Some people don't deserve praise. Aren't you being dishonest by giving it to them?"

With some people, you have to *search* for something to praise.

Watch for anything the individual does right, then praise that. "It's likely you'll see more of the behavior you complimented," says Ken Blanchard.

Praise motivates. Provide it, and watch the changes take place.

Perceptions are Key

What we think of ourselves, and of others, means a lot. In Chapter 3, Zig Ziglar told us how sales trainer P. C. Merrill's belief in him helped the young salesman have faith in himself. Here he tells more about it. "When I was young, I never thought of myself as becoming 'successful.'

"Then Mr. Merrill comes along and says, 'You could be a sales champion. You could go all the way to the top.' Nobody had ever said those things to me. I made a dramatic change in performance as a result."

Ziglar also talks about Harvard University researcher Dr. Robert Rosenthal. In one well-known study, Rosenthal told a group of teachers they'd be working with geniuses who could solve any problem.

He told another group of teachers that the kids in their classes were average, and they could expect average performance from them.

At the end of the year, the classes had performed just as Rosenthal predicted. The geniuses were one full year ahead of the average students. But there was a catch. *All groups had actually been average students at the beginning of the year.* The attitude of the teachers helped mold brilliant students from average ones.

Perception Molds Minds—Young and Old

Zig also told me how he learned more about the power of praise and perception from his middle daughter.

"When our third daughter was born, we knew we were going to have trouble with our second one because all our friends and relatives insisted the middle child would be a problem.

"Just as we expected, Cindy started developing some real problems. She became a chronic complainer, griper, and a whiner. Of course, I handled it with sheer genius. Because if I said it once, I said it a thousand times, 'Why does Cindy whine so much? Why can't she be like Susie and Julie?'"

So Zig and his wife changed their approach. They realized they needed to change their own perceptions—and how they communicated them to their daughter. At that time, Cindy's nickname was Tadpole. Every time somebody came to see them, Zig began calling his daughter over, saying, "This is the happiest little girl you've ever seen. She's always smiling, and laughing, and grinning, and talking—aren't you, Sweetie; aren't you, Tadpole?" She'd look at Zig and grin. And then he'd say, "Tell them what your name is, baby!" and she'd say, "It's Tadpole."

"One day," Zig told me, "I started the routine again and Cindy said, 'Daddy, I've changed my name.' I said, 'Oh, what's your name now?' She said, 'I'm the Happy Tadpole.'

"The neighbors asked what had happened to Cindy. Something had happened to her, but it didn't happen until we changed the way we saw her. When we saw her as a cheerful, happy girl, she became one."

Harnessing the Power of Praise

One note of caution: Avoid phony praising. If you're faking things to praise, people will know you aren't sincere. Instead, *begin looking for the things people do right,* even if they're few and far between. Then your praise will be real, and you'll get another benefit, too. Your own optimism will rise, and change will be more manageable, as you look for (and find) the good.

SETTING LIMITS

Sometimes we need more than praise. When someone does something wrong or hurts you, a reprimand may be in order. But remember to keep a positive approach whenever possible. Otherwise you become known as a critical person.

Most of the achievers I interviewed said they rarely get angry. When they do though, they let the other person (or people) know. Then they let go and move on.

In *The One-Minute Manager,* Ken Blanchard recommends not only telling the individual exactly what you believe he's done wrong, but also reminding him that you still think well of him, in spite of his performance in the situation.

Ken Blanchard generally practices what he preaches. But like all of us, his successes vary. Several years ago, Blanchard had asked his son, Scott, not to park his pickup truck in the driveway. On several occasions Scott agreed. One day Blanchard came home from work to find the truck in the driveway, blocking his wife's car.

"When Scott arrived home three hours later, I went to meet him in the street to tell him what he did wrong. Afterward, Scott ran in the house after me, saying 'Hey Dad, you forgot the last part of the reprimand—how that's not like me and how you're not mad at me, but my behavior.'"

"I laughed," Blanchard says wryly.

LISTEN UP

In the mid-1980s, Mark McCormack wrote *What They Don't Teach You at Harvard Business School*. In preparing the book, McCormack asked a number of business associates, including top CEO's, what advice they'd give abut succeeding in business. Almost all said, "Learn to be a good listener."

As famed psychiatrist and Menninger Institution founder Karl Menninger said, "Listening is a magnetic and . . . creative force. The friends who listen to us are the ones we move toward. We want to sit in their radius. When we are listened to, it creates us, makes us unfold and expand."

When you listen carefully to someone, that person feels cared for. David L. Olson, M.D., is a successful physician who practices in Sacramento, near one of my offices. Over the past few years, Dr. Olson has referred a number of patients to my group for counseling. All speak highly of him—many say he's the finest physician they've ever been to. Why? They say it's because Olson takes time to *listen*. He truly cares about them, and it shows.

Many people talk too much. They're busy waiting to say something and don't really listen to what the other person says. Then, when it's their turn to speak, they overdo it. As the old saying goes, "If you talk long enough, you're bound to say something stupid."

Quiet people sometimes tune out, too. They're thinking about something else, and miss the words of whomever they're communicating with. Men are often guilty of this. We learned to tune out our mothers and, unfortunately, continue the behavior as adults.

SPEAK UP ... BUT NOT TOO MUCH

Listening is more than half the battle. But we also need to speak, not only to ask questions but also to state opinions. Most successful people are highly articulate. They know how to persuade and move others.

Almost everyone is asked to speak before a group—at least once. Most find it frightening at the beginning. Humor consultant and speaker Jim Pelley says, "A recent poll states that the number one fear among Americans is public speaking, and the number six fear is death. So the next time somebody commits a violent crime, the police should put him on the lecture circuit."

But speaking in public doesn't have to be that punishing. I asked Walter Cronkite, one of America's favorite communicators, why he seems so relaxed and convincing on television.

"I never took any lessons or instruction," Cronkite said. "I really was sincerely involved in attempting to communicate rather than perform.

"At the beginning I deliberately slowed my delivery, which took some of the intensity out of it. That was on the suggestion of a friend, Andy Rooney, when I first went on the evening news back in '61. After Andy saw me, he asked, 'What are you trying to sell?'"

So Cronkite began speaking more slowly. Obviously, it worked. Obviously, we can't all communicate as well as Cronkite, but if you'd like to learn to speak more effectively, Toastmasters (mentioned in the previous chapter) can be very helpful.

It also pays to be careful with *written* communications. In his book, *A Whack on the Side of the Head*, Roger von Oech tells of one classic communications slip-up.

J. Edgar Hoover, then director of the FBI, was reading a copy of a letter he had dictated earlier. He didn't like the way the letter looked, and wrote "Watch the borders," along the bottom. Then Hoover asked his secretary to retype it.

The secretary did as her boss asked, then sent the letter to agents all over the country. For the following two weeks FBI agents along the Canadian and Mexican borders were put on special alert.

HELP, WE NEED SOMEBODY

Helping and loving others fills your world with love. In an Institute for the Advancement of Health study, volunteers said they actually *feel* better when they help. Their reports included increased energy, reduced pain, and even feeling "high."

These benefits probably come from the body's release of endorphins. Psychologist Jack Panksepp, of Bowling Green University, says, "It is our own natural opiates, the endorphins, that produce the good feelings that arise during social contact with others."

These good feelings can translate into good health, too. Allen Luks, author of *The Healing Power of Doing Good* (Ballantine, 1992), studied more than three thousand part-time volunteers. When compared to individuals who volunteered only once a year, those who volunteered weekly were *ten times* as likely to report that they were very healthy.

But the good feelings and good health don't come when helping is forced. Just donating money doesn't have much effect either. Helping needs to be more direct.

In Alcoholics Anonymous, members try to help "the alcoholic who still suffers." Bill Wilson, the cofounder of A.A., found this an important key to his own recovery. When Wilson had been sober just a few months, he took a business trip to Akron, Ohio. There he felt a tremendous desire to drink. Instead of pouring one for himself, he decided to find an active alcoholic to help.

With the help of a local minister, Bill discovered a prominent surgeon whose drinking had been taking him downhill for years. Bill and "Dr. Bob" (as A.A. members call him) met and talked for hours. They realized that they had much in common, and came to believe that together they could stay sober. The two men were the first members of Alcoholics Anonymous. Today there are over 2 million.

When we help people who need it, the results are beautiful, for everyone. As Menninger Institution founder Karl Menninger, M.D., said, "Love cures people—both the ones who give it and the ones who receive it." Many of the high achievers I interviewed know the benefits of volunteering. They do it frequently.

- CEO and author Harvey Mackay spends 25 percent of his time on volunteer work. "Over the past twenty-five years I've counseled five hundred different people on what to do with their lives. That, plus working with the United Way, Heart Fund, Cancer Society, the University of Minnesota, among others."
- Through her company, Lillian Vernon, chairman and CEO of the Lillian Vernon Corporation, donates items to hundreds of charities and other organizations. Gifts include: seven thousand teddy bears to hospitalized children, bedclothes and towels to the homeless in New York City, and a portion of the profits of certain catalog items to charities.
- Jill Eikenberry and Michael Tucker are the official spokespersons for the Susan G. Komen Foundation, an organization working to advance breast cancer research, education, and treatment. Eikenberry also hosted and co-produced a documentary for NBC on breast cancer. Husband Michael Tucker says, "Jill is like a one-woman breast cancer network. She gets calls—sometimes as many as 20 a week—from people who've been diagnosed with breast cancer and just need to talk to someone who's been through it."
- Paula Kent Meehan, chairman and CEO founder of Redken Laboratories, Inc., mobilized her company to help save otters endangered by the Valdez oil spill in Alaska. Meehan received

the SPCA's Paloma Award in 1990 for her work in helping animals.

How to Help

Whomever, whatever, whenever you help, the key, as the story that follows shows, is to do it.

At dawn, an old man walked slowly down a beach. In the distance, he saw a young man run across the sand, bend to pick up a stranded starfish, and gently throw it back into the sea. Again and again, the young man tossed small starfish from the sand to the water.

Finally, the old man walked forward and asked why the other man used such energy doing something which seemed a waste of time.

"The starfish will die if they're left in the sun," the young man replied.

"But there must be thousands of miles of beach and millions of starfish. How can your efforts make any difference?"

The young man looked down at the little starfish in his hand. Then he threw it to the safety of the sea. "It makes a difference to this one," he said.

SUMMARY: COMMUNICATION AND SUPPORT

This chapter is summarized easily: *Help yourself by loving and helping others.* By building support systems you'll feel better, live longer, and handle change more easily. By cooperating, rather than competing, you'll be more productive.

Creating networks can build your business and your enjoyment. And, as you deal with the people around you, remember to emphasize the positive. Praise people more than you think they need.

Listen. One of the greatest gifts you can give another is to show you care by *hearing* what she or he has to say. When you *do* speak, keep it slow and clear.

Finally, build your health and vitality by serving others through volunteer work. Imagine what the world would be like if everyone did.

NOTES

The studies on support and health were summarized in "Beyond Self," by Eileen Rockefeller Growald and Allan Luks, in *American Health*, March 1988.

The data cited on married people appeared in "The Paradox of Happiness," by Dian Swanbrow, in *Psychology Today*, July/August 1989.

The studies on self-centered people were summarized in *American Health*, June 1985.

The information on cancer support groups was reported in the *Auburn Journal* (via UPI), on October 13, 1989.

The rabbit research cited was discussed in the *Self Care Journal*, November/December 1989.

Touching and big babies was covered in "The Magic Touch," by Daniel Goleman, in the *Sacramento Bee*, April 16, 1988.

Hatfield's quote and the research on moods was covered in "Watch Your Moods—They're Catching," by Daniel Goleman, originally published in the *New York Times*, reprinted in the *Sacramento Bee*, November 18, 1991.

The survey cited was adapted from one produced for the California Department of Mental Health, called "Can Friends Help You Stay Well," in 1981.

The studies on competition/cooperation appeared in "How to Succeed Without Even Vying," by Alfie Kohn, in *Psychology Today*, September 1986.

Dr. Williams's observations on blocked arteries were covered in "Beyond Self," listed above.

The study on hostility in lawyers was summarized in "Stress: A Special Report," in *New Dimensions*, February 1990.

Michael Clowes's thoughts about Gertrude Crain were quoted in "The Keeper (and Stoker) of the Company Flame," by Stephan Wilkinson, in *Working Woman* magazine, October 1987.

The research on criticism was summarized in "Workplace Criticism Can Do Great Harm," by Daniel Goleman, in the *Sacramento Bee*, August 7, 1988.

The information on how bosses perceive their feedback came from a book review in *Success* magazine, June 1989.

The research on genius students was covered in *See You at the Top*, by Zig Ziglar, Pelican Publishing Company, 1983.

The story about Blanchard's reprimand appeared in "Life as a One-Minute Management team," by Colin Flaherty, in the *San Diego Business Journal*, December 21, 1987.

Data on the life expectancy of volunteers came from *Beyond Self*, cited above.

Information on volunteers who feel good appeared in "Helper's High," by Allen Luks, in *Psychology Today*, October 1988.

The study of volunteers and their health came from *The Healing Power of Doing Good*, by Allan Luks, Ballantine, 1992.

16

Putting It All Together

Let's review the 12 Steps to Mastering Change:

1. View change as a challenge.
2. Build your commitment through goals and passion.
3. Stay committed when the going gets tough.
4. Know when to control, when to let go.
5. Deal with setbacks and go forward.
6. Be optimistic.
7. Use humor.
8. Learn from mistakes.
9. Maintain perspective.
10. Tune the body.
11. Build self-confidence.
12. Communicate effectively and . . . love.

Like anything positive, the 12 Steps to Mastering Change are best used in moderation. Strive for balance, and you'll reap the rewards, without going overboard into obsession.

- Having a sense of control is vital. Insisting on being in control *all the time* creates stress.
- Humor smooths the way for you and everyone else. Using humor where it isn't appropriate hurts people and may be a form of denial.

- Regular exercise builds endurance and reduces stress. Too much exercise actually causes stress.

THE PROCESS OF CHANGE

Sometimes we resist changing because it's uncomfortable. Here's an experiment I sometimes use in my seminars:

- Try folding your arms in front of your chest in the direction you usually do. Notice how that feels. Now straighten the arms, and cross them again, *putting the other arm on top*. How does that feel?
- Now clasp your hands together, fingers interlaced. Notice how that feels. Then take the hands apart. Put them back together with the opposite thumb on top. How does *that* feel?

Often, when we do something new, it seems awkward and uncomfortable. That doesn't mean it's wrong—just that it's new. Soon it gets easier. I've been doing this exercise above for years. Now it doesn't matter which arm or thumb is on top. I have learned to feel comfortable with either one on top. And you can do the same as you accommodate to change in your life.

As you continue your change process, remember the lesson Harvey Mackay shared in Chapter 1. It takes hundreds of blows for a stone-cutter to split the rock. Each stroke combines with those before, building eventual success. Learning to handle change happens the same way.

THE TOP EIGHT SELF-HELP STRATEGIES

In each chapter of this book, I've recommended strategies you can use to implement the 12 Steps to Mastering Change. Seven strategies were mentioned more than the others. They are:

STRATEGY #1:
Write about what's bothering you. Putting your problems on paper boosts immune system functioning and helps you feel better.

STRATEGY #2:
Find a support group. There are hundreds in most cities, dozens in most towns. To find them, call a local mental health center. Most have a list of groups. Or, contact me at the address listed in

the back of the book. I'll send you a list of self-help groups that are available in most areas.

Strategy #3:
Think objectively. When dealing with pressure-packed change, restructure your thoughts. Use the approach in Step 11 or devise your own.

Strategy #4:
Emphasize your beliefs. You may already be clear about what you believe in. If not, try writing it down. Then use your beliefs to provide a foundation for life.

Strategy #5:
Visualize. Imagine yourself where you want to be and doing what you like. Visualize yourself performing the way you'd like to more often. Use your senses: sight, sound, and feeling.

Strategy #6:
Turn negatives into positives: Negative situations happen to us all. Yet in almost every problem lie the seeds for future good. Look for them. Plant them. Watch them grow.

Strategy #7:
Help others. By helping others you help yourself. (But watch out for going overboard into codependency.)

Therapy Can Make a Real Difference

There's one more important method for mastering change. If you still feel stuck after reading and using the strategies in the book, counseling may help.

The most courageous people I know are those who look honestly at their lives. Sometimes honest appraisal reveals a part of ourselves that we need to change. True courage allows us to do what's necessary to make those changes. And sometimes what's necessary is to enlist the aid and support of someone who specializes in helping us to make our lives work better. Several of the peak performers I interviewed talked about how therapy had helped them.

The easiest way to find a therapist is through referral. Ask your family doctor for names of good therapists, or talk to friends who have been to counselors they found helpful. As in any profession, some counselors are better than others. Talk to a therapist on the telephone before you go in. Ask such questions as:

- How do you structure your counseling sessions—What are they like?
- What is your orientation?
- How long do most people come to see you?
- How do your clients feel when they are through?
- What is your background?

If the therapist can't or won't answer such questions, find someone else. And if you don't like the way the counselor sounds, it probably isn't a good match. Try another.

When you've found someone who seems right, arrange an initial appointment. When you meet, assess again whether this is the right person to work with. Does he or she seem supportive but willing to confront you when necessary? Will you mind seeing that person once a week for a while? Does the counselor seem to have a good understanding of the issues that concern you?

If the answer to these questions is "yes," you've probably found someone who can help. Then, give the counseling a chance to make a difference. Even brief therapy requires at least four or five sessions for marked change shifts in behavior. And, if you want to work in depth, counseling will probably take quite a bit longer, sometimes months or even years. But it's often worth the investment—most people report that working with the right therapist helps them handle change and pressure much more effectively.

HOW TO USE WHAT YOU'VE LEARNED

If you don't feel you need therapy, you don't really *need* to do anything besides reading this book. The power of **stories, modeling,** and **motivation** will continue to work.

But there are ways to supercharge your growth. One method is to reread the book. By doing so, you'll continue to program your mind positively. Using some of the strategies described will become automatic.

Or, if that seems like too much, pick a chapter, any chapter. Read it again. Focus on it. If you read a part of the chapter before bed each night, your unconscious mind will integrate it while you sleep. Set a goal to incorporate a particular skill or strategy in your life.

Finally, to further enhance your ability to handle change—practice. As John Johnson said, "Everything gets better with practice. Musicians rehearse. People taking an examination cram. Concentrate and practice."

When you practice, sometimes you'll make mistakes. That's

great. With each mistake you'll learn more about how to do better. You'll be closer to transforming pressure-packed change into productivity and happiness.

Now, before we close, take a moment to imagine yourself the way you want to be. How would you like to be a year from now? (Use whichever senses you can—sight, sound, and/or feeling.)

- How will you look?
- How will things look to you?
- How will you sound?
- How will things sound to you?
- How will you feel?

Imagination can make your dreams come true.

THE ESSENCE OF THE ESSENCE

This book contains the best of over 1500 pages of interviews. The following quotes briefly summarize the vision of *12 Steps to Mastering the Winds of Change*. First, professional speaker and former NFL referee Jim Tunney:

"If you treat change as an enemy, if you try to keep it from touching your life, it will penetrate more and you'll be under greater pressure.

"But if you look at change as a friend, as something that's going to happen to you anyway, things are different. Ask, 'How can I make the best of this situation?' Look at it as an opportunity.

"I walk onto the football field saying to myself, 'This is going to be an exciting game. A lot of pressure, but an exciting game, and I'm looking forward to doing my best.' This game, this speech, this situation, will make me better at what I do."

Ann Rudin, former Mayor of Sacramento: "The changes that produce stress are the very things that give life color and enjoyment. The things that have enriched my life are often found in situations I might have avoided if I were afraid of change and challenge. Dealing with the challenges has made me stronger and better able to withstand pressure."

Pilot and executive Bob Hoover: "Relax ... tomorrow will be better. Things are going to change, so don't dwell on what the problems are right now. Let's think about how great it's going to be downstream."

And, finally, *One-Minute Manager* coauthor and speaker Ken Blanchard: "We're just a speck in time. Next time you're stressing yourself out, ask as if anybody will care in a hundred years. They won't. Because it won't really matter."

Each of us is a potential peak performer. Each of us is capable of being cool, calm, and collected when pressure-packed change occurs. And, through the power of stories, modeling, and motivation each of us can build energy and serenity.

You truly *can* master the winds of change. You've already begun. Do it!

Index